ACTA UNIVERSITATIS UPSALIENSIS
Studia Anglistica Upsaliensia

53

Patricia Phillips

The Adventurous Muse:

Theories of Originality
in English Poetics
1650–1760

UPPSALA 1984

Distributor:
Almqvist & Wiksell International
Stockholm

Doctoral thesis at the University of Uppsala, 1984

ISBN 91-554-1512-1
ISSN 0562-2719

Abstract

Phillips, P. The Adventurous Muse: Theories of Originality in English Poetics 1650–1760. Acta Universitatis Upsaliensis. *Studia Anglistica Upsaliensia* 53. xii + 163 pp. Uppsala. ISBN 91-554-1512-1.

For those who aspired to literary fame in the period 1650–1760 originality was not an uncommon goal. Whereas many of the more eminent literary figures of the time regarded themselves as the loyal custodians of the classical tradition they had inherited, to a large section of the reading public and those authors who sought to gratify its demands, the secular and aristocratic bias of this legacy, its elements of fantasy and outworn folktale, and its cosmopolitan, non-English inclination were unacceptable. Often ill-equipped by either education or tradition to understand or appreciate the languages and literatures of Greece and Rome, this new group of readers and authors sought a poetry which would reflect their immediate concerns and interests. Gripped with a desire to assert their own identity, they preferred to exploit more accessible resources. To this end they looked to the Bible and related religious themes, the discoveries of science, a new appreciation of nature and, lastly, the very mind of man itself. Their preoccupation with the originality of these subjects found a frequent airing in Prefaces, Apologias and Treatises, as well as in the poetry itself. These theories of originality are discussed and illustrated. It emerges that the urge to be original, to cast off the burden of the past, was expressed, not, of course, by a consolidated group, school or movement, but by a multitude of individuals. Their achievement may have fallen short of their ambition but they were far from being a few eccentric revolutionaries. Indeed, their efforts were greeted with interest and pleasure by an enthusiastic public. Their theories of originality and contempt for the practice of literary imitation were taken up and further explored by the "popular press", an influential arbiter of public taste. Consequently, it may truly be said that the Neo-Classical Age was equally, an Age of Experiment.

Patricia Phillips, Department of English, Uppsala University, Box 513, S-751 20 Uppsala, Sweden

Printed in Sweden by
Borgströms Tryckeri AB, Motala 1984

iv

For My Mother
May Phillips
who showed the way

Contents

Acknowledgements

It was the late Dr. Adina Forsgren who first aroused my interest in the eighteenth century and I deeply regret that she never saw this work completed.

Professor Gunnar Sorelius has been helpful throughout, and I should like to thank him for his patience, advice and support. Dr. Sven-Johan Spånberg kindly read the draft manuscript and made useful comments. At an early stage Dr. Anne Clauss and Dr. Henrik Rosenmeier of the University of Copenhagen read a long and, I'm afraid, dull chapter.

I am indebted to the University of Uppsala for a most generous research fellowship and travel grant without which this book might never have been finished. The librarian at the English Institute, University of Copenhagen, Mr. Gorm Røde, and the library committee proveded me with microfilms and other necessary facilities.

I wish to thank the Bodleian, the British Library, and Oxford University English Faculty Library, Oxford City Central Library and the library of Trinity College Dublin; in California, the Lancaster Public Library, the library of the California Institute of the Arts and especially, the Huntington Library for the scholarly hospitality of its staff and readers.

To Davíd Erlingsson I owe thanks for much robust criticism—not only of my work.

I am especially grateful to my mother-in-law, Betty Mills, who carefully and uncomplainingly read the whole work in proof.

Lastly, to Stephen Mills who helped me proof-read, excised many an ambiguity, always encouraged—and often distracted—thank you.

Preface

The earliest English dictionaries define "original" as simply the first beginning, the fountain head, or, occasionally, as the first draft of a writing. The
familiar modern connotation of independently creative and non-imitative
does not occur—not even in Johnson's *Dictionary*. Indeed, the *OED* itself
dates this meaning to 1756 and the first appearance of the substantive
"originality" to 1787.

Yet, as those short chapters in standard literary histories devoted to
"rebels", "revolutionary tendencies" or "pre-Romantic elements" reveal,
the attractions of the concept had been felt much earlier.

In this study, I wish to examine this interest in originality, to discover
what forms it took and how widely it appealed. To this end I have restricted
myself to those authors for whom the pursuit of originality was a conscious
choice and whose purpose was clearly articulated. The natural conclusion to
the period studied was the publication of Edward Young's *Conjectures on
Original Composition* (1759), the first examination of the subject to use both
"original" and "originality" freely in text and title. Selecting the starting
point was more difficult, since this is a topic of perennial interest. The
choice of 1650 was encouraged by the publication in that year of D'Avenant's
Preface to *Gondibert*, which, in its contemporary appeal on the grounds of
originality, marks at least one satisfactory beginning.

Manifestations of this interest in originality are to be found, not always in
the works of those great figures with whom the age has become closely
identified but in other names, now obscure for the most part, who in their
own day, however, commanded a popular and appreciative audience. Now
relegated, in many cases, to the footnotes of the period, it is in their studied
efforts to achieve something new that the anatomy of the idea of originality
is most clearly evident.

It has not been my intention to question their views, or to assess their
contributions, but simply to highlight their aspirations. In this I have
followed the advice of R. S. Crane. In "On the Writing of the History of
English Criticism 1650–1800", he suggested that the historian's role was to
"exhibit critics speaking for themselves with respect to problems not set for
them, after the event, by the historian but such as they themselves had

formulated in the process of solving them''. Nor, he continued, should he attempt to impose on them criteria of praise and blame based on a "demand for uniformity to a particular idea of excellence in criticism'' but should rest his analysis "solely on an estimate of how much different critics were able to accomplish with the principles, devices, and materials at their disposal''.[1]

In my survey of theories of originality, I confine myself to suggested alternatives to the subjects permitted by classical precedent. These were drawn from religion, science, nature and the mind of man himself. After a very brief appraisal of the conditions which favoured the growing interest in originality, I devote one chapter to each of these topics. In the final chapter, an examination of a selection of literary journals of the period reveals the extent of the general interest in originality. At the same time, the foolhardy nature of any attempt to impose a strict chronological pattern on the ideas examined becomes apparent. No "original school'' or "movement'' can be discerned. These ideas were adopted, exploited and often dropped by some, only to be as enthusiastically revived by others. What is certain, however, is the Age's undiminishing interest in the question of originality and its tendency to single out that quality for the highest praise. Far from merely enticing the demented few—precursors of a new, enlightened age—approval of originality was the stock-in-trade of the commercial journalist, a sure indication of broad popularity.

P. P.
Oxford, December 1983

[1] *UTQ*, 22 (1952), p. 391.

Introduction

In 1710, the third Earl of Shaftesbury examined the health of contemporary poetry and concluded:

... since the Age is now so far advanc'd; Learning establish'd; the rules of Writing stated; and the Truth of Art so well apprehended, and everywhere confess'd and own'd; 'Tis strange to see our *Writers* so unshapen still and monstrous in their Works, as heretofore. ... they perform as ill as ever, and with as little regard to those profess'd *Rules of Art,* as the honest BARDS, their Predecessors, who have heard of no such *Rules,* or at least never own'd their Justice or Validity.[1]

Yet this is the Age that after-generations have regarded as the zenith of Neo-Classicism when knowledge and appreciation of "Learning" and "the Rules of Writing" could be taken for granted—when those who ignored them could be lightly dismissed as ignorant, eccentric or anachronistic.

It is certainly true that many of the great and not a few of the hacks, earnestly recommended the principle of imitation and the practice of the rules as the most perfect, the most successful or the most expedient mode of composition.[2] But, it seems, very many more fought shy of such restraints.[3]

---

[1] *Soliloquy: or Advice to an Author* (1710), pp. 106–107. Shaftesbury's opinion was a popular one. It was even incorporated, unacknowledged, in Thomas Nevile's *Remarks on Mr. Mann's Elfrida* (1752), p. 60.

[2] Two articles that have been especially interesting on the reasons for the popularity of imitation are Bernard Weinberg, "L'Imitation au XVIe et au XVIIe Siècles" in *Actes du Ive Congrès de l'Association Internationale de Littérature Comparée. Fribourg. 1964,* ed. F. Jost (The Hague, 1966) and A. O. Lovejoy, "The Parallel between Deism and Classicism" in *MP,* 29 (1931–32), 281–299. See also C. C. Green, *The Neo-Classical Theory of Tragedy* (Cam. Mass., 1934), pp. 68–75 and C. S. Baldwin, *Renaissance Literary Theory and Practice* (N. Y. 1939). Charles Gildon was one of the better-known hacks who attempted to codify the chaos of the Rules once and for all in *The Complete Art of Poetry,* 2 vols. (1718). See, in particular, I, 130–131 and passim. See also Thomas Rymer's Preface to the Translation of Rapin's *Reflections on Aristotle's Treatise of Poesie* (1674) in *The Critical Works of Thomas Rymer,* ed. Curt A. Zimansky (New Haven, 1956), p. 3; Sir Richard Blackmore, *Preface to Prince Arthur* (1695) in *Critical Essays of the Seventeenth Century* ed. J. A. Spingarn (Oxford, 1908–9, rpt. 1957), III, 234 (hereafter referred to as Spingarn) and *Taste. An Essay. By J. S. D. S. P.,* 2nd. ed. (1739), p. 26.

[3] Opposition to the dictatorship of the Ancients was not an unknown phenomenon. A long established dissent from their authority, based on a lively historical sense of their value, already existed. See the writings of Minturno, Castelvetro, Cinthio, Lope de Vega, and

Shaftesbury believed that these authors were merely giving way to untutored public demand—and indeed, he was right.[4] The Age which he observed so closely, was one of confidence and optimism.[5] The past, it was felt, should no longer dominate the present. When people looked back, they saw not a golden, but a very dark age indeed—a time from which little that was valuable or relevant to the perfection of the present could be gleaned.[6]

The older notion that the passage of time portended the decay of the world was waning in the face of what was felt to be substantial evidence to the

---

Guarnini in *Literary Criticism—Plato to Dryden,* ed. Allan H. Gilbert (N. Y. 1940). See also J. E. Spingarn, *A History of Literary Criticism in the Renaissance* (1899; 2nd. ed. N. Y., 1908), Part 1, Ch. VI; Part 2, Ch. III and Part 3, Ch. IV. Working dramatists e.g. Harrington, Daniel, Ben Jonson, Webster and Dryden in England and Corneille in France, were in the forefront of the opposition. They found the demands of contemporary audiences to be a safer guide to success than the dictates of the past. See, *Elizabethan Critical Essays,* ed., Gregory G. Smith (Oxford, 1904) and vol. I of Spingarn's *Critical Essays of the Seventeenth Century.* See also, Felix E. Schelling, "Ben Jonson and the Classical School," *PMLA,* 13 (1898), 221–249; John C. Sherwood, "Dryden and the Rules: The Preface to *Troilus and Cressida,*" CL, 2 (1950), 73–83; and "Dryden and the Critical Theories of Tasso," *CL,* 18 (1966), 351–359; Mary Thale, "Dryden's Dramatic Criticism: Polestar of the Ancients," *CL,* 18 (1966), 36–54.

[4] *Soliloquy,* pp. 107–108. Many authors and, in particular, dramatists were agreed on the changed nature of the times and the need to experiment. See for example: Sir Robert Howard, Preface to *The Great Favourite* (1668); E. H. [Edward Howard], Preface to *The Woman's Conquest* (1671), sig. A3r-v; John Dryden, *Heads of an Answer to Rymer* (written in 1677 or 1678 and first printed in 1711. See notes to the *Heads* in *The Works of John Dryden, Prose 1668–1691,* ed. S. H. Monk (Berkeley, Los Angeles and London, 1971), XVII, 185–193 and 411–417; Abraham Cowley, Preface to *Pindaric Odes* (1677), p. 19; Samuel Butler, *Upon Critics who judge Modern Plays etc.* (1678); Charles Gildon, "An Essay at a Vindication of Love in Tragedies, against Rapin and Mr Rymer. Directed to Mr Dennis" in *Miscellaneous Letters ... on Several Subjects* (1694), pp. 145–171. (In this essay Gildon was much more of a "Modern" than in his later advocacy of the rules in *The Complete Art of Poetry.* See note 2 above); George Farquhar, *A Discourse upon Comedy* (1702) in *Works,* 2nd. ed. (1711), II, 72–73; John Hughes, "Remarks on The Fairy Queen" in *The Works of Edmund Spenser* (1715), I, lix-lxi; *Some Remarks on the Tragedy of Hamlet, Prince of Denmark* 1736 (Augustan Reprint Society, September 1947, Series 3, no. 3); John Campbell, *The Rational Amusement* (1754), pp. 257–58; Richard Hurd, *Letters on Chivalry and Romance* (1762), ed. E. J. Morley 1911), p. 154.

[5] See, for example, the weekly Whig newspaper, *The Honest Gentleman* No. XVII (Wednesday, February 25 1718).

[6] See, for example, Sir Thomas Pope Blount who used both God and Nature to twist the arguments of the conservatives and prove the contrary of the "Opinion so universally believed" that "the World doth daily decline": Essay V, *"Whether the Men of this present AGE, are anyway Inferiour to those of former Ages etc."* and Essay IV, "Of the Ancients: The Respect that is due to 'em: That we should not too much enslave ourselves to their Opinions" in which Blount proposes that Truth and the Ancients are not synonymous. Both essays are in *Essays on Several Subjects,* 3rd. ed. (1697), pp. 144–145; p. 121; see also Joshua Poole, *The English Parnassus* (1657). The preface by one "J. D." is a staunch defence of contemporary English poetry on the grounds that the Moderns possess as much genius and wit as the Ancients.

2

contrary.[7] It seems certain that the growing ignorance and indifference to the classics, to be detected among the fast increasing reading public, in no small measure contributed to this nonchalance.[8]

In addition, the fact that much that concerned the Rules had received the French imprimatur was enough to alienate those committed to the national character. This was an Age of Pride—English pride. All that was foreign and, in particular, French, was fast becoming anathema to John Bull.[9] He rejoiced in his independence, both political and literary, and revelled in his sense of superiority.[10] It was his pleasure to proclaim himself a true original, firmly rooted in native English tradition, gloriously free of the shackles of the past and indifferent to the enervating winds that blew across the Channel.[11]

[7] For the belief in the theory of the decay of the world see, R. F. Jones, *Ancients and Moderns. A Study of the Background of the Battle of the Books,* (St. Louis, 1936); Gordon L. Davies, "The Concept of Denudation in Seventeenth-Century England," *JHI,* 27 (1966), 278–284.

[8] Attempts were made to remedy or improve this classical ignorance. One such effort was Dr. William King's *An Historical Account of the Heathen Gods and Heroes; Necessary for the Understanding of the Ancient Poets* (1711). This was a handbook especially designed for those who were obliged to read the classics in translation. In his preface, Dr. King took into account another objection to the classics, "The Heathen Pretences to Divinity are sufficiently expos'd by the Fathers, and therefore it is not to be expected that they should be confuted here, it not being the Business of the Place" (p. 1).

[9] For a cross-section of this opinion see, Charles Gildon, *Modern Poets against the Ancients* (1694) in *Critical Essays of the XVIIIth Century,* ed. W. H. Durham (New Haven, 1915), pp. 16–17; William Congreve, *An Essay Concerning Humour in Comedy to Mr. Dennis* (July 10, 1695); Ambrose Philips, *A Reflection on our Modern Poesy* (1695); Elkanah Settle, *Farther Defence of Dramatick Poetry* (1698); Thomas Purney, Preface to *Pastorals* (1717) in *Works,* ed. H. O. White (Oxford, 1933); Matthew Prior's patriotic "I had rather be thought a good Englishman, than the best Poet, or greatest Scholar that ever wrote" in the Preface to the equally patriotic *Solomon or the Vanity of the World* in *Poems on Several Occasions* (1718); Corbyn Morris, *An Essay towards Fixing the True Standards of Wit, Humour, Raillery, Satire, and Ridicule* 1744 (Augustan Reprint Society, 1947); Joseph Warton, *Adventurer* 133 1754 (Augustan Reprint Society, 1946); Adam Smith, "A Letter to the Authors of the *Edinburgh Review*" in *The Early Writings of Adam Smith,* ed. T. R. Lindgren (N. Y., 1967); Isaac Hawkins Browne, *The Immortality of the Soul* (1754), p. 7; Roger Comberbach, *A Dispute; consisting of a Preface in Favour of Blank Verse* (1755), Preface, p. ii. On the other hand, André Rouquet maintained that the English tended to be more "confined to the rules of reasoning", adept at science and commerce but with limited imaginations. See, *The Present State of the Arts in England* (1755), p. 21.

[10] David Hume, *A Treatise of Human Nature* (1739), p. xxi.

[11] For strong opinions on the differences between English and French creativity see, [Thomas Baker], *Reflections upon Learning,* 3rd. ed. [1700], p. 47; Elkanah Settle, *Farther Defense* etc. (1698), p. 33, quoted in *The Critical Works of John Dennis,* ed. E. N. Hooker (Baltimore, 1939, 1943), II, 454 (hereafter referred to as Hooker) see also Hooker, I, 482 and Thomas Purney, *Works,* p. 47 (see note 9 above). For opinions on innate English originality see Congreve and Warton, note 9 above. See also: E. L. Mann, "The Problem of Originality in English Literary Criticism 1750–1800," *PQ,* 18 (1939), 97–118.

The principle of literary imitation was founded on that well-known belief that nature was universal and immutable; that it had been best observed and represented by the Ancients; that it was, therefore, reasonable to follow their example closely.[12] But doubts as to the validity of this definition of nature were increasing. A new theory of nature was posited—one that allowed for endless variations and permutations.[13]

---

[12] The equation of Nature and the Ancients was the cornerstone of the theory of imitation and was repeated incessantly by all who aspired to the name of critic. Dryden wrote, " . . . both the poets and the painters in ancient times, and in the best ages have studied her [Nature] and from the practice of both these arts the rules have been drawn by which we are instructed how to please, and to encompass that which they obtained, by following their example", *A Parallel of Poetry and Painting* (1695) in *Essays of John Dryden*, ed. W. P. Ker (1900; rpt. N. Y. 1961), II, 139 (hereafter known as Ker); *Preface to Albion and Albanius* (1685) in *The Works of John Dryden*, ed. H. T. Swedenberg, Jr. et. al. Berkley, L. A. London, 1976), XV, 4 (hereafter known as *Works*). (But for a much freer and more generous analysis of the role of imitation in literary creation, see the "Heads of an Answer to Rymer" (1677), *Works*, XVII, 185–193; Dedication to *Love Triumphant* (1694) in *Works*, VIII, 374; Dedication of the *Æneis* (1699) in Ker, II, 199–200. See also his justification of the originality of the figure of Caliban in Preface to *Trolius and Criseida* (1697), Ker, I, 219.) See further the references to Dryden in Note 3 above. John Dennis also, on occasion, insisted on the justificaion of the rules on the grounds of Nature. For example, "The Rules are nothing but an observation of Nature. For Nature is rule and order itself", *Letters upon Several Occasions* (1696). See also, John Oldmixon, *An Essay on Criticism* (1728): "The Rules laid down by those great Criticks are not to be valu'd, because they are given by *Aristotle, Horace* etc. but because they are in Nature and in Truth . . . for we do not judge so because *Aristotle* and *Horace* did so judge; but because it is in Nature and in Truth, and they first showed us the way to find it out" (p. 3); *An Essay Concerning Critical and Curious Learning*, 1698 (Augustan Reprint Society, 113, 1965), pp. 26–27 and pp. 31–32; Charles Gildon, *The Complete Art of Poetry* (1718), I, 112 and 124 and passim; John Constable, *Reflections upon Accuracy of Style* (1731), p. 79. The best known formula is, of course, 11. 88–89 in Pope's *An Essay on Criticism*. For a discussion on the multifarious definitions of "Nature", consult A. O. Lovejoy's "'Nature' as Aesthetic Norm," *MLN*, 42 (1927), 444–450 rpt. in *Essays in the History of Ideas* (Baltimore, 1948), pp. 69–77). For the ways in which Aristotelian mimesis was transmuted into Neo-Classical imitation, see J. W. Draper, "Aristotelian Mimesis in England," *PMLA*, 36 (1921), 372–400.

[13] See, for example, Henry Felton, *A Dissertation on Reading the Classics and Forming a Just Style* (1709, publ. 1713), p. 44; Samuel Cobb, *A Discourse on Criticism* from *Poems on Several Occasions 1707* introd. Louis I. Bredvold, (Augustan Reprint Society, 1946); John Armstrong, "Of Imitation", Sketch XIII in *Sketches; or Essays on Various Subjects by Launcelot Temple, Esq. In Two Volumes*, VIII (*Harrison's British Classicks*, 1787), p. 15; William Melmoth the Younger, *Letters on Several Subjects, By the late Sir. Tho. Fitzosborne Bart.* (1748), pp. 5–6. The authority of *Longinus: On the Sublime*, an influence in English criticism at least since the time of Dryden's Preface to *Trolius and Criseida* (1697), not only permitted a new theory of the passions to evolve, but encouraged the equation between literary merit and the quality of the individual mind which attempted to produce it. For the popularity and the history of English translations of Longinus, see A. F. Clark, *Boileau and the French Classical Criticism in England* (Paris, 1925), pp. 364–369. See also, S. H. Monk, *The Sublime: A Study of Critical Theories in XVIII-Century England* (New York, 1935), pp. 18–22. All quotations from Longinus in my text are from *Longinus: On the Sublime* in *Classical Literary Criticism*, tr. T. S. Dorsch. Harmondsworth, England, 1965.

It needed only the growing suspicion of the genesis of the rules and a concomitant impatience with the restraints imposed by the principle of imitation to persuade authors to look in new directions for inspiration.[14] Writers of this frame of mind were as confident of their own abilities as the oft-quoted spider whose entrails supplied the materials with which to spin.[15]

In this new scheme of things, the faculty of the Imagination played an influential role. Traditionally distrusted and feared, it was now regarded as equal, or occasionally, superior to Reason and Judgment.[16] The ascendancy of the Imagination had its roots in a literary tradition, as venerable as the tradition of imitation, that regarded the poetic Imagination as God-like.[17] It was this tradition which conspired to undermine the position of the Ancients

[14] See, for example, Henry Felton, pp. vii-viii; Joseph Trapp, *Lectures on Poetry Read in the Schools of Natural Philosophy at Oxford* (1711, trans. 1742), p. 263, Leonard Welsted, *A Dissertation Concerning the Perfection of the English Language prefixed to Epistles, Odes, etc. Written on Several Subjects* (1714, 2nd. ed. 1725), p. xvii and passim.; Henry Pemberton, *Observations on Poetry, especially the Epic* (1738), pp. 1–2, quoted by Swedenberg, "Rules and English Critics of the Epic, 1650–1800," *SP*, 35 (1938), 566–587; see also Joseph Spence's letter to Samuel Richardson in *The Correspondence of Samuel Richardson* (1804), II, 319–27 quoted in Austin Wright, *Joseph Spence. A Critical Biography* (Chicago, 1950), p. 122; Oliver Goldsmith, *An Enquiry into the Present State of Polite Learning* (1759), p. 22. See also, R. S. Crane, "A Neglected Mid-Eighteenth Century Plea for Originality and its Author," *PQ*, 13 (1934), p. 22.

[15] Bacon's use of this image was probably responsible for its popularity. See, *Novum Organum* in *Works*, ed. James Spedding et al. (1870; rpt. N. Y., 1968), IV, 92–93. Swift's uncomplimentary reference to the spider in St. James's Library is well-known. See *A Full and True Account of the Battel . . . between the . . . Books . . .* (1710) in *A Tale of a Tub with Other Early Works 1696–1707*, ed. Herbert Davis (Oxford, 1939), pp. 147–150. Leonard Welsted, on the other hand, compared the original poet who draws his inspiration from himself to the silkworm who "spins out of her own bowels that soft ductile substance which is wrought into so great a Variety of Ornaments" (*A Dissertation*, p. xxxviii).

[16] See, e.g., Margaret Cavendish, Duchess of Newcastle, "The Mine of Wit" in *Poems and Fancies* (1653), p. 154; Howard's Preface to *The Duke of Lerma* (1668) quoted in Bonamy Dobrée, *English Literature in the Early Eighteenth Century 1700–1740* (Oxford, 1959), p. 335; Spence's letter to Richardson in Note 14 above; *Taste. An Essay. By J. S. D. S. P.*, 2nd. ed. (1739), p. 24. Fear of the imagination is well summarised in Robert Burton's *The Anatomy of Melancholy*, 2nd. ed. (Oxford, 1624), pp. 78–83. For the debate on the imagination during the eighteenth century and earlier, see M. W. Bundy, *The Theory of Imagination in Classical and Medieval Thought*, XII, (University of Illinois Studies in Language and Literature, May-August, 1927), nos. 2–3; Bundy, "'Invention' and 'Imagination' in the Renaissance," *JEGP*, 29 (1930), 535–545; Louis I. Bredvold, "The Tendency toward Platonism in Neo-Classical Esthetics," *ELH*, 1 (1934), 91–119; D. F. Bond, "'Distrust' of Imagination in English Neo-Classicism," *PQ*, 14 (1935), 54–69; Bond, "The Neo-Classical Psychology of the Imagination," *ELH*, 4 (1937), 245–264; F. R. Johnson, "Elizabethan Drama and the Elizabethan Science of Psychology," *English Studies Today*, eds. C. L. Wrenn and G. Bullough (Oxford, 1951), pp. 111–119; William Rossky, "Imagination in the English Renaissance: Psychology and Poetic," *Studies in the Renaissance*, 5 (1958), 49–73.

[17] See the definitions of poetic genius in, e.g., Samuel Wesley, *Epistle to a Friend Concerning Poetry 1700* (Augustan Reprint Society, 1947), p. 2 and in Shaftesbury, *Soliloquy* (1710), p. 54.

as models for imitation for all succeeding generations. It disputed the narrow definition of truth and the superior role assigned to Reason in poetry that imitation of their works was thought to involve.[18] In this tradition, the Imagination suffers none of the limitations imposed by the joint forces of Reason and Judgment, but enjoys a perfect autonomy.[19] Its careful nurture eventually becomes the key to the development of that typically eighteenth-century phenomenon—the original genius.

It needed very little to persuade the reading public that it was solely the exercise of the Imagination that counted in the appreciation of literature. Within twelve months of Shaftesbury's pronouncement on the shortcomings of author and audience, another literary spokesman of the Age, Joseph Addison, was inculcating his readers with a distaste for the order and regularity which the principle of imitation imposed.[20] In their place he offered the cultivation of an indefinable "something more essential" which would work on and pleasingly disturb the emotions of the reader. Neither his Reason nor his Judgment was to be involved. Learning and the rules of writing are lightly dismissed.[21]

What was it, then, that the new readers wanted? Who were these authors, who, as Shaftesbury acidulously put it "would be *all* Genius" and in which directions did they turn in order to satisfy the inclinations of their readers and of themselves.[22]

Some of the answers will be found, hidden among the fumbling intentions expressed in the "prefix'd Apologies", "Epistles Dedicatory, Prefaces and

[18] The kind of poetry abhorred by authors of this stamp was that covered by Dryden's famous definition of wit: "A propriety of thoughts and words, or, in other terms, thoughts and words elegantly adapted to the Subject", *The Author's Apology for Heroic Poetry and Poetic Licence* prefixed to *The State of Innocence* (1677), Ker, I, 190. (Dryden defined wit differently on other occasions. See Gunnar Sorelius, *The Giant Race before the Flood* (Uppsala, 1966), pp. 97–99). Addison thought this definition was more appropriate to Euclid, *Spectator* 62 in *Spectator*, ed. Donald F. Bond, 5 vols. (Oxford, 1965) (referred to hereafter as Bond), I, 267. See also the comments of Corbyn Morris, *An Essay towards Fixing the True Standards of Wit, Humour, Raillery, Satire and Ridicule* 1744 (Augustan Reprint Society, Series 1, No, 4, November, 1947), p. xi-xv. See the introduction by James L. Clifford for the importance of this essay.

[19] See for example, Thomas Warton, *Observations on the Faerie Queene* (1754), pp. 12–13; Joseph Warton, *Essay on the Writings and Genius of Pope,* Part I (1756), pp. ii-iii; John Gregory, *A Comparative View of the State and Faculties of Men* (1761, publ. 1765), pp. 128 ff.

[20] In particular in the essay on the differences between the natural and imitative genius in *Spectator* 160 (1711) and also in the essays on the Imagination, *Spectator* 411– (June 21, 1712)—*Spectator* 421 (Juli 3, 1712), Bond, III, 535–582. See below, pp. 122–127.

[21] *Spectator* 409, Bond, III, 530.

[22] "Miscellany V" in *Characteristics of Men, Manners, and Opinions*, III (1711), 258–259.

Addresses to the Reader" to which Shaftesbury took such exception.[23] Other clues can be gleaned from that most telling source of all—the popular press. From these it will be possible to construct at least a partial picture of the early beginnings of a new aesthetic in literary criticism.

[23] *Soliloquy*, p. 48.

Chapter 1

Divine Poetry: "an unattempted Course"

"Neo-Classical" poetry was not the characteristic expression of the age that bears this label. It was the voice of the small, but exclusive and influential, elite which had inherited the classical legacy of the Renaissance—a legacy that was secular, esoteric and aristocratic. At least since the time of Elizabeth, their literary efforts had revelled in the poetry and fables of the Ancients. This intemperance did not go unnoticed or uncriticised. In his history of the period, Thomas Warton noted disapprovingly that "everything was tinctured with antient history and mythology", so much so that the "perpetual allusions to antient fable were often introduced without the least regard to propriety".[1]

It was not only the lack of propriety that offended. The poetry of scintillating satire and brilliant wit that the new Ancients produced did little to assuage the longings of those cut off by birth, religion or inclination from this literary tradition.[2] Their distaste for it is aptly summarised in the title of one G. Potter's "A commendacion of true poetry and a discommendacion of all baudy, pybald and paganizde poets etc." (1594).[3] For poetry to be acceptable at all in these circles, it had to be *true* poetry, that is, poetry which concerned itself with Christian themes and man's search for salvation. It alone escaped the censure of serious men.[4] Even in the eighteenth

---

[1] *The History of English Poetry from the close of the 11th to the Commencement of the 18th Century,* (1781), III, 492 and 494.

[2] Numerous books and translations of the Ancients were banned by Whitgift and Bancroft during Elizabeth's reign; efforts were made by her Privy Council to substitute acceptable works such as Christopher Ocland's *Anglorum Praelia* and *Elizabetha* for some of the classical poets in the school curriculum. Thomas Sternhold and John Hopkins made the translation of the Psalms that provoked the wrath of John Dennis, Isaac Watts and many others. The trend continued during the seventeenth century when the opportunity arose. After the brief halcyon period of the Restoration, the controversy resumed with Jeremy Collier, see Spingarn, I, lxxxi-lxxxvii and III, 253–291.

[3] *The History of English Poetry,* III, 448.

[4] Sir Leslie Stephen attributed this interest to a thirst for spiritual solace which could not be quenched by the acceptable, but emotionally arid, religion of the established church: "Every creed decays, or certainly the creed decayed in this instance, as it became incapable of satisfying the instinct of various classes of the population, and the perception of its logical defects was the consequence, not the cause of its gradual breakup. It was not that men

century what pleased most generally was poetry with a religious theme. Milton's shorter poems were neglected, but there were over 100 editions of *Paradise Lost* compared with 50 of Shakespeare and 7 of *The Faerie Queene*.[5] Isaac Watts's *Horae Lyricae* reached 50 editions and his *Hymns* were still selling at a rate of 50,000 copies a year at the beginning of the nineteenth century. The works of such long forgotten names as Thomas Ellwood, Benjamin Keach and John Mason went into several editions, and the divine poems of that butt of the Wits, Sir Richard Blackmore, moved the hearts of great men from Addison to Dr. Johnson.[6]

This popular inclination was soon accompanied by a growing awareness of the purely aesthetic qualities of sacred scripture.[7] In his hierarchical arrangement of poetry, Sir Philip Sidney had assigned as the greatest poetry "both in antiquity and excellence" that which "did imitate the inconceivable excellencies of God". He had judged the psalms of David as one of the most perfect examples of this high genre. Significantly for what was to come, he had grouped these divine poets with the other group of "right poets", they "which most properly do imitate to teach and delight, and to imitate, borrow nothing of what is, hath been, or shall be; but range, only reined with learned discretion, into divine consideration of what may be and should be". Both share the honour of the title of *vates*.[8]

---

perceived a new method of meeting Hume's scepticism, or the deistical arguments of Shaftesbury or Tindal; but that the Deism and Scepticism were alike unable to supply satisfactory answers to the questions which men asked or a satisfactory language in which to clothe their emotions", *History of English Thought in the 18th Century*, 3rd. ed. (1927), II, 382.

[5] R. D. Havens, *The Influence of Milton on English Poetry* (Cambridge, Mass., 1922), pp. 4–5; 403.

[6] See note 21, p. 16 below.

[7] See Israel Baroway, "The Bible as Poetry in the English Renaissance: An Introduction," *JEGP*, 32 (1933), 447–481. For French interest in the Bible as literature see René Bray, *La Formation de la Doctrine Classique en France* (Paris, 1931), pp. 289–302 and R. A. Sayce, *The French Biblical Epic in the Seventeenth Century* (Oxford, 1955).

[8] *The Defence of Poesie* (1583) in *Literary Criticism from Plato to Dryden*, ed. A. H. Gilbert (N. Y., 1940), pp. 414–415. Sidney considered those poets who wrote of what scientists were subsequently to dub as "truth", or, in Sidney's words, "Matters philosophical; either moral ... or natural ... or astronomical ... or historical", as inferior to those "who having no law but wit, bestow that in colours upon you which is fittest for the eye to see". Not everyone agreed: see below Ch. 2, pp. 46 ff. Among the extensive bibliography of divine poetry the following were most helpful: A. A. Perdeck, *Theology in Augustan Literature* (Groningen, Den Haag, 1928); Thomas F. Mayo, *Epicurus in England 1650–1725* (Dallas, Texas, 1934); Sister M. K. Whelan, *Enthusiasm in English Poetry in the Eighteenth Century* (Washington, D. C., 1936); Basil Willey, *The Seventeenth-Century Background* (1936); Hoxie Neale Fairchild, *Religious Trends in English Poetry*, 2 vols. (N. Y., 1939, 1942); J. B. Broadbent, *Some Graver Subject* (1966). On the poetry of the literary elite see A. O. Lovejoy, "The Parallel of Deism and Classicism," *MP*, 29 (1931–32), 281–299; George Williamson, "The Restoration Revolt against Enthusiasm," *SP*, 30 (1933), 571–603; James Sutherland, *English Literature in the late Seventeenth Century* (Oxford, 1948; rpt. 1962).

The more conscious men became of the imaginative qualities of the Bible, the more they compared it favourably with the standard of literary excellence represented by the classics. To the advocates of this view the Bible appeared as a veritable treasure house of subject matter, verse forms, images and the rhetorical sublime. Enfranchised by their conviction that God's word was itself poetry, poets like Cowley, Woodford, and Watts took a determined stand against those who distrusted all poetic expression as well as those representatives of the literary establishment who disapproved of or disliked religious poetry. They professed a determination to restore to poetry something of its original integrity and power, to re-enlist it in the service of religion and to shake of the dross of classicism and hedonism which seemed to them to mark the writings of their more secular brethren. They insisted that theirs was the greater poetry because its themes were more serious and "truthful" than classical subjects; (their popularity in their own time and later, attests to the fact that their devoted readers agreed).

They also made another and, for literary history, more important claim. Whatever may have been their spiritual motives in choosing to write divine poetry, many authors were not unaware of its attractions as a new and original field. For poets who sought freedom and originality, for whom the burden of classicism was too great, divine poetry was one of the earliest and most important ways in which they could assert their individuality and declare themselves independent of tradition. Their choice was deliberate and selfconscious. Self-styled "divine" poets often wished to be regarded as original poets.

Before examining those authors who sought originality in divine poetry it may be helpful to review the opinions of Milton who did not share their concern with originality, but whose great epic, the noblest divine poem of the age, was long regarded as a worthy example by the champions of originality. Milton differs from his admirers in that he was able, without apparent difficulty, to combine with his Puritan beliefs, a profound knowledge and love of classical literature and an elevated notion of the dignity of the poet. His conception of the function of the poet may explain this paradox, for unlike many of those adhering to the Platonic-Renaissance tradition of the *vates*, who emphasised the aspect of inspiration, he chose to stress the civil elements. In his well-known Preface to the second book of *Reason of Church Government,* this is what takes precedence. The poet's function is to inculcate virtue by precept and example; to calm and direct the passions and emotions of the mind; to sing the glory of God; to celebrate the deeds and sufferings of his true followers; and lastly, Milton's own contribution to the tradition, "Whatsoever in religion is holy and sublime, in vertu amiable, or grave, whatsoever hath passion or admiration in all the changes

10

of that which is call'd fortune from without, or the wily suttleties and refluxes of mans [sic] thoughts from within, all these things with a solid and treatable smoothnesse to paint out and describe".[9] By omitting any reference to purely literary qualities in this uncompromisingly severe account of the function of the poet, Milton would have gone far in placating the wariest of his Puritan readers.

Contrary to what might have been expected of a Puritan apologist, Milton does not weigh classical literature against the Bible, at least not in this early Preface.[10] He was too much of a classicist for that. At this, admittedly early, stage in his career, he displays none of the antipathy towards classical writings evident in other writers of divine poetry. Instead, he appears to judge the merits of the Bible and the Ancients as equal, though different. In his discussion of the literary kinds, he takes his examples not only from the classics, but also from the Bible and sixteenth-century Italian Christian poetry. Though this may have been to soothe the suspicions of his Puritan readers, it is more likely that Milton regarded all these as examples of the Ideal Genres of Epic, Tragedy and the Greater Ode.[11] These Ideals exist independent of specific cultures or periods. Milton did not believe that any one culture or country could lay claim to superiority. Such diverse literatures as the Hebraic, Graeco-Roman or the Renaissance Italian could all produce examples of the Ideal.

The same sense of perspective is evident when Milton sets himself the question "whether the rules of Aristotle ... are strictly to be kept, or nature to be follow'd, which in them that know art, and use judgment is no transgression, but an inriching of art" (p. 813). It becomes a matter of choice. In Milton there is neither a superstitious reverence for the code of rules nor an outright rejection of it. Subject matter, not preconceived restrictions, dictates the form.

Abraham Cowley and his followers

Though *Paradise Lost* became and remained the perfect model of a divine poem, Milton's complex view of tradition and the individual talent made

---

[9] *Complete Prose Works*, I (New Haven, 1953), p. 817. The Preface was written in January or February 1642.

[10] But see *Paradise Regained*, Bk. IV, ll. 331–342.

[11] Some modern scholars appear to suspect Milton's motives. See, for example, William R. Parker, "On Milton's Early Literary Program," *MP*, 33 (1935–36), 49–53.

little impact on the eighteenth century, if, indeed, it was known at all.[12] It was the theories of Abraham Cowley that inspired poets to turn to divine themes to find new scope for originality. Cowley's prestige was high during the late seventeenth and early eighteenth centuries, and his opinions and poetic practice are frequently cited by his admirers.[13] Though never completed, his Christian epic, *Davideis* (1668) was fairly popular for a time, but it is his remarks on the new genre that had greatest significance for later theorists.[14] Their clarity and simplicity is such that it is not difficult to understand why they were seized on and transformed into a literary programme to be repeated by one divine poet after another throughout the period.

Cowley aknowledges Virgil as the undisputed master of the epic form, and in so doing is as docilely imitative as the staunchest Ancient.[15] He tells the reader in his Preface that he planned his *Davideis* in twelve books, "not for the *Tribes* sake but after the *Patern* of our Master *Virgil*", and that modern authors would "do ill to forsake" the examples of Homer and Virgil "to imitate others" (pp. 86, 87). In the subject matter of epic, however, he declares himself independent of the Ancients. He takes issue with the excessive paraphernalia of classical myth and tale which, he believes, clogs to no purpose so much contemporary poetry. Not only irrelevant and out-moded, it is also responsible for the currently low reputation of poetry. For poetry, he claims somewhat dramatically, is now in bondage to the

---

[12] *The Reason of Church-Government Urg'd against Prelaty* is thought to have been published around the end of January 1642. It made little impact then and was re-issued in 1654 without even its original title page being cancelled. No allusions seem to have been made to it then, or subsequently, and its lack of significance is attested to by the fact that no separate editions occur. See John T. Shawcross, "A Survey of Milton's Prose Works" in *Achievements of the Left Hand: Essays on the Prose of John Milton,* eds. Michael Lieb and John T. Shawcross (Amherst, 1974), pp. 294–295. The influence of *Paradise Lost* was great and immediate. See, for example, Samuel Slater, Preface to *Poems in Two Parts* (1679). R. D. Havens deals with the question of Milton's influence in *The Influence of Milton on English Poetry* (1922).

[13] See Jean Loiseau, *Abraham Cowley's Reputation in England* (Paris, 1931).

[14] In Preface to *Poems* (1656), Spingarn, II, 77–90. See the enthusiastic remarks of contemporaries and later authors, for example: Daniel Baker, "On Mr Abraham Cowley's Works" in *Poems upon Several Occasions* (1697), pp. 1–2; Charles Gildon, *The Complete Art of Poetry* (1718), p. 109; Sir John Denham, "On Mr Abraham Cowley His Death, and Burial amongst The Ancient Poets" in *Poems and Translations,* 7th ed. (1769), p. 48. See also *The Present State of Poetry. A Satyr addres'd to a Friend.* By B. M., (1721), p. 6; John Husbands, *A Miscellany of Poems* (1731), sig. P3ʳ. Cowley differs from other divine poets in his Stuart loyalties. His interest in Biblical epic was probably stimulated by the controversy on the subject in France where he spent his exile during the early years of the Commonwealth.

[15] Typical "Neo-Classical" assessments of Virgil's stature as a poet are Joseph Addison's *An Essay on Virgil's Georgics* (1697) and Richard Blackmore's *Preface to Prince Arthur* (1697).

Devil who manipulates it for his own ends, as he does most of the less savoury aspects of modern society (p. 88). The results are obvious. No longer devoted to serious and other-worldly matters, poetry is degraded by sensual and libidinous themes: "The wicked and beggarly *Flattery* of great persons", "the unmanly *Idolizing* of *Foolish Women*", "the wretched affectation of scurril *Laughter*" or "the confused antiquated *Dreams* of senseless *Fables* and *Metamorphoses*" (p. 88). To restore poetry to its former greatness it will be necessary to abandon its current stock, in particular, "the *whole Body* (or rather *Chaos*) of the *Theologie*" of classical times. Modern authors, more fortunate in being of the true religion, can only "deride their *folly*" and be "wearied with their *impertinencies*". They can, therefore, be no more an inpiration to true poetry than can "their worthy *Successors, the Knights Errant*" (p. 89).

Cowley is the first influential figure in England to urge the choice of Biblical themes for their originality as well as their morality. To eschew classical myth is not only virtuous, it is also a necessity for the original poet. "For", he says feelingly, "it is almost impossible to serve up any *new Dish* of that Kinde. They are all but the *Cold-Meats* of the *Antients,* new-heated, and new set forth". Though there may once have been vitality in these themes, "the heat of the *Soil* was not then wrought out with continual *Tillage*". To the Moderns who foolishly "come a *Gleaning,* not after the first *Reapers,* but after the very *Beggars*" little remains. But, Cowley assures his readers, literary merit awaits those who choose the way to truth. After the "Regeneration" of Poetry, he promises, poets "will meet with a wonderful variety of new, more beautiful, and more delightful *Objects*", and after the bondage of the old ways they will experience a new sense of freedom and liberty; for they will never "want *Room*, by being *confined to Heaven*" (p. 88).

The immediate and extensive influence exerted by Cowley on his contemporaries is evident in the work of Samuel Woodford. An admirer of Cowley, like him a Fellow of the Royal Society and an enthusiast for divine poetry, Woodford gained a considerable reputation for himself as a poet. *The Athenian Oracle* placed him high on a list of prescribed reading, giving him precedence over both Cowley and Milton.[16] Encouraged by Cowley's work, Woodford followed his example and undertook a paraphrase of the psalms of David and the Canticles. Many of Cowley's opinions are reflected in his prefaces to these poems. Like his mentor, he claims that to identify poetry and religion is to admit its true nature:

---

[16] *The Athenian Oracle,* 3rd. ed. (1728), II, 37.

Theology and Poesy have in all ages of the World gone hand in hand, nor is there really such a disparity between their natures, as is generally, though without any reason, imagined. For if one has been lookt on as containing the Will and Pleasure, the other no less has been reckoned the Stile and Language of Heaven. Musick and Numbers, the chiefest of the Liberal Arts, serve but as Hand-maids to this great and All-commanding Mistress.[17]

A surfeit of classicism and a contempt for the ignorance of the Ancients is also evident in Woodford. But, in advocating the Bible as a source of original and, therefore, superior subject matter, he goes somewhat further than Cowley in espousing the cultivation of its purely literary aspects. He believes that a utilisation of biblical themes, to an extent equivalent to the exploitation of classical mythology, will generate a new fruitfulness of the imagination:

The Holy Bible doubtless is an excellent Soil and of such kindly nature, that if it were cultivated either as it ought, or only as the barren sand of Antiquity and all the tedious tales of the Heathenish Superstition too often have been, it would produce the greatest and most rich increase. For, besides that like them it has never yet been thoroughly broken up, the most unfruitful part of it, at least that which may seem so, abounds with inexhaustible Mines, which could plentifully reward any that should labour in them. And it were beside unreasonable to think that Palestine alone, which was so fruitful of all things else, should be barren only of Laurels.[18]

Woodford's interest in the Bible as subject matter was clearly one in which the literary implications of originality dominated any purely evangelical mission. Like many others before and after him, he found these unexploited resources both challenging and attractive.

The same is true of Samuel Wesley. A typical virtuoso in many ways, his interests were many and wide-ranging. He delved into the new science, was interested in British antiquity, and knew something of the customs, architecture and languages of the Holy Land. Reckoned a "dunce" by the Scriblerians, he had a place in the *Dispensary,* the *Battle of the Books* and the first version of the *Dunciad.* In his defence it must be said that he was possessed of a charming and refreshing disregard for traditional literary practice. In his Preface to *The Life of Our Blessed Lord and Saviour* (1694) these qualities are evident in his brief for the biblical and Christian epic in

---

[17] Preface to *A Paraphrase upon the Psalms of David* (1687), sig. A2^v.

[18] Sig. B2^v. The Bible was frequently compared favourably with the writings of the Ancients. See, for example, Benjamin Keach, Proem to *The Glorious Lover. A Divine Poem upon the Adorable Mystery of Sinners Redemption* (1679); *Spectator* 339, (1712), Bond III, 254–261; Alexander Pennucuik, Preface to "A Morning Walk to Arthur's Seat" in *Streams from Helicon,* 2nd. ed. (1720), unpag. See below, pp. 35–38.

14

which he also upheld the propriety of Christian machinery in epic.[19] This Preface, an early example of historicism in action, disputes the right of the Ancients to remain as unassailed models of perfection:

To begin with Homer, he wrote in that manner, because most of the ancient Eastern Learning, the Original of all others, was Mythology. But this being now antiquated, I cannot think that we are oblig'd superstitiously to follow his example, any more than to make Horses speak, as he does that of Achilles''. (p. 4)

Like Dennis later, he takes issue with the long-standing tradition that fiction is an essential part of the main action of epic. This outworn shibboleth is countered with the weighty argument that the truths of Christianity must surely be superior to the fables of the Ancients—even in poetry.

Wesley reserves his admiration for poets whom he deems to merit the accolade of originality. Spenser is singled out as "Natural and Lively", although "Irregular" (p. 22).

As for Milton's *Paradise Lost*, it's an Original, and indeed he seems rather above the common Rules of Epic than ignorant of them. (p. 23)

He himself espouses the cause of originality with a wholehearted enthusiasm. Anything which tends to pervert the natural inclinations of the poet is condemned with the greatest severity. In *An Epistle to a Friend Concerning Poetry* (1700), he demands:

Why should we still be *lazily content*
With threadbare *Schemes,* and nothing *new* invent?
All *Arts* besides *improve, Sea, Air* and *Land*
Are every day with *nicer Judgment* scan'd
And why should *this* alone be at a stand?
Or *Nature* largely to the *Ancients* gave
And little did for *younger Children* save;
Or rather we *impartial Nature* blame
To hide our *Sloth,* and cover O'er our *Shame*;
As sinners, when their *Reason's* drown'd in *Sense*;
Fall out with Heav'n, and quarrel *Providence*. (pp. 7–8)

His optimism and confidence mark Wesley out as a true Modern. Not all those who advocated the originality of divine poetry can be so simply described. Richard Blackmore and John Dennis are, and were, familiar figures in the period. Their different interpretations of the theory of imitation set them at loggerheads for a time, for each reckoned himself as closer

[19] For a brief and very helpful summary of the question of Christian machinery in epic poetry see Hooker, I, 462.

to the great Ancients, but their subsequent thoughts on the originality of divine poetry almost certainly contributed to their eventual friendship.

Richard Blackmore and John Dennis

The closing years of the seventeenth century coincided with a new mood in English society. Disenchanted with the Catholic and absolutist pretensions of James II, the nation turned to the House of Orange and the new political and social era it initiated. The licentious days of the Restoration were nothing but a dim memory. Now the crown took an active and concerned interest in the moral welfare of its people. Collier spoke out and won support; societies for the Reformation of Manners sprang up; William spoke from the throne on the desirability of a higher moral tone.[20] The royal plea did not fall on barren soil. That prolix soul, Sir Richard Blackmore, responded with alacrity. If the King wanted verse of a more moral hue, Blackmore was delighted to oblige. Though wanting in poetic talent, at least to the modern reader's mind, Blackmore forms an important and influential link in the development of the belief in the originality of divine poetry. His tedious expansiveness notwithstanding, the commentary which forms a preface to his first essay in the genre reflects the opinions of many of those stalwart souls who were busily defying the literary establishment and the contumely of the Scriblerians in order to attempt new things in what they fondly hoped was a new way.[21] Nor should it be forgotten that they were also satisfying a deep and profoundly felt need.

Divine poetry was something of a *volte face* for Blackmore. He had started out as a convinced Ancient and cast his *Prince Arthur* in the best and, he felt, most accurate classical tradition. But the moral danger of his country and the royal appeal could not be ignored. Blackmore turned his willing hand to *A Paraphrase on the Book of Job* (1700). Although his evangelical lucubrations tend to smother all other thoughts, it is possible to discern quite an elaborate theory of originality in the essay. To begin with, he is pleasantly conscious of the adventurous nature of his undertaking:

[20] Preface to *A Paraphrase on the Book of Job (1700)*, unpag.

[21] Two particularly devastating attacks on Blackmore were, *A Satyr upon a late Pamphlet Entitled A Satyr against Wit* (1700) and *Commendatory Verses on the Author of the Two Arthurs and the Satyr against Wit; By some of his particular Friends* (1700). Blackmore is addressed in such unfriendly terms as "incomparable Bard and Quack". But, on the other hand, John Locke and his correspondent William Molyneux admired *Prince Arthur* and Addison, Dennis and Dr. Johnson were lavish in their praises of *Creation*. See Johnson's Life of Blackmore in *Lives of the English Poets,* ed. Birkbeck Hill, (Oxford, 1905), II, 244. See also, Albert Rosenberg, *Sir Richard Blackmore* (Lincoln, Nebraska, 1953). See also Ch. 2, Note 47, p. 64 below.

It has been observ'd by great Judges, and I find Mr. Le Clerk of the same Opinion, that the Moderns have wholly form'd themselves on the Models of the Ancients, and that we have scarce any thing but the Greek and Latin Poetry in the World. We have no Originals, but all Copiers and Transcribers of Homer, Pindar, and Theocritus, Virgil, Horace, and Ovid. Their Design, their Phrase, their Manner, and even their Heathen Theology, appear in all the Poems that have since their Time been published to the World, especially in the Learned Languages. 'Tis therefore to be wish'd that some good Genius, qualify'd for such an Undertaking, would break the Ice, assert the Liberty of Poetry, and set up for an Original in Writing in a way accommodated to the Religion, Manners, and other Circumstances we are now under. But however we write, I think 'tis high time to leave out our Allusions to the Pagan Divinity; for how beautiful soever they might be in the Pagan Authors, who wrote to a People that believ'd in those Deities, 'tis the most ridiculous and senseless thing in the World for a Christian Poet to bring in upon all Occasions the Rabble and Riffraffe of Heathenish Gods; and yet if we reflect on our Modern Poems one would think we were all Pagans to this Day. What have we to do with Jupiter and Juno, Mars and Venus, and the rest? We know they are a Jest, and yet they are brought into all our most grave and chastest Poems . . . than which there cannot be a more intollerable [sic] Absurdity. (sig. B1ʳ⁻ᵛ)[22]

As was to be expected, Blackmore also takes issue with those who, in the raging controversy over the use of Christian machinery in epic, maintain that the intervention of God or his Angels precludes suspense and surprise. He scorns such literary timidity: "Are our Poets then so dry and barren", he demands, "have they so little learning, and so poor a stock of Images, that they are not able to furnish themselves with proper Allusions, surprizing Metaphors, and beautiful Similes, without reviving the old exploded Idolatory of the Heathens?". He suggests that they should look to the Bible for inspiration. There, in the Book of Job, for example, they will find a poem "that is indeed an Original, and not beholding to the Greek and Latin Springs". They will also find, if, he adds modestly, his paraphrase has not obliterated it, "a sublime Stile, elevated Thoughts, magnificent Expressions

----

[22] Blackmore's conviction that religious subjects were original persisted. See his Preface to *Redemption* (1722), p. v. An opinion of Blackmore not often quoted is Henry Needler's *To Sir Richard Blackmore, on his poem, entitled, Creation* (*Works*, 1724). All quotations from Needler are from the 2nd. ed. (1728). In this poem Needler praises Blackmore for his daring originality. For example:
    These beaten Paths thy Loftier Strains refuse
    With just Disdain, and Nobler Subjects chuse:
    Fir'd with Sublimer Thoughts, thy daring Soul
    Wings her aspiring Flight from Pole to Pole,
    Observes the Footsteps of a Pow'r Divine,
    Which in each Part of Nature's System Shine,
    Surveys the Wonders of this Beauteous Frame,
    And sings the Sacred Source, whence all Things came. (pp. 33–34)
In the quotation in my text, Blackmore is probably referring to Jean Le Clerk's *Parrhasiana* (1700), in particular, Ch. I, "Of Poets and Poetry" in which this popular author castigated the imitative practices of the modern poets.

where the Subject requires them, and great richness and abundance throughout the whole, without the Aids of the Pagan System of Divinity" (sig. B1ᵛ).

We do not know John Dennis's reaction to Blackmore's Preface, but in the light of their subsequent friendship, it is likely to have been one of approval. Dennis may well have found Blackmore's changed opinions so soon after his own damning criticism of *Prince Arthur* very gratifying indeed.[23] At any rate, Blackmore's thoughts are akin to Dennis's own, for the role of religion in modern literature was one of Dennis's favourite themes.

In his most important critical works, The *Advancement and Reformation of Modern Poetry* (1701), and its unfinished sequel, *The Grounds of Criticism in Poetry* (1704), Dennis explores the relationship between religion and literature and examines their reciprocal importance. Although by no means a new departure in criticism, his own conviction of "the Newness and Boldness" of his views should not be dismissed too summarily, for in these works, Dennis succeeds in formulating a literary aesthetic founded solely on the basis of emotion.[24] Its implications for Dennis's otherwise profound reverence for the Ancients and his willing acceptance of the principle of imitation in certain respects were far-reaching. His fears regarding the decay of taste and literature made him a stern advocate of the discipline of the rules and the restraint of tradition.[25] Yet his aesthetic inclinations often led him in other directions, to positions where subjectivity counted more than tradition and where emotion was more important than decorum. Furthermore, in the theory of the emotions and divine poetry which he evolves in *The Advancement*, he opens the way for a greater scope for originality which he promised to develop more fully in *The Grounds of Criticism*.

In the conflict which persisted concerning the relative merits of the Ancients and Moderns, Dennis sided with the Ancients. But being a true whig at heart, he also believed in the possibility of progress and improvement. Indeed he belies his standing as an Ancient in the very title of his first major critical work, *The Advancement and Reformation of Modern Poetry*. In it he attempts an assessment of the poetry of his contemporaries and proposes a plan for the improvement and furthering of modern talent, of whose existence he is never in doubt. His aim is, he says, to "set the Moderns upon an equal Foot with even admired Antiquity" (I, 200). The treatise is a lengthy comparison of the conditions, both internal and exter-

---

[23] For an assessment of their relationship, see Hooker, I, 448.

[24] "The Epistle Dedicatory" of *The Advancement*, Hooker, I, 197–198. See also I, 508–509.

[25] See, for example, his attack on Leonard Welsted's *Dissertation* in *The Causes of the Decay and Defects of Dramatic Poetry* (1725?), Hooker, II, 275–299 and 502–508.

nal, which may be responsible for the superiority of the Ancients and the inferiority of the Moderns. After a detailed examination, he concludes that the ancient authors have had no specific advantages over the Moderns. They enjoyed neither greater mental abilities nor a more congenial society. Their superiority in literary matters, which Dennis does not question, is the result of two factors neglected or ignored by the Moderns. They have chosen a "regular" way of writing, and have made their religion the main subject of their poetry. These two points constitute, at this stage, Dennis's plan for reform. Later, he was to dispense with regularity and advocate the use of religion as the sole criterion for achieving excellence and parity. But in *The Advancement* he continues to insist on the general efficacy of the rules and declares that "[t]he necessity of observing Rules, to the Attaining of a Perfection in Poetry is so very apparent . . . [that if] anyone should pretend to succeed alone by the natural Force of his Fancy, that Man would certainly be esteem'd a very impudent and impertinent Person" (I, 201). The combination of regularity and religion results in the excitement of both the ordinary and the extraordinary passions. It is this that produces the greatest poetry:

A Poet is capacitated by that which is commonly call'd Regularity, to excite the ordinary Passions more powerfully by the Constitution of the Fable, and the Influence which that must necessarily have, both upon the Words and Thoughts; and Religion, besides the Influence it will have upon the ordinary Passions, will be to a Poet, who has Force and Skill enough to make his Advantage of it, a perpetual Source of extraordinary Passions, which is commonly call'd Enthusiasm, for the Sentiments and Expressions [sic]. (I, 201)

His plan for the improvement of modern authors then, at this stage, is to exhort them to combine poetry and religion, thus promoting each. "The ultimate End of the ensuing Discourse", he declares, "is to shew, That the Intention of Poetry, and the Christian Religion, being alike to move the Affections, they may very well be made instrumental to the Advancing each other" (I, 207).

Passion is "the Characteristical Mark of Poetry" and should infuse the whole poem. Sacred subjects are the most conducive to passion, especially those exalted or "Enthusiastick" passions whose cause remains mysterious and inexplicable. It follows, therefore, that sacred subjects are more truly poetical than profane ones. Indeed, "the nearer Poetry comes to Perfection, the more agreeable it is to the Design of the True Religion, and . . . consequently, Poetry is much more noble, and more instructive, and more beneficial to Mankind, than either History or Philosophy" (I, 252). Moreover, the design of Poetry is the same as that of "True Religion". They both propose "to exalt the Reason, by exalting the Passions, and so make Happy the whole Man, by making Internal Discord cease" (I, 265). In Dennis's opinion, it must surely be clear to all rational people that poetry has much more in common with "True Religion" than it can have with "Paganism or Philosophy, or Deism, whose Designs have been shown repugnant to it". Although Dennis believed in the power of the poet's imagination to transcend time and animate the long dead fictions of the past, he still thinks that modern poetry would be better off ridding itself of the "Grecian Revelation" which has been so long "utterly exploded and contemn'd by the very Boys" (I, 266). It would then make its appeal to "the Generality of Readers" which is one of its main obligations.

A child of his time, Dennis accords to Reason its full due. Since the Graeco-Roman myths and the philosophy of ancient times are both wantonly at odds with the truth as it is known to modern reason, these should be discarded in favour of the superior truths of Christianity, which, Dennis confidently believes, fulfill the requirements of Reason:

The Christian Religion alone, can supply a Poet with all that is sublime and majestick in Reason; all that is either soft or powerful, either engaging or imperious in the Passions; and with all the Objects that are most admirable to the Senses; and consequently, most delightful. (I, 266)

He concludes, therefore, "that the Moderns, by joining the Christian Religion with Poetry, will have the Advantage of the Ancients; that is, That they will have the Assistance of a Religion that is more agreeable to the Design of Poetry, than the *Grecian* Religion" (I, 278). His reasons are not those of simple faith, but are founded on his theory that emotion is the heart of poetry.[26] Only a subject of high seriousness can engender the superior type of emotion which he calls "enthusiastick passion". It is this passion which is the mark of great poetry. Religion is the only subject capable of exciting this passion. Therefore only religious poetry is great.

In order to prove his point he compares Milton with Virgil. Still a staunch believer in "regularity" and with a strong predilection for the poetry of the great Ancients, his comparison favours Virgil. His only concession to Milton is his superior choice of subject:

When I say that *Milton* excels *Virgil,* I mean, that he does so sometimes, both in his Thought, and in his Spirit, purely by the Advantage of his Religion. But at the same Time, I am very far from thinking, that he so much as equals him either in the continual Harmony of his Versification, or the constant Beauty of his Expression, or his perpetual Exaltation. He writ in a Language that was not capable of so much Beauty, or so much Harmony; and his Inequality proceeded from his Want of Art to manage his Subject, and make it constantly great. For it would be an easy matter to prove that none of the Moderns understood the Art of Heroick

---

[26] For an analysis of Dennis's thoughts on emotion in poetry and his position in relation to other critics of the period, see Hooker, II, xciii-xcix.

Poetry, who writ before *Bossu* took Pains to unravel the Mystery. But nothing can make more for my Subject, than to shew that *Milton,* who lay under these vast Disadvantages, very often excell'd, even the Prince of the *Roman* Poets, both in the Greatness of Thought, and his Spirit. (I, 271–272)

Milton owes his "Greatness" and his "Elevation" to the excellence of his religion, but Virgil excells him in art. This was Dennis's position at the end of *The Advancement.* He had pointed the way to the improvement of poetry, by the adoption of regularity and religion, but, so far, remained silent on the originality of divine poetry.

It is this, however, which is his main preoccupation in *The Grounds of Criticism in Poetry* (1704). Unfortunately, this work is little more than a proposal for a much larger project, which, through want of popular support, remained unfinished. It is, nevertheless, the most important and original critical treatise of its day. In it, the relationship of great poetry and religion, expounded in *The Advancement,* takes on a new dimension. Now it is its potential for originality in poetry and the intrinsic merit of that originality that takes precedence.

It seems possible that Dennis's growing acquaintance with the theory of the sublime facilitated the connection he made between the passions, subjectivity and originality. In his book on the sublime, Professor S. H. Monk noted:

By investigating the emotions consequent to sublimity, men began to learn that art is a matter, not of the rules, but of the individual's response to an object or an experience, and this knowledge led them gradually to that subjective view of art out of which an aesthetic was evolved. Incidentally, the habit of studying the emotional effect of art was certain to emphasize the belief that the individual emotion is more valid than all the rules, and such a belief firmly held and clearly undertood produces the poetry of a Wordsworth and not of a Pope.[27]

The sublime, the mind of the poet and the concept of originality are inextricably linked. It will be recalled that two of the five sources of the sublime as described by Longinus were innate and depended on the quality of the mind of the poet.[28] This subjectivity is evident in the expanded definition of the "Enthusiastick Passions" presented by Dennis in *The Grounds of Criticism:*

Enthusiastick Passion, or Enthusiasm, is a Passion which is moved by Ideas in Contemplation, or the Meditation of things that belong not to common life. Most of our Thoughts in Meditation are naturally attended with some sort and some degree of Passion; and this Passion, if it is strong, I call Enthusiasm. (I, 338)

---

[27] *The Sublime,* p. 50. For a general discussion of Dennis and the Sublime, see pp. 46–54. Professor Monk does not, however, link the Sublime with originality.
[28] *Longinus: On the Sublime,* p. 108.

Not only is this enthusiasm meditative it is also violent. It is, consequently, inseparably linked with religious emotion: " ... the Enthusiastick Passions in Poetry are truly admirable, when the greater and more violent they are, the more they show the Largeness of Soul, and Greatness of Capacity of the Writer" (I, 340). "[A]s great Passion only is the adequate Language of the Greater Poetry", Dennis reasons, "so the greater Poetry is only the adequate Language of Religion, and ... therefore the greatest Passion is the Language of that sort of Poetry, because that sort of Poetry is the worthiest Language of Religion' (I, 340).

Not content with the Longinian definition of the sublime, Dennis set himself to prove that ideas that are truly sublime are religious ideas. He does this by analysing the characteristic marks of the sublime and finding that all these marks are to be found pre-eminently in religious ideas. At this point, it becomes evident that both the sublime and the Christian religion share an important characteristic—originality. One of the features of the sublime is that "which makes us think". This Dennis says, is the equivalent of the fact that "the Wonders of Religion are never to be exhausted; for they are always new, and the more you enter into them, the more they are sure to surprize" (I, 360). Therefore, for the poet to succeed in the greater poetry, he must assure himself that "the Constitution of the Poem be religious, that it may be throughout pathetick" (I, 364).

But it is in his enthusiasm for Milton's *Paradise Lost* that Dennis clearly demonstrates that originality has assumed an importance that it did not have in his earlier work. In his remarks on Milton, the subjectivity and originality of the sublime are combined with the theory of the enthusiastic passions and religious ideas. The result is one of the most outspoken pieces on the originality which inspires divine poetry. Unfortunately, since the work remained unfinished, it reads like a summary of the theory stated in its simplest form. Clearly however, Dennis's position has altered since *The Advancement*. Then, as now, he proclaimed religion as the basis of the greatest poetry because of the enthusiastic passion which it inspired. But, whereas earlier, he had linked religion with regularity as the two marks of great poetry, in this essay he eliminates the latter requirement.

Milton is no longer Virgil's inferior, but "one of the greatest and most daring Genius's that has appear'd in the World". He has made a "glorious present" to his country of "the most lofty, but most irregular Poem, that has been produc'd by the Mind of Man". When Milton decided to write "something like an Epick Poem", he resolved at the same time, we are told, "to break thro' the Rules of *Aristotle,*" not because he was ignorant or scornful of them but because "he had discernment enough to see, that if he wrote a Poem which was within the compass of them, he should be subjected to the same Fate which has attended all who have wrote Epick Poems ever since the time of *Homer*; and that is to be a Copyist instead of an Original'' (I, 332).

With scant respect for the time-honoured tradition of imitation, Dennis curtly dismisses those who have bound themselves by it:

Tis true, the Epick Poets who have liv'd since *Homer*, have most of them been Originals in their Fables, which are the very Souls of their Poems; but in their manner of treating those Fables, they have too frequently been Copyists. They have Copyed the Spirit and the Images of *Homer*; even the great *Virgil* himself is not to be excepted. (I, 333)

It is significant that not even those who rested satisfied with emulating the spirit of the great Ancients are exempt from Dennis's criticism, for even that is an obstacle to originality. Milton is the first and the only figure, according to Dennis, since the time of Homer, who decided ''for his Country's Honour and his own'' to be totally original, that is ''to write a Poem that should have his own Thoughts, his own Images, and his own Spirit''. Neither the Rules, the Practice nor the Spirit of the Ancients were permitted to interfere with his design.

Furthermore, claims Dennis, it was this very originality that inspired Milton to choose the subject he did: ''he was resolved to write a Poem that, by vertue of its extraordinary Subject, cannot so properly be said to be against the Rules, as it may be affirmed to be above them all''. Aristotle had formed his rules on Homeric practice where the action concerned Man against Man. Milton decided therefore, that his subject would be quite different: ''the Devil on one side and man on the other''. The Devil is the Hero because he gets the better of his opponents, and since ''all the Persons in his Poem, excepting two, are either Divine or Infernal'' and very different from ''what *Homer* and *Aristotle* ever thought of'' they ''could not possibly be subject to their rules, either for the characters or the Incidents''.

In the completed version of the treatise, Dennis would have gone on to define Milton's originality more closely:

We shall now shew for what Reasons the choice of Milton's subject, as it set him free from the Obligation which he lay under to the Poetical Laws, so it necessarily threw him upon new Thoughts, new Images, and an Original Spirit. In the next place we shall shew, that his Thoughts, his Images and by consequence too his Spirit, are actually new, and different from those of *Homer* and *Virgil*. Thirdly, we shall shew, that besides their Newness they have vastly the Advantage of those of *Homer* and *Virgil*. (I, 334)

The proposed comparison was never made. We are left with nothing but these tantalising hints of what might have been one of the most dramatic discussions of originality and its connection with divine poetry. It is clear, however, that Dennis's position in this later essay differs greatly from the one he held earlier. Milton's *Paradise Lost* is deemed great and irregular. Furthermore, it is original by virtue of Milton's conscious choice to write in a way different from the classical authors. In other words, choosing a subject unknown and untried by them releases the writer from the obligation of following in their footsteps. Finally, Dennis enlarges the concept of originality by extending it to include not only subject matter, images and sentiments, but also the spirit of the work, in which, traditionally, imitation was permitted. Dennis insisted that the spirit of the work must not be borrowed from another but should be the author's own. This undoubtedly, is the most revolutionary aspect of the essay.

It is impossible to determine the extent or quality of Dennis's influence. It appears, however, that divine poets, even those of an occasional inclination, were often quite familiar with the works of like-minded authors. There are clear echoes of Dennis's thought in Aaron Hill's *Advice to the Poets:*

> Scorn then, the servile Imitator's Name,
> Nor, humbly splendid, wear *Cast Coats* of Fame
> . . . .
> *Lean* not, sustain'd,—a Weight no Muse allows!
> Pilfering the faded Bays, from Classic Brows;
> Nor creep, contented in the Modern Way;
> A dry, dull, soft, slow, languid, tiresome Lay!
> But, strongly sacred, and divinely warm,
> Strike the aw'd Soul, and the touch'd Passions charm:
> Till the stern *Cynic,* soft'ning at your Strain
> Feels himself mov'd, and hugs the pleasing Pain
> While *lazy Lovers* from their Langour start
> And gain a *Conquest,* tho' they lost a Heart.[29]

Thomas Newcomb attributes his inspiration more directly to Dennis's "excellent treatise" and claims originality for his subject:

I had none to follow, none to guide me in those dark and unknown Regions on the other side of the Grave: The Scenes I have drawn, being chiefly laid beyond the Verge of Nature and the Limits of this World . . . .[30]

That there was a sense of continuity and common purpose among many of the divine poets is clear from the writings of the much more important figure of Isaac Watts. He appears to have been well read not only in the work of his

---

[29] *Advice to the Poets, A Poem. To which is Prefix'd, An Epistle Dedicatory to the Few Great Spirits of Great Britain* (1731), p. 24. See Dorothy Brewster, *Aaron Hill, Poet, Dramatist Projector* (N. Y., 1913), pp. 164–69 for a more complete discussion on Dennis's influence on Hill. See also, Fairchild, I, 448. Hill, however, did not admire Blackmore. See *Advice to Poets.*

[30] *The Last Judgment of Men and Angels. A Poem in twelve Books after the Manner of Milton* (1723), sig. C1^{r-v}.

immediate predecessors, but also Racine and Corneille. John Dennis must surely have been consoled that such an influential contemporary regretted that his proposal to propound *The Grounds of Criticism* was not permitted to bear fruit.[31]

Originality and the Inspired Poet

It is in the theory and practice of Isaac Watts that exhortations such as Dennis's to modern authors can be seen to have had greatest effect. Watts was a Dissenter and his religious inclinations made him a rebel against the literary as well as the ecclesiastic authorities. A conscious and over-riding desire to be original informs his work and is the explicit subject of many of his poems. He belonged to that group of divine poets who accepted the Platonic notion of the inspired poet, suitably refurbished in the light of Christianity.[32] He was, however, not content with the simple statement that divine poetry was the result of divine inspiration. He contended that poetry should be the immediate outpouring of the inspired soul, beginning when the inspiration strikes and ending when it wanes. In fact, since divine poetry is the only kind which is completely the result of inspiration, it is what the original and inspired poet should always attempt:

If the heart were first inflamed from Heaven, and the muse were not left alone to form the devotion and pursue a cold scent, but only called in as an assistant to the worship, then the song would end where the inspiration ceases; the whole composure would be of a piece, all meridian light and meridian fervor; and the same pious flame would be propagated and kept glowing in the heart of him that reads.[33]

Apparently unimpressed by the powerful dictum that judgment should rule the imagination, Watts claims that this "Sedate" faculty need play very

[31] Preface to *Horae Lyricae* in *Eighteenth-Century Critical Essays*, ed. Scott Elledge (Ithaca, N. Y., 1961), I, 154.

[32] The question of inspiration preoccupied many divine poets. Cowley had expressed suspicion of such claims, but the influential Fénèlon had entertained no such doubts. According to him, it is this quality that distinguishes the sacred from the profane writers. See *Dialogues Concerning Eloquence,* tr. William Stevenson (1722), p. 155. The priest-poet or *vates* of ancient times is frequently mentioned as a worthy precursor for modern divine authors. See Meric Casaubon, *A Treatise Concerning Enthusiasm* (1665), pp. 8–9 and Samuel Cobb, *Of Poetry* (1710). The direct inspiration of God was held responsible for the gloriously poetical language of the Bible. See Samuel Woodford, Preface to *A Paraphrase upon the Psalms of David* (1667), sig. A2ᵛ; Aaron Hill, Preface to *The Creation* (1720). Edward Philips summarised what this meant to divine authors. He maintained that Poetry was "a Science certainly of all others the most noble and exalted, and not unworthily termed *Divine,* since the height of Poetical rapture hath ever been accounted little less than *Divine Inspiration*", Spingarn, II, 259.

[33] Preface to *Horae Lyricae* in *Eighteenth Century Critical Essays,* I, 158. This edition is used for all subsequent quotations from Watts's Preface.

little part in limiting the bold excursions of the superior genius whose imagination is "lavish" in its outpourings. The poetry that results has the power to transform and transcend the mundane and to elevate and enrapture the soul in a sort of religious ecstasy. Indeed, Watts is certain, at some time prior to its corruption by secular and heathen influences, it was not uncommon for men to find that "a divine and poetic rapture lifted their souls far above the level of that economy of shadows, bore them away far into a brighter region, and gave them a glimpse of evangelic day" (p. 148).

Watts found the superiority of divine poets self-evident. By a kind of comparative analysis, he demonstrates that the poets of the Old Testament, because they were directly inspired by God, far outstrip even the greatest of the great Ancients in excellence. The writings of Isaiah, David and Habbakuk are incomparably superior to the works of Homer, Virgil and Pindar who, being earthbound, can never reach the summit of the sublime. The Biblical poets have access to a wealth of images and sentiments not available to the classical poets. Furthermore, because they were directly inspired they were aware of themes and ideas denied the heathen poets:

Nor did the Blessed Spirit, which animated these writers forbid them the use of visions, dreams, the opening of scenes dreadful and delightful, and the introduction of machines upon great occasions; the divine licence in this respect is admirable and surprizing, and the images are often too bold and dangerous for the uninspired writer to imitate. (I, 154)

Although certainly attracted by the spiritual value of his chosen subject matter, Watts was acutely sensitive to the scope and freedom which divine poetry would permit him as an artist. That he saw himself as an original, and ambitious, poet rather than a "divine author" is clear from his advice to others aspiring to write religious verse. He emphasises to them that this form provides the best opportunity to fulfill "an ambition to exceed all modern writers" (I, 155). In order to achieve this, the poet must educate himself in the books of the Bible, reading them day and night, for herein will be found all that is needed for the "greater ease and surer success of the poet". It is noteworthy that the typical Augustan advice to the aspiring poet, to acquaint himself with the works of the great Ancients and acquire learning, is ignored by Watts. His comparison of the relative difficulties of divine and profane poetry is also interesting. He assures his novice poet that his task, if he chooses to write religious poetry, is much less arduous, because the fact that "the Christian mysteries have not such need of gay trappings as beautified, or rather composed, the heathen superstition" gives him a great advantage over the profane poet who must labour to regarnish the wellworn fabric of classical myth.

It is clear that these "gay trappings" were without much appeal to Watts.

He did not confine his Dissenter's abhorence of the ornate and lavish to the ritual and traditions of the Established Church, but extended it to all that was merely ornamental and custom-ridden in literature. His antidote to such decadence was a truly Christian poetry. "The wonders of our religion, in a plain narration and a simple dress, have a native grandeur, a dignity and a beauty in them" (I, 155), he claimed, because "the naked themes of Christianity have something brighter and bolder in them, something more surprizing and celestial, than all the adventures of gods and heroes, all the dazzling images of false lustre that form and garnish heathen song" (I, 156). Furthermore, since these themes are "divinely true", unlike the "medley of fooleries" that comprise the classical mythologies, "the advantage of touching the springs of passion" will fall to the benefit of the Christian poet.

In many of the poems which make up the collection *Horae Lyricae* (1706), the poet's sense of his own individuality, his difference from other men, his yearning for originality and his sense of personal isolation are important themes. It is not surprising therefore, that in the preface, Watts makes no claim for the general truth of his poetry, but admits frankly that these poems are the expression of his own unique way of looking at the world, and that they will appeal only to like-minded people. He describes some of his poems as being "formed when the frame and humour of my soul was just suited to the subject of my verse. The image of my heart is painted in them, and if they meet with a reader whose soul is akin to mine, perhaps they may agreeably entertain him" (I, 159). His poetry is not another version of general and universal truth, and will, on his own admission, not appeal to his "Fellow-Citizens of the Universe, to all Countries, and to all Ages". Instead it will find a small select audience in some few receptive kindred spirits.

His conscious and determined cultivation of individuality is the theme of "Tis Dangerous to follow the Multitude", a poem addressed to his former teacher and mentor, the Reverend Thomas Rowe. As a radical Protestant, tradition held few charms for him. He regarded what some felt to be merely a reverence for antiquity as a mindless enslavement and irrational surrender of self, because such admiration of the past was a paralysis of the present.

> Meer Hazard first began the Track
> Where Custom leads her Thousands blind
>   In willing Chains and strong;
> There's not one bold, one noble Mind
> Dares tread the fatal Error back,
> But Hand in Hand our selves we bind
>   And drag the Age along.[34]

---

[34] *Horae Lyricae* (1706), p. 137. All quotations are from this edition unless otherwise stated.

Watts desires a different fate for himself. As a poet inspired by Heaven, he is able to strike out in new and untrodden ways. He can free himself from the multitude and rejoice in his own individuality:

> Me let some Friendly Seraph's Wing
> Snatch from the Crowd, and Bear Sublime
>   To Wisdom's lofty Tower
> Thence to survey that wretched Thing
> Mankind; and in exalted Rhime
>   Bless the delivering Power.

Watts's delight in the powers of his own mind permitted him an interesting variation on the theme of the dual nature of man. Traditionally, the two elements of body and soul were thought to co-exist in an uneasy and weary alliance, in which the soul is continually thwarted by the perversity of the sensual body.[35] In the end, death intervenes on behalf of the soul which is freed from its material burden. But Watts's interpretation of this event is different. In the poem, "True Riches", death is not the gateway through which the soul must pass in order to attain eternal bliss, but is rather the signal for the release of the "ego"—man's most important constituent. After death the "I" is not subsumed by the immortal soul in Heaven, but expands and becomes greater than the visible universe. The result is one of intense joy:

> When I view my Spacious Soul,
> And survey myself a whole,
> And enjoy myself alone,
> I'm a kingdom of my own.[36]

The thought is both unorthodox and strikingly vainglorious, but this is the prevailing tone of the whole poem. Watts revelled in himself and his individuality. In execrable but explicit verse he goes on to describe his now free soul in terms reminiscent of the Garden of Eden. It is vast, exotic, beautiful and mysterious:

> 'Tis a Region half unknown,
> That has Treasures of its own,
> More removed from publick View
> Than the Bowels of *Peru,*
> Broader 'tis, and, brighter far,
> Than the Golden *Indies* are;

---

[35] One of the more interesting discussions of this popular view of the psychology of man is Henry Barker's translation of the anonymous French work, *The Polite Gentleman: or reflections upon several Kinds of Wit, viz., in conversation, books, and affairs of the world* (1700).

[36] *Horae Lyricae,* 10th. ed. (1750), p. 159.

Ships that trace the watry Stage,
Cannot cross it in an Age,
Harts or Horses, strong and fleet,
Had they Wings to help their Feet,
Could not run it half way o'er
In ten thousand Days or more. (p. 160)

Another poem, significantly entitled "Free Philosophy" and again
addressed to Thomas Rowe, may be said to be Watts's earliest explicit
manifesto of his theory of originality. He felt as strongly about artistic
freedom as he did about religious freedom and came to associate originality
with Dissenting individualism. Both are subsequently combined to form a
literary aesthetic which attacks all that restricts and confines in religion and
art. The specific object of his contumely is identified as "Custom" which
can only be vanquished by the individual genius breaking away into freedom:

Custom, that Tyraness of Fools,
That leads the Learned round the Schools
In Magick Chains of Forms and Rules,
   My Genius storms her Throne:
No more ye Slaves with Awe profound
Beat the dull Track, nor dance the Round,
Loose Hands, and quit th'Inchanted Ground,
Knowledge invites us each alone.
I hate those Shackles of the Mind
   Forg'd by the haughty Wise;
Souls were not born to be confin'd,
And led like *Sampson* Bound and Blind:
I love thy gentle Influence, Rowe,
   Who only dost Advise:
Thy gentle Influence like the Sun
Only dissolves the Frozen Snow,
Then bids our Thoughts like Rivers flow,
And chuse the Channels where they run.
Thoughts should be free as Fire or Wind,
The Pinions of a Single Mind
   Will thro' all Nature fly:
But who can drag up to the Poles
Long fetter'd Ranks of Leaden Souls?
My Genius which no Chain controuls
Roves with Delight, or deep or high;
Swift I survey the Globe around,
Dive to the Centre thro' the Solid Ground,
Or travel o'er the Sky. (pp. 153–154)

Later editions of *Horae Lyricae* contain other poems which refine this
theme. For example, Watts's identification of the established church with

29

outworn tradition and, of Dissent, with free inspiration and genius is made explicit in some lines added to the poem "To her Majesty" which, in the first edition was an encomium on Queen Anne. In those early days, it had seemed that a greater toleration was to be permitted to Dissenters. But by 1721 those hopes had been dashed and Watts's earlier and rosier view of the glories of Queen Anne's reign was much tempered in the later version by the addition of some trenchant lines on the state of religion in England. The simplicity and purity of Dissent is favourably compared with that dying dinosaur, the Church of England:

> Here a solemn Form
> Of ancient Words keeps the Devotion warm,
> And guides, but bounds our Wishes: There the Mind
> Feels its own Fire, and kindles unconfin'd
> With bolder Hopes.[37]

In "Freedom", dated 1697, but not included in the first edition, the poet's independent stance and apartness from lesser men is described by analogy with the qualities of natural phenomena, a device to which original poets frequently resorted:

> I can and will be free;
> Like a strong Mountain, or some stately Tree,
>   My soul grows firm upright,
> And as I stand, and as I go
>   It keeps my Body so;[38]

Because his genius is God-given, to be used only in the service of Heaven he is set apart—superior to the "Slaves and Asses" that "stoop and bow". His "Creation Right" makes him proud and independent as well as original. He will never permit his muse to timeserve: "I cannot make this Iron Knee / Bend to a meaner Power than that which formed it free" (p. 158). In the last stanza of this poem, the Poet, having sung his song of freedom, hangs his harp in a tree and lies down to rest. While he sleeps Nature takes up his theme, and, as if to prove his noble apartness, a storm blows up, making all "the meaner Plants" bend before it. Only "The Iron Oak" on which the harp is hanging, remains unmoved.

In "Two Happy Rivals, Devotion and the Muse", Watts explores an unexpected aspect of the connection between divine poetry and originality. In other poems he had stated his belief that it was only in divine poetry that

---

[37] *Horae Lyricae*, 10th. ed. (1750), p. 124. See John Hoyles, *The Waning of the Renaissance 1640–1740* (The Hague, 1971), pp. 207–208.
[38] *Horae Lyricae*, 10th. ed. (1750), p. 156.

true genius could find original expression. In this rather obscure poem, however, he seems to claim that his poetic genius far outstrips his faith. His muse, unencumbered by the flesh, is free and wild:

> ... Lo she disdains
> The Links and Chains,
> Measures and Rule of vulgar Strains,
> And over the Laws of Harmony a sovereign Queen she reigns.[39]

He is equal to his Muse when she is absorbed in themes of love, nature or earthly glory—sublunary matters—but once divine themes become its object:

> Then she leaves my flutt'ring Mind
> Clogg'd with Clay, and unrefin'd
> Lengths of Distance far behind.

It appears that it is his faith that remains earth-bound, while his poetry soars aloft:

> Faith has Wings, but cannot rise,
> Cannot rise, ... [as] Swift and high
> As the winged Numbers fly,
> And faint Devotion panting lies
> Half way th' Ethereal Hill. (p. 89)

The poem concludes with a dream in which the soul achieves perfect freedom through death when the "cumbrous Clay" has fallen away. In this state it enters a region of perfection hitherto unknown even to the Muse whose "thousand loose *Pindaric* Plumes" are left far behind. The poem concludes with a promise to compose no more until "the gross Organ" has been refined and the Muse can then "trace the boundless Flights of an unfetter'd Mind / And raise an equal Song" (p. 91). Watts's belief in the powers of the Muse is seemingly without reservation, for he appears to claim that the Poetic Genius is so free and original in its inclinations, that even the Soul, for as long as it is linked with the body, is confined and restricted in comparison.

In another poem, the Muse is again described in terms which emphasise her originality and power. "The Adventurous Muse" depicts the original genius rising like a lark heaven-ward (pp. 161–163). "Nor *Rapin* gives her Rules to fly, nor *Purcell* Notes to sing". Free from all burdens of knowledge, acquired learning or fear of the unknown, the Muse is as elemental as

---

[39] *Horae Lyricae*, 10th. ed. (1750), p. 88. H. N. Fairchild remarked on these poems as early pleas on behalf of original genius. See *Religious Trends in English Poetry*, I, 127–129.

Nature itself. "Touch'd with an Empyreal Ray" she "springs, unerring upward to eternal Day" and, relying solely on her own innate prowess, "steers / With bold and safe Attempts" to the celestial sphere. In turning to divine themes the original poet may, unlike imitative poets, rely on inspiration and natural genius and safely disregard the accumulation of literary tradition and rules which is their lot:

> Whilst little Skiffs along the mortal Shores
>   With humble toil in order creep
> Coasting in Sight of one another's Oars
>   Nor venture thro the boundless Deep,
>   Such low pretending Souls are they
> Who dwell inclos'd in Solid Orbs of Skull;
>   Plodding along their Sober Way
> The Snail o'ertakes them in their wildest Play,
> While the poor Labourers sweat to be correctly dull.

Using yet another metaphor, Watts demonstrates the originality of divine poetry:

> Give me the Chariot whose diviner Wheels
>   Mark their own Rout, and unconfin'd
> Bound o'er the everlasting Hills
> And lose the Clouds below, and leave the Stars behind.
> Give me the Muse whose generous Force,
>   Impatient of the Reins,
>   Pursues an unattempted Course,
> Breaks all the Criticks' Iron Chains,
> And bears to Paradise the raptur'd Mind

Milton is his great precursor. Now sanctified, he, when mortal, showed the way to originality. He sang of "Themes not presum'd by mortal Tongue", "New Terrors", and "New Glories". His Muse "trac'd a glorious Path unknown / Thro' Fields of heavenly War and Seraphs overthrown". His genius was truly "adventurous". "Sovereign, she fram'd a model of her own" and, rejecting even the custom of rhyme, chose the untried "Verse Sublime".[40] The poem ends with a panegyric to the original genius who chooses to write divine poetry and, consequently, inspires devotion in others. Though he "Knows no Rule but native fire", he "talks of unutterable Things" while "With Graces infinite his untaught Fingers rise / Across the Golder Lyre".

This is certainly how Watts regarded himself. Despite his repeated acknowledgment of man's lowly spiritual status, his egotistical genius con-

---

[40] For Watts's originality of prosody and metre, see V. de Sola Pinto, "Isaac Watts and the Adventurous Muse", *Essays and Studies* (Oxford, 1935), pp. 86–107.

tinually asserted itself. He saw the poet as his own treasure house and universe and condemned anything that threatened to dilute his personal vision. An aggressive self-confidence reinforces his belief in his own genius and his espousal of originality. The popularity of his poems makes him the most widely heard and determinedly original voice of the time.

After Watts, the pressure to defend and justify sacred poetry appears to have diminished. The fashion persisted but there is a marked decrease in critical discussion. Fewer authors felt the need to preface their poems with apologias for the genre and were often content with an acknowledgment of their masters. Thus Daniel Baker, the Rector of Fincham in Norfolk, noted that his aim in *The History of Job* (1706) was the same as "that learned author", Sir Richard Blackmore. His explanation that the character of Job attracts because it is "not conformable to the Scheme of Homer and Virgil, from whose Model our Modern Criticks have borrowed all their Laws and Rules of Poetry" without considering "that the Case is much alter'd since the Days of those two famous Writers" (sig. A2ᵛ), has the facility of a much-turned commonplace. It is not surprising that in an earlier poem he also saw fit to pronounce Cowley the saviour of English poetry and wit and the happy equal of Homer and Virgil.[41] Thomas Ellwood, the Quaker, followed even closer in Cowley's wake and published yet another *Davideis* in 1712.

Watts too, had his followers. Joseph Mitchell, whose *Jonah* (1720) had at least two editions, addressed the dedication to him, declaring that his greatest endeavour was to emulate him. Elizabeth Rowe was also inspired by him.[42] As late as 1754, the combined influence of the theories of Dennis, Blackmore and Watts is still strong in Samuel Bowden's *Poems on Various Subjects* (Bath, 1754).

The *Spectator* lent its considerable authority to the popularity of divine poetry, particularly in the papers devoted to *Paradise Lost*. That Milton "received but very few Assistances from Heathen Writers, who were Strangers to the Wonders of Creation", that many examples of the Sublime are evident in Holy Writ and that Eastern poets are generally more imaginative than those of cooler, western climes became, with Mr Spectator's assistance, the cornerstones of any discussion on the relative originality of sacred and secular poetry.[43] Nor did the *Spectator* hesitate to suggest that,

---

[41] "On Mr Abraham Cowley's Works" in *Poems upon Several Occasions* (1697), pp. 1–2.

[42] *The History of Joseph. A Poem* (1736) and "To Mr Watts, on his Poems sacred to Devotion" in *Poems on Several Occasions* in *Miscellaneous Works in Prose and Verse,* 2 vols. (1739), I, 70–71.

[43] See Nos. 160 and 339.

since the Christian religion lends itself so superbly to poetic treatment, more sacred poems should be undertaken:

One would wonder that more of our Christian Poets have not turned their Thoughts this way, especially if we consider that our Idea of the Supreme Being is not only infinitely more Great and Noble than what would possibly enter into the Heart of a Heathen, but filled with everything that can raise the Imagination and give an Opportunity for the Sublimest Thoughts and Conceptions.[44]

Another popular divine poem, Edward Young's *The Last Day,* received a commendation in the *Guardian* 51 (1713) while still in manuscript.[45] It is an interesting essay, not only because it summarises many of the themes often broached in the discussion of divine poetry—another indication of how commonplace they had become—but also because the lover of divine poetry is depicted as tender-hearted and emotional. The writer claims that he has a heart "tender and generous, a Heart that can swell with the Joys, or be depress'd with the Misfortunes of others, nay more, even of Imaginary Persons; a Heart large enough to receive the Greatest Ideas Nature can suggest, and delicate enough to relish the most beautiful".[46] It is Dennis's prescription for poetry in a sentimental application. As he had predicted and the *Guardian* attests, the true Lover of Poetry can only find this emotional stimulation in Sacred Poetry, which will last "when Homer's shall decay". Sacred poetry alone is capable of giving true pleasure. Echoing Dennis, the *Guardian* claims "That Poetry gives us the greatest Pleasure which affects us most, and that affects us most, which is on a Subject in which we have the deepest Concern..." (p. 312).[47]

---

[44] *Spectator* 453, IV, 95.

[45] When published in 1714, the poem had two editions in the same year. See Fairchild, II, 134. There is some doubt as to who wrote the essay. One of Young's biographers attributed it to Steele, while the other, Shelley, thought Young himself was the writer.

[46] *The Guardian,* (1714), I, 309–310.

[47] A multitude of other writers offered variations, refinements and endless repetitions of these ideas. See, for example: *The Athenian Oracle,* 2nd. ed. (1704), I, 269 in favour of the aesthetic value of religious poetry; Matthew Prior's Preface to *Solomon* (1718) in which there are echoes of Dennis's belief in the redeeming power of religion for modern poetry; James Ralph, "Of Poetry" in *The Taste of the Town* (1731) suggests the same remedy for the theatre; (the ribald nature of this work probably means the author was not in deadly earnest); Isaac Hawkins Browne, although more strongly influenced by Shaftesbury than earlier theorists on divine poetry, compares the poet with God on the basis of their originality (*Of Design and Beauty,* 1734); in the Preface to his *Miscellany of Original Poems on Various Subjects* (1752), Francis Hawling insists on his originality (see Fairchild, II, 290); Anthony Blackwell led the way to sounder Biblical criticism and asserted the superiority of the Biblical poets over the Ancients in *The Sacred Classics defended and illustrated* (1725). John Hughes, friend and collaborator of Blackmore, displayed in his Preface to *On Divine Poetry* in *Poems on Several Occasions* (1735) and in *Essay on Allegorical Poetry* (publ. 1735, although possibly written before Husbands' *Miscellany*), a similarly lively enthusiasm for the originality of primitive

34

The Last Day, a poem of impeccable Protestant orthodoxy, has something of Watts's sense of individuality and forecasts the central tenet of the *Conjectures,* "Know Thyself":

> Think deeply, then 0 man, how *great* thou art;
> Pay thyself homage with a trembling heart;
> ....
> Enter the sacred temple of thy breast,
> And gaze, and wander there, a ravish'd guest;
> Gaze on those hidden treasures thou shalt find,
> Wander through all the glories of thy mind.[48]

Later Voices

One of the last extensive discussions on the originality of sacred poetry is contained in John Husbands's Preface to *A Miscellany of Poems by several Hands* (1731).[49] Although he does not explicitly acknowledge any of his predecessors, many of the ideas discussed above are evident in his thinking. For example, he defends his inclusion of sacred poetry in the *Miscellany* by arguing that the prevailing taste of the Age for the literary standards of Greece and Rome is now anachronistic and rests solely on custom and familiarity. Far from being a guide to excellence, the narrow insularity of these standards vitiates their usefulness. Their indiscriminate application is absurdly myopic as well as pretentious:

People are apt to form their Notions of Excellence from their own Perfections, and their Notions of Things from Objects with which they are most conversant. Our Art of Criticism is drawn from the Writers of *Rome* and *Athens,* whom We make the Standard of Perfection. But

poetry. In *Letters concerning Poetical Translations etc.* (1739) William Benson suggested that the Bible supplies "the standard of our Language" and for it to diminish in significance would mean chaos (pp. 82–83). It was about this time that Thomas Seaton (1684–1741) endowed at Cambridge a yearly prize for sacred poetry (Fairchild, II, 65). The popularity of divine poetry persisted. See, for example, the Preface to *Poems Divine, Moral, and Philosophical* (Gloucester, 1746). Sacred oratorios also gained in popularity. As well as the *Messiah,* Handel set Samuel Humphrey's *Deborah* to music (1746); William de Fisch wrote the music for John Hoadley's *Judith* (1733).

[48] *The Complete Works of the Reverend Edward Young,* I (London, 1854), 286.

[49] See R. S. Crane, "An Early Eighteenth Century Enthusiast for Primitive Poetry: John Husbands," *MLN,* 37 (1922), 27–36. Professor Crane took Husbands' authorship for granted on the basis of Boswell's remark, "A Miscellany of Poems, Collected by a person of the name of Husbands" (p. 27). In J. H. Burn's *Catalogue, Part I of Ancient and Modern Books* (1822–30), however, the volume is described thus: "This volume is curious from the circumstance of the Preface containing Remarks on the Beauties of the Holy Scriptures especially considered in a Classical View, being written by Dr. Johnson, and the translation of Pope's Messiah inserted in the Work, his first published literary production" (p. 55). A careless statement by an ignorant bookseller, or another of Johnson's many anonymous prefaces?

35

why have not the *Jews* as much Right to prescribe to *Them,* as *They* have to prescribe to the Jews? Yet to this Test We endeavour to bring the sacred Books, not considering that the Genius and Custom of the *Israelites,* were in many things very different from those of the *Greeks* or *Romans.* This is just as if an Inhabitant of *Bantam* shou'd endeavour to adjust our Behaviour, according to the Manners of his own Countrymen. (sig. E1^v)

In order to distinguish the characteristics of the two antipathetic cultures of the east and west, he, too, resorts to the well-known contrast between the natural and the rule-bound genius. Not unexpectedly he decides that "the Genius of the *East* soars upon stronger Wings, and takes a loftier Flight, than the Muse of *Greece,* or *Rome*" (sig. E3^r). Echoing the distinction made by Sir William Temple and Mr Spectator, among others, he compares the differences between "the *Oriental* and *European* Poetry" in horticultural terms. European gardens may well display "greater Elegance, Order and Regularity" (Sig. F1^v), but the gardens of the East consist of "inartificial Beauties" and an "agreeable Rudeness" because there Nature "appears in all her Charms", and "unsubdu'd by Art" can offer "a wild, and perhaps more forcible, Pleasure to the Mind" (sig. F2^r).

Hebrew poetry reveals qualities more natural, vigorous, and by implication, more desirable than those to be found in classical works. This enviable extravagance makes it a more suitable vehicle for the expression of the passions, in particular a reverence for God, than the calm and well-ordered poetry of the west. It is clear that Husbands shared Dennis's belief that passion is the mark of great poetry and that all poetry, but in particular sacred poetry, must have an emotional impact to be effective:

... the Strength and Energy of the Figures, and the true Sublimity of Style, are a natural Effect of the Passions. No wonder therefore that their Diction is something more flourish'd and ornamental, more vigorous and elevated, more proper to paint and set Things before our Eyes, than plain and ordinary Recitals. This sort of Poetry is more simple, and at the same time more worthy of the Majesty of God, than that which is regular and confined, which must with Difficulty express the Dictates of the Holy Spirit, and wou'd be apt to give some Alloy to the Sublimity of the Sense. (sig. C3^r)

He notes and approves of Cowley's commendation of the Bible as a bountiful source of new subject matter. His opinion of the relative merits of the sacred writers and the great Ancients is unequivocal. In his view, the sacred writings "far surpass all human compositions". Indeed, "the Bible in competition with other books is (to use Lord Bacon's comparison) like Moses' rod, which immediately swallowed up those of the magicians". The writings of the Prophets, for example, abound with the "strong Thoughts and magnificent Ideas" of the Sublime and instances from them would far outdo those examples from the Ancients which Longinus selected. This should not surprise his readers, Husbands thinks, for the books of the Bible

36

have the incomparable advantage of divine inspiration and are, consequently, "far superior to any Thing that the Mind of Man, unassisted, cou'd have been able to invent or conceive". Guided "by a Power more than human", the authors of the Bible, according to Husbands, evince "a divine Enthusiasm" and "a Fury something more than Poetical" (sig. L4^r).

Husbands also suggests that instead of attempting to confine the wild enthusiastic fury of the Biblical authors within the restricting conventions inherited from the literatures of Greece and Rome, modern authors should look to these "noble Strains of Poetry" for "new Laws for the Sublime". They are worthier models for they "teach Us Beauties never yet attain'd by the greatest of Heathen Writers" (sig. O3^{r-v}). Although Husbands does not make use of the term "original", he does insist that those who choose to write in the fashion of the Biblical authors may happily ignore all that the Graeco-Roman rules imply, because, unlike those who must follow these rules, they can claim to be as inspired as the writers of Scripture. In this case, the rules, derived from merely mortal and heathen works, are quite irrelevant.

Husbands also touches on another theme which other writers were to exploit more fully. He suggested that divine writers might also turn to Nature, which, in the abundance with which it evinces the benevolent and creative hand of the Deity, is yet another fruitful source of inspiration.[50] Faced with the wonders of God's creation, Man's heart "overflows with love towards the Author of his being and happiness, and he feels a kind of inspiration which tunes his soul for harmony and thanksgiving". Thus, inspired both by the great writers of Scripture and the material evidence of God's own creativity, the divine poet is guaranteed a subject of perpetual originality:

... He has a Subject infinitely superior to all others; a Subject that can never satiate, that can never be exhausted; a Subject which is worthy to employ the Thoughts of all created Beings to Eternity. (sig. B2^v)

Husbands's own contribution to the discussion is his bluntly stated belief that the current indifference to the Bible in Society is simply evidence of its bad taste. The fact that the Bible is no longer a source of admiration and respect to the average man of intelligence and taste "must proceed from a great corruption in his taste, as well as a great depravity in his manners ... Hence that contempt, hence that insensibility to the greatest beauties that ever adorned poetry". This is the first hint of what was to become in later, more irreligious times, a much commoner attitude. Before

---

[50] See below, Ch. 3.

long, although the beauty of its poetry was a subject of general agreement, the spiritual aspects of the Bible were increasingly considered of less significance.

Indeed, by the 1740's, the notion that the Bible could be assessed purely in terms of its value as great poetry had become sufficiently established to permit Robert Lowth to deliver his lectures as Professor of Poetry at Oxford on that very subject.[51] By now, in fact, it is not the poetry but the truth of the Bible that is subject to question. In his second lecture Lowth announced:

Since, therefore, in the sacred writings the only specimens of the primeval and genuine poetry are to be found, and since these are not less venerable for their antiquity than for their divine original, I conceived it my duty in the first place to investigate the nature of these writings, as far as might be consistent with the design of this institution: in other words, it is not my intention to expound to the student of theology the oracles of Divine Truth, but to recommend to the notice of the youth who is addicted to the politer sciences and studious of the elegancies of composition some of the first and choicest specimens of poetic taste. (pp. 50–51)

Lowth's lectures were primarily a literary exegesis of the Bible, but, in the course of his talks, he not only assembles many of the elements which had attracted writers of previous generations to sacred poetry, but also forges in a new way the now traditional link between the concept of sacred poetry as the greatest kind and the concept of poetry as the spontaneous language of the heart. In his first lecture he repeats the adage that poetry has had its origins in religion and that it is most perfect when, true to its origins, it concerns itself with divine themes. In addition, when a poet chooses a divine subject, Lowth's auditors were to hear, he enters a realm of inspiration in which the restraints of convention and rule no longer apply:

In other instances Poetry appears to want the assistance of art, but in this to shine forth with all its natural splendour, or rather to be animated by that inspiration, which on other occasions is spoken of without being felt. (p. 36)

The "ineffable sublimity" of the subject matter of Hebrew poetry and its perfection of language and style are a further testimony to divine inspiration. It is obvious, then, that a poetry of this perfection equals or excels the writings of what Lowth cuttingly describes as the "fabulous ages of Greece". The sophistication and polish of this culture is no substitute.

Many of the other premises in current use in the arguments in favour of the superiority of primitive, unclassical poetry are unhesitatingly incor-

---

[51] *De Sacra Poesi Hebræorum Praelectiones Academicae Oxonii habitae* etc. 1741–1750 (Oxford, 1753). Many editions. English translation, G. Gregory, (London, 1787). Quotations are from this edition.

porated by Lowth in his exposition of the merits of Biblical poetry. He claims, for example, that as well as having its origins in religion, poetry in this prototypical state was essentially a natural outpouring of violent and impetuous emotions. It was only later, in more sedate times, that attempts were made to curb the spontaneous expression of inflamed passion. That feeling of universal decay that prompted a longing for a return to some more perfect pristine state contributes to the belief that the need to express violent emotion had disappeared with the progress of time and the advance of civilization. The growing awareness of historical perspective adds a further dimension. Lowth declared to his students:

Thus, if the actual origin of Poetry be inquired after, it must of necessity be referred to Religion; and since it appears to be an art derived from nature alone, peculiar to no age or nation, and only at an advanced period of society conformed to rule and method, it must be wholly attributed to the more violent affections of the heart, the nature of which is to express themselves in an animated and lofty tone, with a vehemence of expression far removed from vulgar use. (p. 37)

Ideas derived from religion, in particular the concept of the Godhead, can only find appropriate expression in impetuous, uncontrolled and broken language—the language of the heart rather than that of art and rule—because the true language of the emotions is ignorant of "rule and method". Lowth believed that this may be the very reason why the study of the poetry of the Bible has for so long been neglected. Profane poetry, at a remove from true emotion, is circumscribed and finite and therefore, lends itself more readily to study. It is also more easily reduced to rule and order, whereas those writings "which are justly attributed to the inspiration of the Holy Spirit, may be considered as indeed illustrious by their native force and beauty, but not as conformable to the principles of science nor to be circumscribed by any rules of art" (p. 31).[52]

In his seventeenth lecture, Lowth goes further and identifies the greatest poetry as that which reflects the perturbation of the individual mind and which succeeds in the excitation of the emotions. Poetry, he says, is "the effect of mental emotion" and "the agitation of passion":

As poetry ... derives its very existence from the more vehement emotions of the mind, so its greatest energy is displayed in the expression of them; and by exciting the passions it more effectually attains its end. (p. 367)

The poetic process is still one of imitation, but Lowth's definition of imitation is comprehensive: "whatever the human mind is able to conceive, it is

---

[52] See also Lectures III and XXXIII, in which Lowth noted the irrelevance of classical rules to the Bible or to the poetry of any other culture or society.

the province of poetry to imitate". Although this may be merely "things, places, appearances natural and artificial, actions, passions, manners and customs", there is a finer sort of imitation which occurs when the human mind turns its attention inwards and regards itself:

... since the human intellect is naturally delighted with every species of imitation, that species in particular, which exhibits its own image, which displays and depicts those impulses, inflexions, perturbations, and secret emotions, which it perceives and knows in itself, can scarcely *fail* to astonish and to delight above every other. The delicacy and difficulty of this kind of imitation are among its principle commendations; for to effect that which appears almost impossible naturally excites our admiration. The understanding slowly perceives the accuracy of the description in all other subjects, and their agreement to their archetypes, as being obliged to compare them by the aid and through the uncertain medium, as it were, of the memory: but when a passion is expressed, the object is clear and distinct; the mind is immediately conscious of itself and its own emotions; it feels and suffers in itself a sensation, either the same or similar to that which is described. (p. 368)

At a period when poems steeped in subjective emotion, such as Young's prodigious *Night Thoughts,* were enormously popular, Lowth offers a cogent and authoritative explanation for their appeal:

... that sublimity, which arises from the vehement agitation of the passions, and the imitation of them, possesses a superior influence over the human mind; whatever is exhibited to it from without, may well be supposed to move and agitate it less than what it internally perceives, of the magnitude and force of which it is previously conscious. (pp. 368–369)

Although Lowth contends that emotional poetry and religious poetry are one and the same—"by far the greatest part of the sacred poetry is little else than a continued imitation of the different passions" (p. 376)—his remarks make it clear that the time is ripe for a poetry whose main or only interest is the display of emotion for its own sake and whose links with divine poetry become more tenuous, to be replaced with the fascination of the workings of the individual mind.[53]

Sacred poetry stemmed from an earnest desire that imaginative literature should reflect Truth. At the same time, it was recognised as a new and enticing source of originality by many of those for whom the delights of classical imitation, either of fable or genre, had begun to pall. Although by no means a majority of those who undertook divine poetry, these "original" authors were, nevertheless, an influential group. Many of them appealed to the large and attentive audience that was neither equipped nor disposed to appreciate the classical works of a Pope or Swift.

At the outset, it was the subject matter of the Bible that proved most

[53] The religio-meditative poetry of the mid-eighteenth century is well documented. See, for example, Amy Reed, *The Background of Grey's Elegy* (N. Y., 1924; rpt. 1962).

alluring to those in search of new and original themes. Divine writers seized with relief on the "Truths" of Scripture and set about translating them into poetry. The objections were many. Dr Johnson, for example, summarised many earlier arguments when he argued that the feelings that the Scriptures arouse in us are either too reverential or horrifying for "pleasure and terror" to ensue. Furthermore, this reverence eradicates the hope that a mere mortal can embellish the truths of God. "Such events as were produced by the visible interposition of Divine Power are above the power of human genius to dignify".[54]

Johnson was also sceptical of the originality that divine writers believed they found in Biblical subjects:

... these truths are too important to be new; they have been taught to our infancy; they have mingled with our solitary thoughts and familiar conversation, and are habitually interwoven with the whole texture of life. Being therefore not new they raise no unaccustomed emotion in the mind: what we knew before we cannot learn; what is not unexpected cannot surprise.[55]

The apologists for divine poetry either did not know of or chose to ignore these arguments. Indeed, in many cases, as in the work of Cowley, Dennis and Watts, precisely the opposite of these views is expressed.

The growing interest in human psychology had momentous consequences for the theorists who believed in the superiority of divine poetry. They could now offer a new justification for its importance. If poetry is great in proportion to how much it affects the reader, then, went the argument, that poetry is greatest that affects the reader most. What is most affecting is that which most concerns us, and that must be concern for the immortal soul. This concern can be extended to the whole of society, and, since the greatest poetry has always been that which most adequately reflects the preoccupations of the society in which it is written, a poet should turn to the beliefs of his own time and country. If he continues in the shade of the great Ancients, he will never be more than their shadow. In order to equal or excel them, the modern author, agreed the divine writers, must turn to that which most concerns his readers — their own religious beliefs.

As universal agreement on the Bible as the literal word of God began to wane, and, indeed, as the deluge of divine poems continued unabated, the originality of Biblical subject matter was less often trumpeted. The modified legacy of the *vates* which persisted and the growing interest in the emotive

---

[54] *Life of Cowley*, ed. Birkbeck Hill (1905), I, 50. For earlier opposition, see for example, Shaftesbury, "'Tis apparent therefore that the Manners, Actions and Characters of *Sacred Writ* are in no wise the proper Subject of other Authors than *Divines* themselves" (*Soliloquy*, 1710), p. 190.

[55] *Life of Milton*, ed. Birkbeck Hill (1905), I, 182. See also the *Life of Isaac Watts*, II, 385.

qualities of primitive and Hebrew poetry in particular, further diluted interest in the Bible as a fruitful and unexploited source of originality. Instead, the realization of the passionate nature of Biblical verse, the powerful Longinian tradition and the individualism inherent in dissenting Protestantism and coloured by notions of inspiration, prompted the development of the long meditative poem. In it the analysis of the poet's thoughts and emotions in the face of the great imponderables of life and death takes precedence over the earlier fascination with originality. However original they may, in fact, have been, fewer authors lay claim to this distinction. It is as if the pious nature of their undertaking has subsumed such profane ambition.

This movement away from a preoccupation with originality also threatened and was, eventually, to submerge at least to some extent, another source of inspiration often hailed as original—the experiments and advances of natural philosophy.

Chapter 2

Science: "a terra incognita to the Muses"

Around the middle of the seventeenth century, science started to enjoy a popularity somewhat analogous with our modern fondness for ecology. While the flirtation lasted, Society, ever on the look-out for novelty, was handsomely rewarded for its interest.[1] Scientific handbooks and journals for the layman proliferated.[2] Well-attended public lectures were a frequent occurrence in the larger cities of Britain and Ireland.[3] The commercial potential of the new fad was appreciated by enterprising entrepreneurs. As the advertisements in newspapers of the day show, purveyors of microscopes, telescopes, orreries and the other paraphernalia of scientific experiment did a brisk trade.[4] Indeed the popularity of the recreation is nowhere better illustrated than in the extent of the efforts made to render the subject more intelligible to the meaner, female, intellect. Since Fontenelle's successful *Conversations with a Lady on the Plurality of Worlds,* their scientific leanings were treated with great seriousness, at least some of the time.[5] They attended lectures, read literature on the subject prepared especially for them, had scientific works dedicated to them, made journeys (or, more accurately, outings) to places of scientific interest, such as coal mines,

---

[1] See Carl Grabo, "Science and the Romantic Movement," *Annals of Science,* 4 (1939), 191–205; G. D. Meyer, *The Scientific Lady in England 1650–1760,* (Berkeley, 1955), p. 105; J. H. Plumb, *The Commercialisation of Leisure in Eighteenth-century England* (Reading, 1973).

[2] For example, J. T. Desaguliers, *Lectures of Experimental Philosophy* which were copied and edited by Paul Dawson, a protegé of Steele, in 1719 with a second edition in the same year and Henry Baker, *The Microscope Made Easy,* 1742; 2nd. ed. 1743.

[3] For example, the famous Boyle Lectures established by a Codicil to Boyle's will dated July 28th, 1691. In 1711–12 (publ. 1713), these lectures were given by William Derham on Physico-Theology, and proved enormously popular. Derham's blend of science and theology was eagerly appropriated by the devotional poets.

[4] See M. H. Nicolson, "The Microscope and English Imagination" in *Science and Imagination* (Ithaca, N. Y., 1956; rpt. 1962), p. 178.

[5] *Entretiens sur la pluralité des mondes* (1686), tr. Aphra Behn (1688); Joseph Glanvil (1695); W. Gardiner (1715). Fontenelle's ability to popularize science was much admired. Blackmore acknowledged this in his Preface to *The Creation* (1712).

and were exhorted by advertisements to equip themselves with handsome pocket microscopes designed exclusively for their use.[6]

There were, of course, those who remained immune to the charms of change and discovery. To them these early stirrings of scientific interest were simply more evidence of the spiritual and intellectual decay they saw on all sides. In particular, they abhorred what they regarded as the foolish pride in feeble human endeavour that such impertinent curiosity engendered.[7] In its turn, this antipathy spawned that wealth of satire on scientific effort for which the Age is so famous. Shadwell's Virtuosos, Sir Nicholas

---

[6] Nicolson, pp. 182–193; many of these activities were celebrated in the occasional poems of the time, not a few of which were, of course, dedicated to the ladies. See, for example: Richard Savage's compliment to Mrs Oldfield in *The Wanderer* (1729):

Bacon, and *Newton* in her Thought conspire;
Not sweeter than her Voice is *Hendel's* Lyre. (p. 103);

Henry Jones (an Irish bricklayer): *Philosophy, a Poem, address'd to the Ladies who attended Mr Booth's Lectures in Dublin* in *Poems on Several Occasions* (1749) which begins:

To Science sacred Muse, exalt thy Lays;
  Science of Nature, and to Nature's Praise:
Attend, ye Virtuous, and rejoice to know
Her mystick Labours, and her Laws below; (p. 22);

The Reverend Tipping Silvester dedicated *The Microscope. A Poem* to the anonymous "Mrs L—" (*Original Poems and Translations*, 1733); similarly, Moses Browne addressed his "Essay on the Universe" (*The Works and Rest of the Creation*, 1752) to the fair sex in general:

But chief, ye Fair, whose tempted Hand invites
The Rose of Science, while it's Thorn afrights;
Who, by the Poet's Effort, may be won
To read deep Systems, that in Prose ye shun.
For love of Candour, as for Genius prais'd,
Smile on a Muse by generous Motives rais'd,
Cheer her bold Flights th' etherial Tracts along;
For you I meditate the arduous Song; (pp. 4–5)

See also, John Dalton, *A Descriptive Poem addressed to Two Ladies, At their Return from Viewing The Mines near Whitehaven* (1755). This poem has copious footnotes on mining procedures, risks etc. by a W. Brownrigg, who applauds the novelty and originality of the work, but wonders if it will find favour with the public. See "A Letter to the Author", pp. 26, 27. Poems on mines were not new, however, see *News from Newcastle* (1651).

[7] The remarks of Dryden in *Religio Laici* and Pope in *An Essay on Man* (Epistle II) are well-known, but other authors expressed similar views. See, for example: [Thomas Baker], *Reflections upon Learning wherein is shown the Insufficiency thereof, in its several Particulars. In order to evince the Usefulness and Necessity of Revelation. By a Gentleman* (1st. ed. 1699; 3rd. ed. 1700); Alexander Pennecuik, "A Morning Walk to Arthur's Seat" in *Streams from Helicon* (1720); George Woodward, "An Ode" in *Poems on Several Occasions* (Oxford, 1730):

    Man! fond, mistaken Man!
Tho' his capacious Head, the sacred Ark!
Where a whole World of Science does inbark,
    Has steer'd and labour'd all it can,
      As Reason Fill'd the Sail,
Yet what does all this fruitless Search avail?

Gimcrack, the Philosophical Girl, the madmen of the glorious Grand Academy of Lagado and all the other caricatures of the myopic experimenter and collector endure—memorable, if ironic, representatives of this early period of scientific expansion.[8] So sturdy are these embodiments of their

Learn'd Wretch! he fondly would pretend,
His Post is gain'd, his Race is run,
And all his tiresom Voy'ge is done;
Is done! how far? but just enough to shew,
That all his knowledge is but empty Show,
A Pageant Dream! a Point! an End!
No wiser thro' the tedious Course he ran
Fond! mistaken Man!
Than when he first began; (pp. 3–4)

Henry Baker, *The Universe. A Poem intended to restrain the Pride of Man* (?1720): "I thought the readiest way to check this Folly, would be to sketch out a Plan of the Universe; that, by considering the Grandeur of the Whole, MAN might be made sensible of his own Littleness and Insignificance, except in the very place he stands" (p. 6); see G. R. Potter, "Henry Baker. F. R. S.," *MP*, 29 (1931–32), 301–21; Thomas Catesby Paget, *Essay on Human Life* (1734); *Divine Wisdom and Providence* (1736); Mary Leapor, "The Enquiry" in *Poems on Several Occasions* (1748); Henry Jones," An Essay on the Weakness of Human Knowledge and the Uncertainty of mortal Life" in *Poems on Several Occasions* (1749) in which he anticipates Blake in the lines:
The smallest Worm insults the Sage's Hand;
All Gresham's vanquish'd by a Grain of Sand; (p. 65)
Even enthusiasts for science often pondered the comparative insignificance of man. See Sir Richard Blackmore, *The Lay-Monk*, 5 (1713). See also John Dillenberger, *Protestant Thought and Natural Science* (N. Y., 1960); A. D. McKillop. *James Thomson: The Castle of Indolence and other Poems* (Lawrence, Kansas, 1961); Irène Simon, "Robert South and the Augustans," *Essays and Studies* (1975), pp. 15–28.

[8] C. S. Duncan, *The New Science and English Literature in the Classical Period* (N. Y., 1913; rpt. 1972); T. O. Wedel, "On the Philosophical Background of Gulliver's Travels." *SP*, 23 (1926), 434–450; Ralph B. Crum, *Scientific Thought in Poetry* (N. Y., 1931); H. C. Simpson, "The Vogue of Science in English Literature 1600–1800," *UTQ*, 2 (1933), 143–167; Herbert Drennon, "Scientific Rationalism and James Thomson's Poetic Art," *SP*, 31 (1934), 453–471; R. F. Jones, *Ancients and Moderns* (St. Louis, 1936);—, "Science and Criticism in the Neo-Classical Age of English Literature," *JHI*, I (1940), 381–412; W. P. Jones, "The Vogue of Natural History in England, 1750–1770," *Annals of Science*, 2 (1937), 345–352;—, "Science in Biblical Paraphrases in Eighteenth-Century England," *PMLA*, 74 (1959), 41–51;—, "Newton Further Demands the Muse," *SEL*, 3 (1963), 287–306;—, *The Rhetoric of Science* (Berkeley and L. A., 1966); M. H. Nicolson and Nora M. Mohler, "The Scientific Background of Swift's Voyage to Laputa," *Annals of Science*, 2 (1937), 299–334; M. H. Nicolson, *Newton Demands the Muse* (new Haven, 1946);—, *Science and Imagination* (1956; rpt. N. Y., 1962);—, *Mountain Gloom and Mountain Glory: The Development of the Aesthetics of the Infinite* (Ithaca, N. Y., 1959).
The point of view of those conservatives who revered the great thinkers of the past is best illustrated in Book III of *Gulliver's Travels,* where, for example, Aristotle drily remarked that "new systems of nature were but new fashions, which would vary in every age; and even those who pretended to demonstrate them from mathematical principles would flourish but a short period of time, and be out of vogue when that was determined", *Gulliver's Travels* (Penguin English Library, 1967), p. 243. See further, Colm Kiernan, "Swift and Science," *Historical Journal* 14 (1971), 709–22, for Swift's reactions to the developments of science in his day.

creators' disapproval that their puny rivals, the efforts of the satirists on behalf of science, have, not unnaturally, been neglected by later generations.[9]

The impact of science on imaginative literature was not confined to the opportunities it could offer the satirists. There was yet another way in which it contributed to the theory and practice of the authors of the period. It was not long before it was being hailed as a new inspiration to, and potentially rich source for, poets seeking freedom from old ways in original composition.

The Royal Society and Original Composition

When Thomas Hobbes wrote to D'Avenant that the subject of poetry was not natural science but "the manners of men", he was, as usual, somewhat at variance with the opinions of the Age.[10] The example of Lucretius was still a powerful influence.[11] In addition, the efforts of the modern scientist and his successful challenge to authority provoked great admiration among poets struggling with the weight of their own traditions. Not only Newton, but Harvey, Woodward and many other now obscure figures such as Jacob Bobart, Botany Professor at the University of Oxford and Keeper of the Physick Garden, were eulogised by their literary contemporaries for their intellectual freedom and originality of research.[12]

John Norris of Bemerton offered one such compliment, worthy to be placed with Cowley's better known *Ode to the Royal Society.* In his address *To Dr. Plot on the subject of his natural history of Staffordshire,* he contrasts the scientific "Heroic Few" with the lethargic masses who mutely concur with tradition:

> Such drowsie sedentary Souls have they
> Who could to Patriarchal years live on
> Fix'd to *Hereditary* Clay
> And know no climate but their *own*
> Contracted to their narrow *Sphere*
> *Rest* before *Knowledge* they prefer,
> And of this Globe wherein they dwell
> No more than of the Heavenly Orbs can tell

[9] An example of this "pro-science" satire is to be found in Sir Richard Blackmore's journal, *The Lay-monk,* 8 (1713).

[10] He disputed the claims of Lucretius and Empedocles to be poets. See *The Answer of Mr Hobbes to Sir William D'Avenant's Preface Before Gondibert* (1650) in Spingarn, II, 55.

[11] See Spingarn, III, 300.

[12] Abel Evans, *Vertumnus. An Epistle to Mr Jacob Bobart, Botany Professor to the University of Oxford and Keeper of the Physick Garden* (1713).

> As if by Nature placed below
> Not on this Earth to *dwell*, but to take *root* and *grow*. [13]

Norris shares with other writers of like mind an abhorrence for "an over-fond and superstitious deference to Authority, especially that of Antiquity". In his essay, *On the Advantages of Thinking,* he concluded that nothing "cramps the parts and fetters the understandings of men" more than "this strait lac'd humour". [14] Man's tendency to be imitative is disastrous for the human race as well as literature:

Men are resolv'd never to out-shoot their forefathers Mark; but write one after another, and so the Dance goes round in a Circle; out of which, if some had not the Boldness and Courage to venture, the World would never be the Wiser for being older. (p. 117)

Many of the scientists repaid the compliment by taking an active interest in poetry. In fact, not a few combined both vocations. Abraham Cowley was an early enthusiast for science. His interest produced a proposal for forming a scientific Academy that predates the incorporation of the Royal Society. [15] Significantly, this Academy was to further the practices of Baconian empiricism. Abstract theories and hypotheses attracted few of the poet-scientists. Cowley's odes to the Royal Society, to Dr Scarborough and on Dr Harvey sing the praises of their experimental method as well as their independence of authority and their contributions to the furthering of original research. [16] A popular poet, he was noted, not always favourably, for his originality and his disregard of the Rules. [17] It was these qualities which he chose to single out in other poets and, in his commendation, to associate them with the scientific spirit. In his accolade on D'Avenant's *Gondibert,* he noted a new awareness in this epic of truth similar to the search for the truth of matter. The poet, he claimed, had not been content to follow the approved ways of the muse, unlike most others who

> ... their *Fancies* like their *Faith* derive
> And thinking all Ill but that which *Rome* does give.
> The Marks of *Old* and *Catholick* would find
> To the same *Chair,* would *Truth* and *Fiction* bind. [18]

---

[13] *A Collection of Miscellanies* (1678, 4th. ed. 1706), p. 102. For more information on this popular work (9 eds. 1687–1730), see W. P. Jones, p. 38 ff.

[14] *A Collection,* p. 115.

[15] *The Advancement of Experimental Philosophy,* 1661.

[16] See *Poems,* ed. A. R. Waller (Cambridge, 1905), pp. 197–200, 418, 448. See also, "To Mr Hobs", pp. 188–190.

[17] See for example: Thomas Rymer, *Preface to the Translation of Rapin's Reflections on Aristotle's Treatise of Poesie* (1674), Spingarn, II, 173; Earl of Mulgrave, *An Essay upon Poetry,* Spingarn, II, 289; John Dryden, Preface to *Fables,* Ker, II, 158. See also, Loiseau, pp. 40, 43, 55.

[18] "To Sir William Davenant" in *Poems,* pp. 42–43.

D'Avenant has rejected such blind faith. As a child of the new scientific age, he has struck out alone. Disdaining craven imitation himself, he has carved out a path for other, less adventurous, souls to follow:

> Thou in those beaten pathes disdain'st to tred,
> And scorn'st to *Live* by robbing of the Dead.
> Since Time does all things change, thou think'st not fit
> This latter *Age* should see *all New but Wit.*
> Thy *Fancy* like a *Flame* its way does make,
> And leave bright *Tracks* for following Pens to take. (p. 43)

Cowley's predilection for freedom and originality is also evident in his own poetic practice. His preoccupation with the originality of Biblical subject matter has already been noted.[19] In *The Muse* he suggests a wider application of the principle. Originality and not a knowledge of the great works of literature is the foundation of true creativity. Not simply heir and victim of the past, the poet has a closer resemblance to God, the greatest Independent, because both create out of nothing. There are no limitations or restrictions on the poet. He is as free as his abilities permit. In his notes to this poem, Cowley elaborates:

The meaning is, that *Poetry* treats not only of all things that are, or can be, but makes *Creatures* of her own, as *Centaurs, Satyrs, Fairies,* etc. makes *persons* and *actions* of her own as in *Fables* and *Romances,* makes *Beasts, Trees, Waters,* and other irrational and insensible things to act above the possibility of their natures, as to *understand* and *speak,* nay makes what Gods it pleases too without idolatry and varies all these into innumerable Systems, or Worlds of invention.[20]

The connection between poetic originality and scientific discovery is here made clear in the parody of a scientific pandect in which the poet may engage.

Cowley's enormous reputation no doubt popularised this view of the originality of scientific material for the poet.[21] Indeed, it was his staunchest admirer and another poet-scientist, Bishop Thomas Sprat, who made one of the most serious and unusual attempts to resuscitate the art of poetry by a transfusion of the originality engendered by, and inspiring, scientific research.[22]

[19] See above, pp. 12–13.

[20] *Poems*, p. 187. For an unfavourable estimate of Cowley as a scientific poet, see C. S. Duncan, *The New Science and English Literature in the Classical Period,* p. 36.

[21] See Loiseau, p. 21.

[22] Sprat's poetic work includes a poem on Oliver Cromwell published together with poems on the same subject by Edmund Waller and John Dryden (Oxford, 1659) and *The Plage of Athens, which hapned in the second year of the Peloponnesian Warre. First described in Greek by Thucydides; then in Latin by Lucretius; now attempted in English, after the incomparable Dr. Cowley's Pindarick way* (1659). This poem reached its 7th ed. in 1709.

One of Sprat's aims in writing his history of the Royal Society was to win over, or, at least, placate, those opposed to the activities and, indeed, the very existence of that energetic body. He certainly did not take kindly to the barbed scorn of the satirists of the other camp and appears extremely distressed by the efforts of "those Wits and Railleurs". He reproaches them for their ignorance as well as their wit, for, he tells them, they would do better to take note of the efforts of the scientists and exploit the results to the benefit of their own writing. In order to encourage this more advantageous *rapport* he included a chapter in his history entitled "Experiments will be beneficial to our Wits and Writers". In this essay he points the way in which recent developments in the sciences can assist the poet by revealing areas of originality into which poetry has not previously ventured.

He begins by reviewing the eight sources which supply the inventions of wit, in order to find which "are already exhausted, and what remains new and untouch'd, and are likely to be farther advanc'd".[23] Among the categories which he describes as "well-nigh consum'd" are the hackneyed "Fables and Religions of the Ancient World":

They have already serv'd the *Poets* long enough; and it is now high time to dismiss them; especially seing [sic] they have this peculiar *imperfection,* that they were only *Fictions* at first: whereas *Truth* is never so well express'd or amplify'd, as by these Ornaments which are Tru [sic] and *Real* in themselves. (p. 414)

Here Sprat singles out what was the most important claim of the scientific poets over the Neo-Classical. Aware that their original inclinations were not in keeping with the classical tradition, they still insisted with the greatest confidence that a poetry which utilised science must be closer to Truth and, consequently, a greater kind than a poetry based entirely on fiction, however august.

Indeed what makes Sprat's discussion of science and poetry so unusual is his indifference to the demands of the Neo-Classical tradition. He appears to have felt no compulsion to reconcile or match his ideas with what it deemed fitting. This unconformity is particularly obvious when he redefines the hierarchy of genres according to his own scheme of things. The highest kind is no longer the representation of noble actions and the doings of good persons related in narrative or drama, as Aristotle had suggested.[24] As

---

[23] These sources are: "the *Fables,* and *Religions* of the *Antients;* the Civil Histories of all *Countries,* the *Customs* of *Nations,* the *Bible,* the *Sciences,* and *Manners* of *Men,* the several *Arts* of their Hands and the works of *Nature*". See *The History of the Royal Society of London, For the Improving of Natural Knowledge* (1667), p. 413.

[24] *Aristotle's Theory of Poetry and Fine Art,* tr. S. H. Butcher (1895, 412 ed. 1927), ch. IV, p. 17.

scientist and modern man and, therefore, in possession of a hitherto inconceivable degree of truth, Sprat simply states that the "greatest sort of poetry" is that which is inspired by the "Arts of Men's hands". It is "masculine and durable" and is great because it consists of images "that are generally observ'd, and such visible things which are familiar to men's minds" (p. 415). A clue to what Sprat means by this may be found in his famous description of the programme to improve the use of language undertaken by the Royal Society. Comprehensibility and familiarity was their avowed goal; to that end they were

... most rigorous in putting in execution ... a constant Resolution to reject all amplifications, digressions, and swellings of style; to return back to the primitive purity and shortness, when men deliver'd so many *things* almost in an equal number of *words*. They have exacted from all their members a close, naked, natural way of speaking, positive expressions, clear senses, a native easiness, bringing all things as near the Mathematical plainness as they can, and preferring the language of Artizans, Countrymen, and Merchants, before that of Wits and Scholars.[25]

Furthermore, this "the first sort" of poetry is full of potential for the aspiring poet, because it "is still improvable by the advancements of *Experiments*" (p. 415).

Closely related to this poetry of "mechanical things"—in merit as well as in its common scientific basis—is another sort, that which springs from the inspiration of "Working Nature". Because of the great advances made by science in uncovering the secrets of Nature, it has been, and will prove to be "one of the best and most fruitful Soils for the growth of Wit". In this respect, the Moderns have a clear advantage over the Ancients to whom Nature offered little that was original or inspiring. This lack of originality is directly related to the ignorance of scientific matters which prevailed at that time:

Those few things which they knew, they us'd so much, and apply'd so often, that they even almost wore them away by their using. ... They had tir'd out the *Sun* and *Moon*, and *Stars* with their Similitudes, more than they fancy them to be wearied by their daily journeys round the Hevens [sic]. (p. 416)

Such ignorance is out of place in the new world of scientific knowledge which Sprat offers as grist to the mill of modern poets. They are in a position to increase and amplify general understanding of nature by showing the truth of the senses in concrete and comprehensible poetry, to the especial pleasure and profit of the common man:

[25] From The Second Part, Section XX, *Their Manner of Discourse* in Spingarn, II, 117–118.

50

It is now therefore seasonable for *Natural Knowledge* to come forth, and to give us the *understanding* of new *Virtues* and *Qualities* of things; which may relieve their fellow-creatures that have long born [sic] the burden alone and have long bin vex'd by the imaginations of *Poets*. This charitable assistance *Experiments* will soon bestow. The Comparisons which these may afford will be intelligible to all, because they proceed from things that enter into all mens Senses. These will make the most vigorous impressions on mens *Fancies,* because they do even touch their *Eyes,* and are nearest to their *Nature.* (p. 416)

In a final encouraging flourish, Sprat also promises that, because the efforts of science continually reveal new secrets and unravel old mysteries, in the poetry which it will and should inspire, originality is assured. This is made possible by the fact that science deals with the endless detail of Nature whose minutest atom, when examined closely, reveals a universe unto itself. On this point too, Sprat appears casually indifferent to another of the cornerstones of Neo-Classicism, the theory of "generality":

... the variety will be infinite; for the particulars are so from whence they may be deduc'd: These may be always new and unsullied, seing [sic] there is such a vast number of *Natural* and *Mechanical things,* not yet fully known or improv'd, and by consequence not yet sufficiently apply'd. [26]

This variety is not only restricted to subject matter. On the strength of the example of Bacon, Sprat confidently prescribes science as a means to enrich the language of the poet and is, thereby, again at odds with the pundits of Neo-Classicism. [27]

Sprat's discussion of the role that science might play in the resuscitation of poetry introduces three new, but fundamentally unclassical, ideas on the subject of the originality of poetry. In his thought, the anthropomorphic standards of Neo-Classicism have been superseded by concepts which give first place to the new realities as revealed by science, not least because of their immediate relevance and utility. Firstly, science supplies to the poet a foundation of truth which is not simply the universally applicable truths of

[26] P. 416. Cf. *Rambler* 36, "Poetry cannot dwell upon the minute distinctions, by which one species differs from another, without departing from that simplicity of grandeur which fills the imagination; nor dissect the latent qualities of things without losing its general power of gratifying every mind, by recalling its conception". See also: " ... to describe with propriety, minuteness is not so necessary as an enumeration of the more striking, picturesque, and peculiar circumstances: the former is the province of the Naturalist and Philosopher; the latter is the characteristic of a Poet", *Monthly Review,* 18 (1758), 278, quoted by R. A. Aubin, *Topographical Poetry in XVIII-Century England* (1936, rpt. N. Y., 1966), p. 56. Dr. Johnson's predeliction for the general is, of course, not so simple. See Howard D. Weinbrot, "The Reader, the General, and the Particular: Johnson and Imlac in Chapter Ten of *Rasselas,*" *ECS,* 5 (Fall, 1971), 80–96. An extensive bibliography of studies on the theory of generality and particularity is included in this issue of *ECS.*
[27] Hobbes, for example, objected to "the names of Instruments and Tools of Artificers, and words of Art".

human experience, but the seemingly incontrovertible truth of matter. This scientific truth leaves no place for the unacceptable fantasies and benighted ignorance of classical literature. It is evident that the image of the Golden Age held little attraction for men of Sprat's ilk. That which has immediate relevance, which is the result of empirical experiment and which can survive the test of ordinary human sense, must displace the anachronisms of a long dead culture and literature. Secondly, the great genres of epic and tragedy, which celebrate man as noble hero, are subsumed by a new one which celebrates man as mechanic. The Baconian scientist and his painstaking labours have totally overshadowed the exploits and sufferings of the classical giants and their innumerable imitations. Thirdly, and unquestionably of greatest historical significance, Sprat points to a new kind of nature poetry in which the detail and variety of Nature will have an independent and intrinsic importance. He sought to encourage poets to look at the face of Nature in her infinite variety for their inspiration. And indeed, as time passed, a growing number of poets, especially among those who considered themselves "unlearned", found their inspiration in the countryside and the contemplation of the beauties and terrors of nature.[28]

At least one contemporary felt obliged to acknowledge the assistance that the august body of the Royal Society might afford the aspiring poet, thereby gratifying the literary historian at any rate. Samuel Woodford, a fellow member of the Society, and ever on the watch for hints of daring originality, wrote that he would make yet another effort of that kind. His proposal was nothing less than "The History of the first great week of the World" which, he felt was now quite within the bounds of possibility, because recent discoveries had "made the subject more large and comprehensive for verse than ever it has been".[29] As a scientist, he approaches such a subject with some confidence for he feels he can expect "great assistance" from the "unwearied and most successful labours of the *Royal Society*". In his view, they have not only improved "Natural Philosophy in the general", but have also been responsible for "the restauration of decay'd Arts", in particular, "serious, profitable, and sober Poesy" (sig. C2ʳ). His promise notwithstanding, Woodford does not appear to have undertaken such a project, and he was, in any case, soon preempted by the flood of Creation poems which appeared at the turn of the century. The relationship between poetry and science, however, continued to attract attention.

[28] See Ch. 3 below.
[29] Preface to *A Paraphrase upon the Psalms of David* (1667). Woodford was elected to the Royal Society in November, 1664. See pp. 13–14 above.

John Reynolds and Joseph Trapp: Advocates of Science and Original Composition

It was the obscure John Reynolds, Dissenting minister, who produced the first long scientific poem of the eighteenth century. To him also, goes the credit for the first aesthetic discussion of scientific poetry of the century. In the Preface to *Death's Vision Represented in a Philosophical, Sacred Poem* (1709), in which his awareness of past and present scientific poets, from Lucretius to Blackmore, gives continuity to his thinking on the matter, Reynolds examines the state of modern poetry.[30] He finds the dominant genre to be satire, but feels that what was once an effective means of lashing vice and depravity, has become acceptable, fashionable, and, finally, as debauched as that which it would reform. Nobler and more appropriate subjects, such as the Bible might offer, are shamefully neglected, and the prostitution of the art of poetry appears complete. So far Reynolds is simply repeating common enough sentiments, but he now goes further than most of his contemporaries by urging, not only a return to religious subject matter in order to restore poetry to its former dignity, but also to suggest that the same end may be achieved, just as effectively, by resorting to science:

And will Religion Advance and Reform our Poetry, and will not Philosophy do so too? (p.2)

In Reynolds's view, science and religion are closely related. He refutes the not uncommon charge that atheism is the foundation of much scientific thought by insisting that the most recent scientific discoveries take full account of "the Easy and free Constitution of an Almighty Agent" and by reminding his readers that Newton, Whiston and Keil, the most reputable scientists of the day, have accepted as a first premise that everything depends "upon the Arbitrary Appointment of a most wise Architect". It is therefore quite certain, he argues, that scientific poetry must be as serious and elevating as divine poetry and that it merits the same reverence:

Since then these Laws of Motion, founded on Boundless Wisdom, and Arbitrary Determination, reach to all things we see, and Converse with, justly may Appeal be made to the Phenomena of Heaven and Earth, for demonstration of Divine Existence and Perfection. (p. 2)

---

[30] He knows the works of Lucretius, Virgil, Henry More and Cowley. He is aware, too, of the fact that Sir Richard Blackmore is currently engaged on *The Creation,* with which, he declares, his poem cannot compare. He disclaims all knowledge of "the just rules of a Poem, or either the demands or Bounds of the Pindaric Liberty" (p. 8). *Death's Vision* (rpt. 1713) was expanded and published as *A View of Death: or the Soul's Departure from the World* in 1725. See W. P. Jones, *The Rhetoric of Science,* pp. 84–86.

Resuming his argument that science is a fit subject for poetry, Reynolds expresses amazement that in an age so disposed towards, and enriched by, science as the present Age, little has yet found its way into poetry:

Is it not wonder then, that among the numerous Subjects, that are Elaborately Sung, Philosophy in a Philosophical Age (and so Philosophical, that such Problems have been Resolv'd and Discoveries made, as no Ages are known to have been blest with before) shou'd be no more Cultivated by the Sons of the Muses? (p. 3)

He appears to have been conscious of the difficulties such a new departure would precipitate, and is one of the first to come to grips with the problems which the stuff of science presents to the poet. Unlike Bishop Sprat, he does not see science and poetry as natural sister arts. He acknowledges that science is "Restive", "Refractory and Unpolishable Enough"; that "'tis Unactive, Heavy and Dull" and "refuses, Ordinarily, that Metaphorical Cloathing, those turns of Fancy and Wit that almost Essentiate a Poem, and Accomodate [sic] it to Sprightly Minds". He admits, too, that the language of science is reckoned to lack "that Sweetness and Softness" which is commonly felt to be a prerequisite of poetry. Scientific vocabulary is thought of "as Insignificant and Insipid to the Men of Air and Wit", but, he adds, deftly turning the tables, poets are considered in just the same light by "those of Philosophical Thoughts and Study". The solution to the problem is not to bring science closer to poetry but the reverse. Reynolds seems to have thought that it would be in their own best interests if poets set about acquiring a greater knowledge of science. They have the example of the scientists whose greatest achievements are due to their having combined their scientific endeavours with the poetic gifts of Imagination and Fancy:

Certainly there had been a more Easy Conjunction of 'em, had our Poets been furnishd with as much Philosophy, as Philosophers have with Strength of Imagination and Fancy. (p. 3)

It is clear that Reynolds feels that the subject of science in poetry justifies itself. The long tradition of scientific poetry supports his contention. He refers to primitive times when the poets concerned themselves both with "investigating the Mysteries of Nature, and Celebrating them in their Daily Songs of Devotion". He points out that the celebration of science is as old as the celebration of God in nature. Even Lucretius, he notes, called on the assistance of the Muse and thereby ensured that his philosophy would continue to attract subsequent generations. This thought prompts Reynolds to add a new dimension to the claim that scientific poetry embraces a more accurate sort of truth. If the heathen Lucretius could so successfully blend poetry and science, he declares, "a Baptis'd Poet" has good reason to "Sing a better Philosophy to a better End" (p. 7).

In describing the aims of his own poem, Reynolds, although scrupulously insisting on the spiritual aspects, lays great emphasis on the scientific import. He announces that his goal has been the Lucretian one of rendering science intelligible to his readers and he will be satisfied if, by his poem, they should be

... any whit assisted to Remember those more noted Phaenomena of Nature, that either are acknowledged Unaccountable, or that our Theorists are Aiming to Account for; If any of the Newtonian Discoveries shou'd be (as it is meet they shou'd be) more Familiariz'd, and Divulg'd for the Honour of that Great Name; If the Poet shall be invited to Travel and Survey the Modern Philosophical World, so much a Terra Incognita to the Muses; (pp. 12–13)

It is significant that although Reynolds does not neglect the physico-theological aspect of his subject, he is overtly concerned that his poem reveal recent discoveries and point to as yet unexplored scientific mysteries. It was in this way that aspiring poets might turn to his poem as a guide to the possibilities for original composition in the new sphere of scientific endeavour.

By 1715, the aesthetics of science had become respectable enough to merit treatment in a university lecture. In that year, Joseph Trapp, Professor of Poetry at Oxford, devoted part of Lecture 15 of his *Praelectiones Poeticae* to a discussion of the fitness of science as a subject for poetry.[31] Whereas he finds that poems that deal with moral duties cannot be described as true poetry, this is not the case with poetry that has "philosophical speculations" as its subject matter:

... nothing shines more in Verse, than Disquisitions of natural History. We then see the strictest Reasoning join'd to the politest Expression. Poetry and Philosophy are happily united ... (p. 189)

The reasons are clear. Science furnishes the poet with new possibilities for originality. It "affords abundant Matter for Description; it opens a large Field for Fancy, and strikes out new Ideas". Trapp shares with his predecessor, Bishop Sprat, a belief that science can bring the poet closer to the phenomena of nature. The "abundant Matter" includes not only the moon and sun, but also "the Journies of the heavenly Orbs", the origin of the species, astrology, meteorology and seasonal changes, gravity, light and sound, and "innumerable other Wonders in the unbounded Storehouse of Nature". It is in these new directions that the poet should turn his face.

Bishop Sprat would presumably have approved of the secular note which is evident in the Professor's lecture. Not only does Trapp take little account of the use of science for the aggrandizement of the Deity, but he also chooses to treat the poetry of Lucretius as an aesthetic rather than a

---

[31] *Praelectiones Poeticae*. 2 vols (Oxford, 1711–15); 2nd. ed. 1722, 3rd. ed. 1736; tr. as *Lectures on Poetry* (1742). Lecture 15 is entitled "Of Didactic or Præceptive Poetry".

religious problem. Lucretius's atheism, usually a source of suspicion and disapproval, is lightly dismissed as less of a problem than his artistic shortcomings:

He, indeed, is so far from celebrating the Creator that he supposes there is none; but allowing him his Hypothesis, his Poem is truly philosophical. He had deserv'd much greater Praise, had he corrected his Notions in Philosophy, and his style in Poetry, for in this Particular, also, he is often deficient. (pp. 189–190)

It is these shortcomings which must temper any approval of his contribution to scientific poetry. Trapp feels that he must be severely censured for not more thoroughly transforming his subject matter. Scientific poetry should be as undidactic and artistic as any other sort:

It must be owned, this Poet reasons too much in the Manner of the Schools, the Philosopher appears too open, he wants the Gentility to conceal his Beard, and temper his Severity; Poetry and Philosophy, indeed were both to be join'd together, but the one ought to be as the Handmaid to the other . . . (p. 190)

Trapp concludes his discourse with an analysis of the state of scientific poetry at the time. He finds that few poets have exploited the riches of science. He knows of no "modern Poem of this Sort worth mentioning". Although he may only have been referring to the modern Latin poets such as Buchanen, whose *Sphere* he singles out for praise (which would explain why he ignores Blackmore, for example) it is also possible to interpret his remarks as indicating dissatisfaction that no purely scientific poem of any worth has as yet appeared:

But as Natural Philosophy has, by the Help of Experiments, been lately brought to much greater Perfection than ever; this kind of Poetry, no doubt, would have made proportionable Advances, if the same Age that shew'd a Boyle, a Halley, and a Newton, had produc'd a Virgil; or if we had not been so much worse Poets than the Ancients, as we are better Philosophers. We have indeed some poetical Essays on the Circulation of the Blood, the Airpump, the Microscope, and the Telescope, and the like: But these are short Descriptions no ways reducible to the Species of Poetry before us. 'Tis true, they may in some Sense be reduc'd under the Title of Didactic, tho' not of Prescriptive Poetry; they teach by Description, not by Precept. (p. 192)

If this interpretation is correct, Trapp's estimate of the situation is quite accurate. Although there were some intrepid souls who in pursuit of originality, attempted scientific poetry, only a minority were attracted to it on its own merits. John Dennis was one of the few to appreciate the relationship between poetry and science but he inveighed against Leonard Welsted in vain:

He [Welsted] treats Mathematicks, physicks and metaphysicks with the same contempt, and endeavours to make them little in order to make poetry great not considering that poetry is

56

Dependent upon almost evry [sic] one of them, and They are everyone of them Independent of that. If poetry instructs 'tis by them alone it instructs, and if it pleases 'tis by them partly that it pleases.[32]

Science, Teleology and Original Composition

Among the handful of "poetical essays" noted by Trapp was one on the microscope which may well have been a poem of that name by Tipping Silvester.[33] This is a celebration of the new worlds revealed by the microscope and conveys something of the enthusiasm felt by these early users of that revolutionary instrument. The poem is infused with the excitement arising from the discovery of the previously unseen and unsuspected. Silvester confesses to his pleasure in being able to write of the novelty of the unknown. His muse rejoices in the revelations it can make:

Th'egregious Race no more neglected lies,
Once overlook'd, now pleasing with Surprize;
Vain, mortal Wights, deride them now no more,
They raise our Envy, as Contempt before:
Past Nature's Limits through the *Convex* grown,
They wear new Limbs, and Members, not their own. (p. 38)

Each of the phenomena which attracts Silvester's attention, from a head louse to the crystalline structure of salt, is described in terms of what it resembles in the normal-sized world. Thus, the acorn reveals the shape of a fully grown oak while the Nettle at such close quarters appears to the poet as "A vegetable Porcupine".

The telescope was responsible for a very different propensity. To those poets who cultivated the sublime, its discoveries offered welcome imagery and novel thoughts. Lady Mary Chudleigh explains the attractions of these distant views in her Preface to *The Song of the Three Children Paraphras'd:*

I have made use of the Cartesian Hypothesis, that the Fixt Stars are Suns, and each the Center of a Vortes, in order to heighten the sublimity of the Subject, because it gives me a noble and

---

[32] *Decay and Defects of Dramatick Poesy* (?1725) in Hooker, II, 297; see also *The Grounds of Criticism in Poetry* in which Dennis claims that science is "absolutely necessary to a Poet" (Hooker, I, 350).

[33] In *Original Poems and Translations* (1733), pp. 35–54. The Preface contains the information that *The Microscope* had originally been written in Latin and published with companion poems as the *Musae Anglicanae* which had "gone through two or three editions" (p. v). Another poem on which the microscope made an impression was Robert Gambol's *The Beauties of the Universe* (1732). This poet refers to the butterfly as "a beauteous Bird", since "whoever examines this Creature with a Microscope will find, that the Mealy Substance, which is so easily rubb'd off from their Wings, ... is a curious variety of Feathers, which seem wisely dispos'd to answer the Purposes both of Use and Beauty" (p. 14).

sublime Idea of the Universe, and makes it appear infinitely larger, fuller, more magnificent, and every way worthier of its great Artificier.[34]

John Hughes, whose interest in science has already been noted, prefaced *The Ecstasy* with an apology for the poem in which he acknowledges the influence of science on the poet in pursuit of originality.[35] He admits that the first part of his poem is an imitation of a popular model, Casimire's *E rebus Humanis Excusus,* but goes on to claim that the second part unites science and originality:

... the latter Part, which attempts a short View of the Heavens, according to the Modern Philosophy, is entirely Original, and not founded on any Thing in the Latin Author.[36]

The theme is the well-known one of the cosmic voyage. The reader is entertained, as Bishop Sprat and Professor Trapp thought they should be, with descriptions of the moon, the earth, the planets and the milky way. Cowley too, had imitated the same model, but Hughes succeeds in more skilfully incorporating the fruits of scientific exploration. Cowley's Columbus was St. Paul, but Hughes chose Newton as his intrepid explorer of the universe. He is "The great Columbus of the Skies" (p. 7). It is to him that the poet appeals to be his guide "thro' all th'unbeaten Wilds of Day":

> Here let me, thy Companion, stray
> From Orb to Orb, and now behold
> Unnumber'd Suns, all Seas of molten Gold;
> And trace each Comet's wand'ring Way,
> And now descry Light's Fountain Head,
> And measure its Descending Speed;
> Or learn how Sun-born Colours Rise
> In Rays distinct, and in the Skys
> Blended in yellow Radiance flow
> Or stain the fleecy Cloud, or streak the Watry Bow;
> Or now diffus'd their beauteous Treasures shed
> On ev'ry Planet's rising Hills, and ev'ry verdant Mead (p. 8)

Newton was not the only scientist to whom the poets made pleas for assistance and inspiration.[37] Thomas Cooke addressed the famous naturalist and antiquarian, Dr. Woodward, to compliment him on his contribution to poetry and to beg for continued support.[38] With the aid of Woodward's

---

[34] *Poems on Several Occasions* (1703), sig. K3r.

[35] *The Ecstasy. An Ode* (1720).

[36] *Advertisement* to the poem.

[37] For panegyrics to Newton, see W. P. Jones, *The Rhetoric of Science,* pp. 97–105.

[38] "To Dr. Woodward" in Richard Savage's *Miscellaneous Poems and Translations* (1726), pp. 169–172.

scientific discoveries, poetry is assured constant originality and the poet is enabled to accomplish greater feats of creativity:

> Nor should the Muse the ardent Work decline,
> Would'st thou assist the Poet's great Design,
> Through unfrequented Paths her Flight to wing,
> Where never Muse before would dare to sing;
> She, with the Morning Sun, should mount the Sky,
> And round the Globe, in Search of Knowledge, fly.
> Boldly she wou'd the glorious Race pursue,
> And by thy Doctrines trace all Nature through. (p. 170)

The poet hopes that Woodward may be granted a long life in order to "find new Subjects for the Poet's Song", for it is from him alone that such advances in knowledge, and gains for poetry, may be expected (pp. 171–172).

Another of the few purely scientific poems was *The Copernican System* (1728) by the obscure Samuel Edwards who was also attracted by the daring originality of such a theme. In the poem he urges his "Adventurous Song" into the previously "unfrequented paths" of scientific theory. Indeed, Edwards is so preoccupied with the originality of his theme that he exercises a scrupulous nicety in avoiding themes already touched on by other poets. Thus, he declines to describe the climate of winter and, instead, acknowledges his greater precursor, Thomson:

> ... But stay my Muse
> Urge not a Theme already so well Sung
> Smooth, as the Ice they Sing, thy Numbers flow,
> Great Bard we quake, and shudder at thy Frost. (p. 8)[39]

In Mark Akenside's *The Pleasures of the Imagination* (1744), the marriage of poetry and science is one of the most important themes. Although what he has to say has been said before, his application of the principle in his own poetry is of great interest. He contends that the divorce of the two arts has been detrimental to both and was only possible in unenlightened times now past. Science was then the esoteric pursuit of a few sequestered souls while poetry was wholly given over to idolatry and supersition. Their consequent mutual antipathy is well illustrated by the fact that at the Revolution, Locke was among the leaders of one party while Dryden spoke for the other. But, in the new spirit which has since prevailed,

---

[39] Of course, winter was a well-sung theme even before Thomson. See, for example, "A Rural Complaint of the Approach of Winter, October 28 1684" in *Miscellany Poems and Translations by Oxford Hands* (1685) in which the effects of winter on plants are analysed.

poets and scientists now rejoice in a greater intimacy—of advantage to both:

But the general spirit of liberty, which has ever since been growing, naturally invited our men of wit and genius to improve that influence which the arts of persuasion gave them with the people, by applying them to subjects of importance to society. Thus poetry and eloquence became considerable; and philosophy is now of course obliged to borrow of their embellishments, in order even to gain audience with the public.[40]

In the poem itself, however, Akenside's description of the benefits which accrue to poetry from science is much more extravagant. The effect which a knowledge of science has in the apprehension of the pleasures of the Imagination is awesome and far exceeds the already exquisite pleasure to be gained when more than one sense is involved, because science reveals truth, the ultimate source of pleasure:

> Or shall I mention, where celestial Truth
> Her awful light discloses, to bestow
> A more majestic pomp on Beauty's frame?
> For man loves knowledge, and the beams of Truth
> More welcome touch his understanding's eye,
> Than all the blandishments of sound his ear,
> Than all of taste his tongue. (p. 26)

This "pure delight" is the end to be achieved when "the lamp of science" illuminates "the jealous maze / Of Nature". Akenside's own testimony of the enrichment which science has offered him as a poet would surely have gladdened the heart of Bishop Sprat:

> Nor ever yet
> The melting rainbow's vernal-tinctured hues
> To me have shown so pleasing, as when first
> The hand of Science pointed out the path
> In which the Sunbeams, gleaming from the west,
> Fall on the watry cloud, whose darksome veil
> Involves the orient; and that trickling shower,
> Piercing through every crystalline convex
> Of clustering dewdrops to their flight opposed
> Recoil at length where, concave all behind,
> The internal surface of each glassy orb
> Repels their forward passage into air;
> That thence direct they seek the radiant goal
> From which their course began; and, as they strike

---

[40] *The Poetical Works of Mark Akenside,* (undated rpt. of the Aldine ed., ed. Rev. Alexander Dyce 1834), p. 71. See Note 34, p. 85 below. Akenside also wrote *Hymn to Science* (first published in the *Gentleman's Mag.* for October, 1739) in which science is depicted as the great benefactress of both the individual and society, but not as an inspiration to originality.

In different lines the gazer's obvious eye,
Assume a different lustre, through the brede
Of colours changing from the splendid rose
To the pale violet's dejected hue. (p. 26)

Such revelation bespeaks an originality at odds with "the cobweb fashion of the times" and "Opinion's feeble coverings". Only the voice of passion is appropriate:

Then Nature speaks
Her genuine language, and the words of men,
Big with the very motion of their souls,
Declare with what accumulated force
The impetuous nerve of passion urges on
The native weight and energy of things. (p. 27)

One of Akenside's avowed models in *The Pleasures of the Imagination* was Virgil's Georgics. It was a Kind that ought to have attracted the poet-scientists but perhaps Addison's assessment of the scientific georgic acted as an effective deterrent:

Natural Philosophy has indeed sensible objects to work upon, but then it often puzzles the Reader with the intricacy of its notions, and perplexes him with the multitude of its disputes.[41]

A hardy few did seek originality in refurbishing the georgic with new themes directly related to the latest developments in scientific theory, but they are not of great interest, for they seem not so much poets, as purveyors of the latest techniques quaintly presented in verse. They are almost always less excited by the originality of their efforts than by their potential public use. Dr John Armstrong, Akenside's keenest rival in didactic poetry, wrote *The Art of Preserving Health* (1744) in order to improve the physical well-being of the nation.[42] In his invocation to Hygeia, he certainly notes the originality of his venture, but, subsequently allows the didactic nature of his mission to absorb his interest. But he too, was conscious of the difficulties inherent in the task of uniting science and poetry:

'Tis hard, in such a strife of rules, to chuse
The best, and those of most extensive use;
Harder in clear and animated song
Dry philosophic precept to convey.
Yet with thy aid the secret world I trace
Of Nature, and with daring steps proceed
Thro' paths the muses never trod before. (p. 4)

---

[41] *Essay on Virgil's Georgics* in *Joseph Addison's Miscellaneous Works,* ed. A. C. Guthkelch (1914), II, 4. This essay was reprinted several times. See p. 2.
[42] See *The Daily Post,* 12 April, 1744.

Robert Dodsley, who turned to modern agricultural theories in Canto I of his georgic, *Public Virtue* (1753), was also keenly aware of the difficulty involved in the job of expressing the precepts of a craft or trade in verse. He too was indebted to science for assistance in exploring the mysteries of Nature:

Then hear the Muse, now entering Hand in Hand,
With sweet Philosophy, the secret bowers
Of deep mysterious Nature; there t'explore
The causes of Fecundity. (p. 19).

At least one other poet did, however, turn to science for inspiration. In 1750, J. Fortescue, D. D. wrote *Science* in which he traces the relationship between poetry and science throughout history.[43] In line with the thought of those who had preceded him, he acknowledges that poetry, although the matrix of all intellectual activity, stands in great debt to science. Such was the effect of the barbarism of the dark ages, that it was only after science, in a more enlightened time, had been restored to its true place that it was then possible to revive the other arts:

Now the same arts, which gave to science birth,
Revive, and gain new beauties from the Earth.
By time enhanc'd it's [sic] precious value shews
The rare antique, and with more lustre glows.
Thus the sweet flow'r, from earth extracts perfumes,
Shoots with new life, and with more beauty blooms. (p. 10)

Fortescue also reviews the course of English science and notes the fierce independence and originality of its pioneers. They were giants, unafraid to step out into the unknown. Bacon began by pointing the way while Boyle "the maze unravell'd, and the Mystery view'd", but the greatest was Newton, who

with a more than mortal ken,
Pierced the obscure, and taught us to be men;
Th'untrodden paths of science to explore,
Where lay the dross, and where the burnish'd ore. (pp. 14–15)

But this obscure poem is another isolated example, for by mid-century, the authors who sought the originality of science for its own sake, were rare indeed. The concern of the early poet-scientists had been the revitalization

---

[43] Its full title is *Science: an Epistle on it's Decline and Revival With a Particular View to the Seats of Learning, and a virtuous, philosophical Life.* A sequel, or perhaps, another version dated 1751 appeared in *Essays Moral and Miscellanous*, (Oxford, 1754). Fortescue also wrote *On the Passions* (1752), another long didactic poem.

of poetry through science, and their attitude had been, for the most part, unselfconsciously secular. But the taste for divine poetry prevailed. Those ideas and images which had so inspired their early advocates to strike out in a new vein were put to another use by authors apparently indifferent to the attractions of original composition. It is not surprising that the revelations of science, although certainly arousing suspicion of atheism in some breasts, merely confirmed to many, the goodness, wisdom and generosity of the Creator. As one scholar has observed, "It seemed to be axiomatic with the eighteenth century that if technicians would provide England with a sufficient supply of microscopes, that nation would reap a plentiful harvest of good Christians".[44] It was this "teleological" inclination that transformed an impulse to purely secular and original poetry into the traditional devotional habit. The earlier interest in the purely scientific poem was soon subsumed under the overwhelming numbers of divine poems that used science generously but without much interest in its originality.

If Sir Richard Blackmore did not actually begin this trend, he is responsible for one of the most popular poems in the genre, *The Creation* (1712). But more than any of its subsequent imitations, this poem is firmly based on the originality of scientific subject matter. Sir Richard's enthusiasm for scientific progress was unequivocal. It was a great shame, he felt, that when the authority of Aristotle had been routed in science, the same had not happened in poetry:

And if men, from a generous Principle of Liberty, would renounce the unjust, tho' prevailing Power of Authority, and claim their natural Right of entering into the Reason of Things, and judging for themselves, it is highly probable that the Art of Poetry might be carry'd on to greater Degrees of Perfection, and be improv'd, as Philosophy has been.[45]

It is, therefore, no surprise to discover that some of the most illustrious men of the day, who held Blackmore in high esteem, should have thought that he alone was capable of "A natural history of the great and admirable phenomena of the universe".[46] Blackmore complied, with *The Creation,* announcing his aim in such a way as to leave in doubt whether his purpose was devotional or aesthetic:

I would th'Eternal from his Works assert,
And sing the Wonders of Creating Art. (p. 4)

---

[44] Meyer, *The Scientific Lady in England,* p. 87.
[45] "An Essay upon Epick Poetry" in *Essays upon Several Subjects* (1716), p. 12.
[46] See William Molyneux's letter to John Locke, May 27th, 1697 in *Some Familiar Letters between Mr Locke, and Several of his Friends* (1708), p. 219.

63

It is certain that he gloried in the originality of his task:

> How abject, how Inglorious 'tis to lye
> Groveling in Dust and Darkness, when on high
> Empires immense and rolling Worlds of light
> To range their Heav'nly Scenes the Muse invite?
> I meditate to Soar above the Skies,
> To Heights unknown, thro' Ways untry'd to rise. (p. 3)[47]

But Blackmore's paean to the originality of science is one of the last. Although scores of poets followed his example, it is almost always the religious significance of the subject that is accorded primary importance.[48] In view of the preoccupation with originality that characterised many of the divine writers, it is striking that so few of these physico-theological poets laid similar claims. It seems that such an interest may have simply reeked of the profane. These poets happily accepted that they wrote in the age-old tradition of devotional poetry in which pious intentions were more acceptable than authorial ambition. Furthermore, so numerous had these poets become that pretensions to originality in this field could hardly be sustained. A further reason why the originality of science was ceasing to attract as it had done in the early stages was that the interest in science itself among the upper echelons of society was beginning to dwindle. J. H. Plumb has shown that by the end of the eighteenth century a strong sense of conservatism was developing among the upper classes. They now tended to sacrifice their earlier interest in science and Baconian philosophy to a growing suspicion of critical attitudes and a need to justify and defend traditional institutions.[49] Just how far this waning of interest had gone, at least in the question of the assistance science might lend poetry, is evident in the anachronistic claims

[47] For praise of Blackmore as a poet, see: Charles Gildon, *The Complete Art of Poetry* (1718), I, 108; Henry Needler, "To Sir Richard Blackmore on his Poem, entitled, *Creation*" in *Works* (1724, 2nd. ed. 1728) pp. 33–35. See also, Ch. I, notes 20 and 21, p. 16.

[48] See, for example, Edward Young, *A Paraphrase on part of the Book of Job* (1719) where a keen naturalist interest is subjected to the theme of man's inferiority to God; Henry Needler, "On the Beauty of the Universe" in *Works* (1728), pp. 63–76; [Henry Brooke], *Universal Beauty. A Poem* (written 1728, publ. 1735). See Helen M. Scurr, "Henry Brooke" (Diss. The University of Minnesota, 1922). Bevill Higgons, *A Poem on Nature: In Imitation of Lucretius* (1736); Elizabeth Rowe (whose attitude to nature and science is revealed in the line "And read thy name in ev'ry spire of grass" which evokes much nineteenth-century devotional poetry), "On the Works of Creation" in *Miscellaneous Works* (1739), I, 142–143; Jane Brereton, *Hymn to the Creator* (1744); Mary Leapor, "The Enquiry" in *Poems upon Several Occasions* (1748); *An Hymn to the Creator of the World* (1750); *A Philosophical Ode on the Sun and the Universe* (1750).

[49] "Reason and Unreason in the Eighteenth Century: The English Experience" in *Some Aspects of Eighteenth-Century England*. Introd. Maximillian E. Novak (Los Angeles, 1971), pp. 18–22.

made by Moses Browne in his Preface to *An Essay on the Universe* (1739). Browne appears blithely unaware of his numerous predecessors:

I know of none (besides Sir Richard Blackmore in his *Creation*) who have published any Thing of this Kind, and his proceeds upon a wide and different Plan from mine.[50]

He offers the public a long poem (which was sufficiently pleasing to run to at least two editions). In three books it deals with the Earth, the Planets and the Sun respectively, and is heavily larded with digressions on current scientific theory. His enthusiasm is as great as his ignorance:

It is indeed a Wonder no Sublime Genius has been excited to give us some finished Poem upon this great and delightful Theme, for which, Monsieur Fontenelle very ingeniously observes, the Physical Ideas are in themselves most proper; being so happily contrived that . . . at the same time [as] they convince and satisfy the Reason, they present to the Imagination a Prospect which looks as if it was made on purpose to please it.

But more in keeping with current practice than he knew, he made sure to claim that the aim of his poem was an improved apprehension of the Supreme Being:

The best and wisest Use of *Philosophy* is to direct it to such attainable Purposes, in preparing the Mind with raised and enlarged Apprehensions of the great and wonderful Creator.

Science had attracted the attention of original poets for several reasons. Its monopoly of a verifiable "Truth" was irresistible. The manner and method of the scientists, their calm disregard of the past, offered a model to poets who sought freedom from the restraints of tradition.

The subjects which science offered struck many as exciting and novel beyond anything that classical precedent could offer. Explorations of matter, new theories of the universe or the revelations of the new and increasingly sophisticated glasses, delighted and enthralled these authors.

But, in the end, although Bishop Sprat's injunction to poets had been the more adventurous, it was John Reynolds's cautious assessment of the potential of science as subject matter for verse that proved more accurate.

The example that the spirit of scientific endeavour could set for original poets was to find one last—and vigorous—advocate, the Reverend Edward Young.[51] But some time before that, original poets had left science to the scientists and had turned, perhaps "tinctured" with the same enquiring spirit, to another subject which they regarded as original—the natural world around them.

---

[50] *Poems on Various Subjects* (1739), sig. T8ᵛ.
[51] See Ch. 4 below.

Chapter 3

Originality in "the wide Fields of Nature"

Poets who heeded Bishop Sprat's suggestion that "Working Nature" offered "one of the best and most fruitful Soils for the growth of Wit" confronted special difficulties if what they sought was originality. Nature poetry, in the form of traditional pastoral, occupied a long established, if inferior, position, in the hierarchy of the Kinds.[1] It was generally agreed that the novice poet should spend some time in this Kind in order to perfect his craft before attempting higher things—that is, if it was not his fate to be merely,

> By Nature Fitted for an humble Theme,
> A painted Prospect, or a murmuring Stream.[2]

As a result, a body of conventions and rules drawn up to aid the youthful poet accumulated and produced not so much poetry as pedagogy.[3]

To the original poet, one of the most inhibiting of these conventions was that which dictated that the nature depicted in the pastoral should be "an image of what they call the golden age".[4] The poet was not required to represent a close and detailed image of nature as it actually existed, but to

[1] One of the best known divisions of poetry occurs in Thomas Hobbes, *Answer to Davenant's Preface to Gondibert* (1650). Hobbes described "three sorts of Poesy": "Heroique", "Scommatique" and "Pastorall", Spingarn, II, 55. See further, J. E. Congleton, *Theories of Pastoral Poetry in England. 1684–1798* (Gainesville, 1952), pp. 13–17.

[2] Thomas Tickell, *Oxford* (1706). See R. E. Tickell, *Thomas Tickell and the Eighteenth Century Poets 1685–1740*, (1931), p. 16. Many pastoral poets were careful to assure their readers that their pastorals were merely a prelude to higher things. Ambrose Philips wrote that he had begun with the genre that Virgil and Spenser had undertaken "as a prelude to Epic Poetry" (Preface to *Pastorals* (1708) in *Poems* (Oxford, 1937), p. 3); Pope's hints were more subtle: see footnote to 1. 431 of *Windsor-Forest*, in *Poems*, I, 194. Gay was an exception. See: Adina Forsgren, *John Gay. Poet "Of A Lower Order"* (Stockholm, 1964), pp. 47–55.

[3] Rules for pastoral are to be found in, for example, *Tatler* 9 (1709) and *Guardian* 22, 23, 28, 30, 32, together with Pope's ironic comments in no. 40. See also, Congleton, pp. 75 ff.; Forsgren, pp. 110–113. Edward Heuston, "Windsor Forest and *Guardian* 40," *RES*, 29 (1978), 160–168 is also of interest.

[4] Pope's words in *Guardian*, 40, 1713. See *Pastoral Poetry and An Essay on Criticism*, eds. E. Audra and A. Williams, Vol. I, Twickenham ed. (London, 1961), p. 26.

idealize and perfect it. Indeed, the powers of the true poet were thought to far exceed the creativity of nature.[5] Furthermore, the permitted images of this golden world were already limited and defined. Nature had but one face:

The large *Idalian* World, was then all Pasture-Ground, enrich'd with Rivulets, with undulating Streams, and limpid Fountains, and the Nemæean Forest (there being an unintermitted Jubilee of Birds) was a wide Labyrinth of Groves, embellish'd with Honey Trees, with Palms, and with Cedars; and altho' the roseate Dews wou'd often liquify the verdant Plain, yet this did not any Ways molest the shepherds, or in the least Prejudice the Nymphs, but on the contrary render'd 'em the more vegete, lively, and the fitter to attend Diana upon the Chace . . .[6]

The casual indifference of the shepherds and nymphs to changes in temperature illustrates the pastoral poet's lack of interest in natural detail. In the eighteenth-century version of pastoral, details of seasonal change, the world of plants and animals and the other constituents of Sprat's "Working Nature" could not be accommodated. The idyllic landscape which it permitted was nothing more than a decorative backdrop against which the swains might enact their little dramas of love and loss.

The sterile images it did allow were frequently criticised. In *An Essay on the Different Stiles of Poetry* (1713), Thomas Parnel depicts this poverty in an allegory in which the poet, mounted on Pegasus, views his kingdom and sees it for the desert it has become. In the fields of pastoral he observes that all is contrived and vacuous, while the true face of nature is neglected:

There all the graceful *Nymphs* are forc'd to play,
Where any Water bubbles in the way:
There shaggy *Satires* are oblig'd to rove
In all the Fields, and o'er all the Grove;
There ev'ry Star is summon'd from its Sphere,
To dress one Face, and make *Clorinda* fair:
There *Cupids* fling their Darts in ev'ry Song,
While Nature stands neglected all along:
'Til the teiz'd *Hearer,* vex'd at last to find
One constant Object still assault the Mind,

---

[5] Sir Philip Sidney had described the redemptive, idealizing function of the poet thus: "Onely the Poet, disdayning to be tied to any such subiection [to Nature], lifted up with the vigor of his owne invention, doth growe in effect into another nature, in making things either better than Nature bringeth forth, or, quite anewe, formes such as never were in Nature . . . Nature never set forth the Earth in so rich tapistry, as divers Poets have done, neither with so pleasant rivers, fruitful trees, sweete smelling flowers, nor whatsoever els may make the too much loved earth more lovely. Her world is brazen, the Poets only deliver a golden", *Defense of Poesie,* ed. Albert Feuillerat (Cambridge, 1923), p. 8. For Pope's belief in this redemptive potency of poetry see, M. C. Battestin, "The Transforming Power," *ECS* (1969), 183–204.

[6] *Essays upon Pastoral* (3rd. ed. 1730), p. 15.

Admires no more at what's no longer new,
And hastens to shun the persecuting View.[7]

In many quarters a sturdy anthropology resisted any attempt to regard nature as other than a fitting context for humanity. What attracted poets of this frame of mind to country scenes was not an interest in external nature for its own sake, but the evidence that could be gleaned therefrom of the superiority of man. Man's success in taming and subduing the wildness of nature was often praised. In the view from Mount Caburn, admired by William Hay in 1730, it was not the natural landscape that excited his pleasure, but the abundant traces, in the iron works, buildings and forestry plantations, of the transforming powers of man. Hay felt that the prospect afforded a view of the new harmony of Nature. What was once wild and dangerous had now been ordered and controlled by human technology:

Then Industry, Earth's Handmaid, threw apart
Her rural Attire, and dress'd her Charms with Art.
From second Chaos, order did produce,
From useless Things Things of the noblest Use.[8]

Another poet, Thomas Newcomb, took this neglect of natural beauty so far, that in viewing a fine landscape he could only "see" the military and naval might of England.[9]

---

[7] *Miscellaneous Poems,* ed. Matthew Concanen (1724), p. 284. However, there seems to have been as many different thoughts on pastoral as there were writers. So, for example, in his Preface to his translation *Amintas* (Tasso's Aminta), (1698), John Oldmixon thought he detected an unfortunate waning of interest in the genre. Yet, at the other end of the period under review, it is still possible to find a keen enthusiasm. See, for example, the anonymous and unashamedly traditional and imitative *Four Pastorals* (1751) and note that the traditional criteria continued to exert their influence: Goldsmith and Newbery, *The Art of Poetry on a New Plan* (1762) in the section on "Descriptive Poems". In "Nature's Threads", *ECS,* (Fall 1968), 45–57, Raymond Williams noted that the changes in rural England in the century are reflected in the nature poetry of the period, but rightly qualified this assertion by agreeing that the older structure of the reflective pastoral tradition held until about mid-century.

[8] *Mount Caburn* (1730), p. 8.

[9] "On a beautiful prospect from Goodwood Park in Sussex" in *A Miscellaneous Collection of Original Poems* etc. (1740), p. 162. See Aubin, p. 193. The anthropomorphic view of nature is a powerful one and makes itself felt in many ways. See, for example, "To the Nightingale" in *Poems by Several Hands and on Several Occasions collected by Nahum Tate* (1685) and Soame Jenyns, "An Essay on Virtue" in *Poems,* pp. 50–51. Indeed, even the efforts of the early natural historians were often strongly anthropomorphic. See the histories of Oxfordshire and Staffordshire by Dr. Robert Plot. See also Professor Sutherland's view that in eighteenth-century poetry man must always come first. *A Preface to Eighteenth Century Poetry* (1948; rpt. Oxford 1962), pp. 111–112. But cf. the works of Henry Baker, in particular, *The Microscope Made Easy* (1743) and *The Universe A Poem intended to Restrain the Pride of Man* (1720? or 1734). See further, Ch. 2, note 7, pp. 44–45 for other references on the theme of man's inferiority.

Attitudes to external nature, such as these, are not surprising at a time when many found the sight and experience of the untamed landscape an unattractive thought. Not all were as extreme as Charles Cotton who saw the mountains of the Peak district "Like Warts and Wens" and "imposthumated Boyles" on the site of sinful Sodom and Gomorrah. This region is, he declared, a "Country so deformed the Traveller / Would swear those Parts Nature's pudenda were".[10] To many men in the eighteenth century, nature could seem inhospitable, uncomfortable and even dangerous. The reality of the circumstances in which they lived makes their predilection for keeping the hardships of country life at a safe distance, preferably outside the confines of a comfortable mansion such as Pomfret's chosen abode, very understandable.[11]

But other ideas were undermining this persistent contempt for "Working Nature". The increasing respect for the Bible as poetry, the growing awareness of the advances being made by science and the advancing cult of the sublime presented a successful challenge to the older notion, and facilitated the elevation of nature as a subject worthy of regard in its own right. As attitudes changed, the attractions of nature as an original subject were revealed.

Changing Attitudes to Nature

Many parts of the Bible celebrate the beauties of Creation. To see nature as a manifestation of the power and plenitude of the Creator, and, therefore, a

---

[10] *The Wonders of the Peak,* (Nottingham, 1725), p. 13. Professor Marjorie Hope Nicolson has shown that throughout most of the eighteenth century mountains were regarded as hideous and useless blemishes upon the earth's surface: *Mountain Gloom and Mountain Glory: The Development of the Aesthetics of the Infinite* (Ithaca, N. Y. 1959). They were, as Gabriel Plattes observed in 1639, often likened to the "Warts, Tumours, Wenns, and Execrescensies" which grow upon the human body: *A Discovery of Subterraneall Treasure* (1639), p. 5. See also, G. L. Davies, "The Concept of Denudation in Seventeenth-Century England", *JHI,* 27 (1966), 278–84.

[11] John Pomfret, *The Choice* (1700). It went through four editions in 1701 and was included in a second edition of *Poems on Several Occasions* in 1702. See also, John Dyer, *Grongar Hill* (1726); Matthew Green, *The Spleen* (1737); Isaac Hawkins Browne, *The Fire Side: A Pastoral Soliloquy* (1735). Pomfret's predecessors and successors are discussed at length by Maren-Sofie Røstvig in *The Happy Man: Studies in the Metamorphoses of a Classical Ideal* (Oslo, 2 vols, 1954 and 1958). A more realistic approach to life in the countryside is to be found in, for example, "A Rural Complaint of the Approach of Winter" in *Miscellany Poems and Translations by Oxford Hands* (1685); Soame Jenyns, "An Epistle to the Rt. Hon. the Lord Lovelace in Town" (1735) in Dodsley's *Collection of Poems* (1748), III, 153–160, also in *Poems* (1752), pp. 33–42; Mary Leapor, "Winter" in *Poems by Eminent Ladies* (1755), II, 93. In this poem the youthful poetess finds that this time of the year in the country offers little inspiration to the poet.

legitimate source of beauty and pleasure was an approach at odds with the view that regarded external nature as evidence of man's original sin. It also permitted and encouraged a tendency to examine nature and to rejoice in it for its own sake. As the numerous efforts in eighteenth-century miscellanies and collections show, the Psalms were a favourite subject of paraphrase.[12] To the eighteenth-century mind, they appeared to defy the most fundamental tenets of the Ancients and yet to succeed admirably in arousing the higher emotions. Rhapsodic invocations of natural beauty and grandeur, they stress the glory and wonder of nature:

> The heavens declare the glory of God; and the
> firmament sheweth his handywork. (xix, 1)
> The works of the Lord are great, sought out of all
> them that have pleasure therein. (cxi, 2)

Such themes were not, of course, new in the Restoration and eighteenth century. They had always been popular and, indeed, often fused naturally with the themes of classical pastoral, such as the idea of beneficial rural retirement. But towards the end of the seventeenth century, it is possible to discern a tendency to linger on the external beauty of God's works, rather than their significance as divine reflections.

This pure delight in nature is particularly obvious in *Theologia Ruris sive Schola et Scala Naturae* (1686). As its modern editor notes, it is an eloquent expression in a Christian context of some of the main attitudes towards external nature at the end of the seventeenth century and the beginning of the eighteenth. But in its absorption in natural beauty and its expatiation upon the pleasure to be derived from contemplation, it also marks the new departure in attitudes towards nature.[13]

The beauty of Creation, its justification as a reflection of the power and creativity of God, and the powerful poetry these feelings brought forth in the Bible, made it easy to effect a natural link between the beauties of nature and the poetic inspiration of the soul. The ultimate aim was still to praise the Creator, but many poets proclaimed that nature had been their inspiration. In a poem in which he described in some detail the birds and flowers encountered on his journey from Patapsco to Annapolis, a Mr. Lewis testified to this fact:

[12] See, for example, S. Patrick, *Paraphrase on Ecclesiastes, and the Song of Solomon* (1685); Lady Mary Chudleigh, *Poems on Several Occasions* (1703; 4th ed. 1722); "The XIXth Psalm Paraphras'd" and "Upon the Glorious Works of Creation" in *Poems Divine, Moral and Philosophical* (Gloucester, 1746), pp. 12, 36–38.

[13] Introduction by H. S. V. Ogden. Augustan Reprint Society. No. 56 (1956), pp. 1–2. See also Henry Needler's words, "The very Idea of the Country transports my Soul with a Mixture of agreeable Passions!", (*Works*, 2nd. ed. 1728), p. 80; see also pp. 63–76, 92–94.

70

Ten thousand Beauties rising to my View;
Which kindle in my Breast poetic Flame,
And bid my *Creator's* Praise proclaim;
Tho' my low Verse ill-suits the noble Theme.[14]

Another poet soliloquised on the verse from the *Canticles,* "Come, my Beloved, let us go forth into the Field, let us lodge in the Villages" and drew attention to the inspiration to be had from the countryside. In the poem the poet moves easily from the simpler, sensuous joys of the country to a higher plane of inspired poetic originality. In this higher state it is the hidden anatomy of nature which is the object of the poet's attention. By comparison with simpler pleasures this constitutes a "more solid Bliss" in the contemplation of which the poet more nearly resembles the true creativity of God:

There undisturb'd thy Thoughts shall grow more bright,
Thy tow'ring *Muse* shall take a loftier Flight,
And all thy Studies meet with fresh Delight.
When each created Substance that you find,
New scenes of Thought shall open to the Mind;
With Pleasure inexpressible to know
The Reasons *why* and *how* all things do grow.
    How the same Matter diff'rent *Forms* assumes,
And how those *Forms* are wove in diff'rent Looms;
How *Earth* to *Earth*, and *Clods* to *Clods* combin'd,
And Particles of *Stone* to *Stones* are join'd;[15]

The poet's Muse continues to explore the whole of nature, examining in turn the constituency of trees, the anatomy of plants, the interplay of light and colour in nature, and the secrets of water, fish, air, minerals, shells, fossils and astronomy. Such an abundance is irresistible. The poet's only course is immediate retreat to the country where, inspired by the plenitude of nature, his muse will be sated:

Muse strive no more in vain, but take thy Lyre,
And quickly to those peaceful Shades retire:
Where, with a thousand Beauties fir'd, thy Song
Shall brighten, as thy Subject moves along. (p. 18)

---

[14] *Description of the Spring. A Journey from Patapso in Maryland to Annapolis,* April 4, 1730 in *The Gentleman's Magazine,* March 1732. See also [J. G. Cooper], *The Power of Harmony* (1745); Joseph Addison's *Ode,* "The Spacious Firmament on high" (Spectator 465, (1712), Bond, IV, 144. See E. L. Tuveson, *The Imagination as a Means of Grace* (Berkeley, 1960), pp. 69–70; J. Pittock, *The Ascendancy of Taste* (London, 1973), p. 60.

[15] *The Country Life; or, A Passionate Invitation of the Soul to Retirement Being A Divine Soliloquy on Cant. VII, ii* (2nd. ed. 1721), pp. 4–5.

71

The growing awareness of the "thousand Beauties" of Nature was in no small part due to the efforts of the early natural historians. The remarkable and seemingly inexhaustible discoveries of the microscope and the telescope, together with the experiments, observations and hypotheses of scientific men radically altered earlier shibboleths. The old theories of the decay of the world were soon scientifically, and shortly thereafter, fashionably unacceptable.[16] Men learned to rejoice in what they saw around them. An enthusiasm and delight in nature reduced considerably the allure of the myth of the antediluvian world. A subtle realignment of priorities was also taking place. Man was no longer lord of all he surveyed. The belief that he occupied a middle ground between spiritual and brute creation persisted, but some of the confidence in his stature that this belief encouraged began to suffer the erosion of doubt.[17] An admonishing tone appears in many natural histories, in particular, the popular ones. Not infrequently man is chastised for his vainglorious belief in his own superiority. The discoveries of the microscope and the telescope had revealed new perspectives.

It is also possible to detect the early stirrings of an ecological conscience.[18] His cruelty and bloodthirstiness are strongly condemned. In *The Seasons*, James Thomson stands forth as a fervent member of the anti-blood sports lobby: "This falsely cheerful barbarous game of death" (*Autumn*, 1. 384). His brief for vegetarianism is part of his censure of the propensity of "ensanguined man" to dip "his tongue in gore" (*Spring*, 11. 336–378).

That it behoved man to accept his reduced status and to look with greater love and charity on his fellow creatures was a common feeling among those of the new persuasion. It was agreed that he could no longer regard the rest of his creation as merely part of his behest. Something of this deference to the autonomy of nature is evident in a letter by William Melmoth the

[16] See Gordon L. Davies, "The Concept of Denudation in Seventeenth-Century England", *JHI*, 27 (1966), p. 281.

[17] See, for example, Robert Gambol, *The Beauties of the Universe* (1732):
Can we believe the Moon was made so bright,
The Stars to twinkle with that brilliant Light,
Only to gratify our wanton Sight? (p. 4)
and also *Nature, a Poem* (1747), the design of which was "to shew that Complaints against Nature are groundless" (Preface).

[18] See, for example, Anne Finch, Countess of Winchilsea, "A Nocturnal Reverie" (1713): during the night peace reigns:
Their shortliv'd Jubilee the Creatures keep,
Which but endures, whilst Tyrant-*Man* do's sleep;
(*Oxford Book of Eighteenth-Century Verse*, p. 46); see also, M. M. Fitzgerald, *First Follow Nature* (N. Y., 1947), pp. 99 ff., 192 ff.

younger, written to accompany a gift of snail-eaten peaches. Melmoth is clearly one of the first advocates of pesticide-free farming:

To confess the truth then, I have some scruples with respect to the liberty we assume in the unlimited destruction of those lower orders of existence. I know not upon what principle of reason and justice it is, that mankind have founded their right over the lives of every creature that is placed in a subordinate rank of being to themselves . . . I cannot indeed discover why it should be thought less inhuman to crush to death a harmless insect, whose simple offense is that he eats that food which nature has prepared for him; than it would be were I to kill any more bulky creature for the same reason.[19]

The views of the recipient are not recorded.

Conservation of a sort was also advocated by Elizabeth Carter. In a poem addressed to a gentleman who proposed to sacrifice a small wood to that prevailing taste in landscape gardening, the open prospect, she linked the preservation of nature with the inspiration of poetry. Although she is content to adopt the persona of a "Hama Dryad" and makes copious use of the allusions of classical pastoral, it is clear that the destruction of wild and untamed nature is a subject of great concern to her. The loss of such a spot spells deprivation for the poet's inspiration which always owes more to nature than to art. The poem ends with an impassioned plea from the Dryad to the landowner:

Reflect, before the fatal ax
    My threaten'd doom has wrought;
Nor sacrifice to sensual taste
    The nobler growth of thought;

Not all the glowing fruits that blush,
    On *India's* sunny coast,
Can recompense thee for the worth
    Of one idea lost.

My shade a produce may supply,
    Unknown to solar fire;
And what excludes *Apollo's* rage,
    Shall harmonize his lyre.[20]

---

[19]Letter VIII, in *Letters on Several Subjects. By the late Sir Thomas Fitzosborne. Bart* (1748), p. 29. See also Pope's attack on cruelty to animals in the *Guardian* 61, 1713.

[20] "To a Gentleman. On his intending to cut down a Grove to enlarge his Prospect" in *Poems by Eminent Ladies* (1755), I, 177–178. It is interesting to compare this poem with two other well-known poems concerning tree-felling: William Cowper, "The Poplar Field" in which the poet sees the disappearing trees merely as an image of "the perishing pleasures of men" and Gerard Manley Hopkins, "Binsey Poplars" where the destruction of the trees stirs the poet to plead for conservation of "the growing green".

The opposition between art and nature during this period is well-known.[21] That figures such as Addison and Pope approved of the wildness of nature and its resistance to order constituted a particularly influential support for the growing interest in the details of external nature. Equally important was the familiar cult of the sublime.[22] It seems that few ultimately remained immune to its statutory elements. The beauty and terror inspired by the actual or imagined sight of craggy mountains, blasted heaths, turbulent seas and unending deserts is frequently cited in informal letters, works of criticism and in the literature of the period. Shaftesbury's confession of his fascination with the wild and terrible is a fitting summary:

I shall no longer resist the passion growing in me for things of a natural kind; where neither art, nor the conceit or caprice of man has spoil'd their genuine order by breaking in upon that primitive state. Even the rude rocks, the mossy caverns, the irregular unwrought grotto's, and broken falls of waters, with all the horrid graces of the wilderness itself, as representing Nature more, will be the more engaging, and appear with a magnificence beyond the formal mockery of princely gardens.[23]

It was this enthusiasm for nature, sanctioned by the example of the Bible and, in some quarters at any rate, complemented by the advances of science, that facilitated the breakdown of the conventions of pastoral and the opprobrium of fundamentalists.

The Poet and "Working Nature"

Bishop Sprat's injunction to poets to seek inspiration in the cycles and functions of nature—what he called "Working Nature"—the reality of nature rather than the glossy surface permitted in pastoral, was reiterated in

---

[21] See, Addison's *Spectator* essays 411, 412, 414, 477, 589 and Pope's *Guardian* essay 173; see also Fitzgerald, p. 127. See also the attack on "all the Cant of *Nature* and of *Art*" beloved by the well-meaning fool, who:

Fancies those Wits, like Women, are the best,
Where Nature stands all shameless and undrest.
Shakespear comb'd *Weel* [sic]—and on that hopeful Ground
He thinks no Diamonds but on Dunghils [sic] found;
Some Village Bard he finds, whose Muse affords
Verse fit for Milkmaids, Footmen, and their Lords;

. . . .
'Tis true this Genius cannot read—what then?
But none alive can have so quick a pen;

in *The Present State of the Literati: A Satire* (1752), p. 17.
[22] S. H. Monk, *The Sublime* (N. Y., 1935).
[23] Treatise V, *The Moralists* in *Characteristics,* ed. John M. Robertson (London, 1900), II, 125.

different ways by two eminent figures in the early eighteenth century, Joseph Addison and Thomas Tickell.

Addison offered some practical advice to the aspiring poet in *Spectator* 421. Just as the scientist endeavours to train and strengthen his understanding, so it should be the poet's chief consideration to cultivate and refine his imagination. One of the principle ways in which this programme might be managed was by acquiring "a due Relish of the Works of Nature" and becoming "thoroughly conversant in the various Scenary of a Country Life". This was Addison's suggestion in *Spectator* 417. In the unpublished manuscript version of this paper, however, he described exactly how this should be achieved. Although the advice is couched in fairly typical Neo-Classical terms, its burden is to urge the poet to an immediate and direct contact with the countryside itself. He should study the detail and variety of nature to find inspiration:

He must love to hide himself in Woods and to Haunt the Springs and Meadows. His head must be full of the Humming of Bees, the Bleating of Flocks, and the Melody of Birds. The Verdure of the Grass, the Embroidery of the Flowers, and the Glistring of the Dew must be painted strong on his Imagination.[24]

In thus steeping himself so thoroughly in the phenomena of nature, the poet is equipping himself with a veritable treasure of allusions and illustrations which are superior to any that can be derived from elsewhere because their appeal is immediate and vivid: "For the generality, the most entertaining ones be in the Works of Nature, which are obvious to all Capacities, and more delightful than what is to be found in Arts and Sciences" (*Spectator* 421).

When Thomas Tickell took over as Professor of Poetry at Oxford during Joseph Trapp's absence in 1710–1711, he too made the natural alliance between poetry and nature the theme of his lecture *De Poesi Didactica* (1711). With Addison saying much the same thing at the same time in the popular *Spectator,* it is not surprising that the curmudgeonly Thomas Hearne accused Tickell of a lack of intellectual incisiveness and originality of thought.[25]

Hearne was unduly harsh, however, for Tickell's reasons why nature makes a better subject for poetry than morals, the sciences or the other arts, if not particularly original, are nevertheless expressed with an engaging

[24] Footnote in Bond, III, 563–64.

[25] Hearne described the lecture as "a very silly indiscreet Performance" and characterised Tickell thus: "he has no Learning, but is an empty, vain Pretender", R. E. Tickell, *Thomas Tickell and the Eighteenth-Century Poets,* pp. 21–22. The quotations from Tickell's lecture are from the reprint in this work, pp. 198–209.

enthusiasm which may have stirred the interest of his auditors. As far as he was concerned moral conduct was a completely unacceptable subject, even, notably enough, of didactic poetry. Science possessed greater advantages, "for it has an Image for every created thing, whence can be fashioned the most exquisite Pictures in infinite variety" (p. 202). But these exquisite images of the sun, the moon and the stars, when described scientifically, are anathema to true poetry.

In truth, so far is Philosophic speculation from possessing Variety, that it embraces a Horde of Images before our eyes, in a universal and abstract nature, and concentrates thousands of objects into a single Concept. At first sight, what subject could be more fertile than the vast structure of the Universe, the Elements, the formation of Bodies, and the variety of Tastes, Flavours, and Colours? What could be more productive of Ideas? Yet when these very topics are reduced, by Lucretius, to the septem of Epicurus, to a concourse of wandering Seeds and diverse configurations of Bodies, what could be more simple, what more barren? (pp. 202–203)[26]

Scientific themes are, moreover, disfigured by their obscurity and the need which arises for a "tiresome and indefatigable labour of the mind". But a poetry which relies on the charms and mysteries of nature may easily incorporate ideas from other spheres without detriment, "for it exhibits gathered together in itself Charms scattered in every direction, it is not confined within limits, and it is not oppressed by Poverty of Ideas". Tickell's approval of nature poetry expresses itself in a rhetorical flourish:

Why should I prove on the authority of the greatest Bards that, above all, country scenes smile upon Poetry, when the facts themselves make it evident? There is an unpolluted simplicity to commend Moralizing, there is a joyous Variety of Imagery to adorn Philosophical obscurities, there are Arts to soften hard labours, and hopes of Profit not illfounded. There is a nimble Darting about, that is continually reviving the Languid mind: timely excursions away from precepts into story telling: illustrations of Nature's inner secrets by the most charming outward show of things: a sprinkling of wit for the out-of-date: and a constant transference from business to pleasure and back again. There, in fine, whatever Excellence Teachers have counselled, Philosophers have proclaimed, and Artists have fashioned, has been endowed by the hand of Nature, the master craftsman, with sweetness and splendour together. (p. 206)

His rejection of the scientific approach to nature would hardly have found favour with the poet, William Diaper. Anticipating in many respects the ideas of the more illustrious James Thomson, Diaper was one of the poets who regarded the advances made by the study of natural history as the most effective remedy for the ills induced by the archaic pastoral. In *Dryades* (1713), he claims that science alone is capable of breathing some new life into the atrophied genres of pastoral and georgic. The poem takes the form

---

[26] Cf. with Dr. Johnson's views expressed in *Rambler* 121 on the unsuitability of science as a subject for poetry. See also Note 26, Ch. 2, p. 51, above.

of an account of a midnight forum held by the fairies of the English country-side, a far-from extinct race in Diaper's opinion. At the beginning of the meeting there is disagreement among the lesser fairies on the present state of nature poetry. Nape, the autumn fairy, insists that all is well with the genre:

Succeeding Bards in rural Secrets skill'd
Shall teach the Swain t'enrich the barren Field. (p. 11).

But Psecas, "the Sylvan Pow'r / That shapes the Leaf, and paints the woody Flow'r" takes a less optimistic view. The pastoral is at present little more than a slavish imitation of the now sterile genre inherited from the Ancients. It cannot flourish in the harsh realities of modern society and must soon disappear for good:

Who ... would sing of bleating Flocks
Or hanging Goats that brouse on craggy Rocks?
When ancient Bards have rifled all the Store
And the drain'd Subject can afford no more. (p. 12).

At this point, Egeria, the noblest Dryad, intervenes and addresses the assembly authoritatively. There is an implicit rejection of the classical genres in her description of the subject matter that will supplant the old themes in nature poetry. She promises that the gradual revelations of nature by the efforts of science will produce a new and greater genre:

New Beauties show themselves to nearer Views
And Themes untouch'd expect the skilful Muse
The vegetable Worlds neglected lie
And Flow'rs ungather'd fall and nameless dye.
Thousands escape hid in the pressing Throng,
Unknown in *Macer's* or to *Cowley's* Song. (p. 22)

The subject is a new and original one. Hitherto, "The num'rous Natives of the shelt'ring Wood" and the "unnumber'd Kinds" that adorn the Field have been neglected by "th'ingrateful Bard". But now, poets should seek in nature untouched themes which will refurbish their song. The list of likely subjects is comprehensive and, interestingly, it inclines to the minute rather than the sublime. One may speculate whether this reflects Diaper's own preference for the small and secret, the "Strange, puny Shapes, unknown to vulgar Eyes" or whether he had, like so many others, fallen for the magic of the microscope. A partial quotation must suffice:

A thousand Kinds unknown in Forests breed,
And bite the Leaves, and notch the growing Weed;
Have each their Several Laws, and settled States,
And constant Sympathies, and constant Hates,
Their changing Forms no artful Verse describes,

Or how fierce War destroys the wand'ring Tribes;
How prudent Nature feeds her various Young,
Has been (if not untold) at least unsung.
To th'Insect Race the Muse her Pain denies,
While prouder Men the little Ant despise
But tho' the Bulky Kinds are easy Known,
Yet Nature's Skill is most in Little shown;
Besides that Man by some kind Daemon taught
Has secrets found, that were of old unsought. (pp. 23–24)

The modest claims for a poetry of the minute so quaintly put by Diaper are in sharp contrast to the impressive flamboyance of his better known the best equipped to be nature poets. His reasoning has a logic all of its own. Like the other inhabitants of the "Northern Isles", these stalwarts are unruffled by the notorious inclemency of the climate, and are, therefore, much more likely to engage in a minute and particular observation of nature, which is the cornerstone of the new nature poetry. It is this personal exploration which will guarantee originality to the nature poet, for so much lies, as yet, undiscovered:

Matter is infinite, and still descends
Man cannot know where lessening Nature ends. (p. 25)

The modest claims for a poetry of the minute so quaintly put by Diaper are in sharp contrast to the impressive flamboyance of his better known successor, James Thomson. Like many poets concerned with the state of poetry at the time, Thomson believed that a reform of poetry was long overdue and that it could best be effected by turning to the mysteries and beauties of nature. It is among these that the poet will find a new inspiration and a welcome originality:

I know no subject more elevating, more amusing, more ready to awake the poetical enthusiasm, the philosophical reflection, and the moral sentiment, than the works of nature. Where can we meet with such variety, such beauty, such magnificence? All that enlarges and transports the soul! What more inspiring than a calm, wide survey of them? In every dress nature is greatly charming—whether she puts on the crimson robes of the morning, the strong effulgence of noon, the sober suit of evening, or the deep sables of blackness and tempest. How gay looks the Spring! how glorious the Summer! how pleasing the Autumn! and how venerable the Winter!—But there is no thinking of these things without breaking out into poetry; which is, by the by, a plain and undeniable argument of their superior excellence.[27]

---

[27] Preface to *Winter*, 2nd. ed. (1726) rpt. in *Eighteenth Century Critical Essays*, I, 408. The quotations that follow are taken from *The Complete Poetical Works of James Thomson*, ed. with notes by J. Logie Robertson (1908, rpt. 1963). It should be noted that I have restricted discussion of Thomson to his interest in the originality which themes from nature encouraged. There is already a voluminous bibliography of criticism dealing with his relationship with nature and science. Among the more interesting are: Louis. I. Bredvold, "Sensibility in Nature

One of the most striking characteristics of *The Seasons* is its unalloyed "poetical enthusiasm" for nature. Those pious, and often prosaic, hopes expressed by other authors that nature might prove a fruitful soil for originality are transformed into fervent and forceful verse as Thomson moves about his natural landscape. Nature may still be a victim of the ravages of ignorant man:

O man! tyrannic lord! how long, how long
Shall prostrate nature groan beneath your rage
Awaiting renovation. (*Autumn*, ll. 1189–1191)

But for Thomson, of course, this renovation is already complete. In his view, nature, divorced from humanity, possesses an unquestionable superiority. This superiority is evident in its morals and code of conduct as well as in its boundless creativity. In this last respect, nature far excels the limitations of humanity including the modest efforts of the nature poet:

who can paint
Like Nature? Can imagination boast
Amid its gay creation, hues like hers?
Or can it mix them with that matchless skill,
And lose them in each other, as appears
In every bud that blows? If fancy then
Unequal fails beneath the pleasing task,
Ah, what shall language do? ah, where find words

Poetry: Thomson," *The Literature of the Restoration and Eighteenth Century 1660–1798*, III (*A History of English Literature*, ed. Hardin Craig, 1950 rpt. 1962), 98–104; C. A. Moore, "A Predecessor of Thomson's *Seasons*,"*MLN*, 34 (1919), 278–81; John Butt, *The Augustan Age* (1950, rpt. 1966), pp. 75–95; John Chalker, *The English Georgic* (Baltimore, 1969), pp. 90–140; Ralph Cohen, "Thomson's Poetry of Space and Time", *Studies in Criticism and Aesthetics 1660–1800*, eds. Howard Anderson and J. S. Shea (Minneapolis, 1967), pp. 176–192; *The Unfolding of the Seasons* (Baltimore, 1970); J. W. Corder, "A New Nature in Revisions of *The Seasons*," *N&Q*, 211 (1966), 461–64; P. K. Das, "James Thomson's Appreciation of Mountain Scenery," *ES*, 64 (1929), 65–70; Herbert Drennon, "James Thomson's Contact with Newtonianism and his Interest in Natural Philosophy," *PMLA*, 49 (1934), 71–80; "Scientific Rationalism and James Thomson's Poetic Art," *SP*, 31 (1934), 453–471; "Newtonianism in James Thomson's Poetry," *ES*, 70 (1936), 358–372; for a review of these articles see *PQ*, 14 (1935), 175–76; Dwight L. Durling, *Georgic Tradition in English Poetry* (N. Y. 1935), pp. 43–58; Douglas Grant, *James Thomson: poet of "The Seasons"*, (1951); Jean H. Hagstrum, *The Sister Arts: The Tradition of Literary Pictorialism and English Poetry from Dryden to Gray* (Chicago, 1958), pp. 243–267; R. D. Havens, "Primitivism and the Idea of Progress in Thomson," *SP*, 29 (1932), 41–52; Alan D. McKillop, *The Background of Thomson's Seasons* (Minneapolis, 1942); Martin Price, *To The Palace of Wisdom: Studies in Order and Energy from Dryden to Blake* (N. Y., 1964); James Thomson, *The Seasons*, ed. James Sambrook (Oxford, 1981), pp. xx-xxxi; Patricia M. Spacks, *The Poetry of Vision* (Cambridge; Mass. 1967), pp. 13–45; *The Varied God: A Critical Study of Thomson's "The Seasons"*, (Berkeley & L. A. 1959); Jeffrey B. Spencer, *Heroic Nature: Ideal Landscapes in English Poetry from Marvell to Thomson* (Evanston, 1973), pp. 253–295.

Tinged with so many colours and whose power,
To life approaching, may perfume my lays
With that fine oil, those aromatic gales
That inexhaustive flow continual round. (*Spring*, ll. 468–479)

Deciding that his poetic powers can cope with this burden of perfection, Thomson finds that nature provides not only an inspiration but also a paradigm of growth:

As rising from the vegetable world
My theme ascends, with equal wing ascend
My panting muse . . . (*Spring*, ll. 572–574)
Lend me your song, ye nightingales! oh, pour
The mazy-running soul of melody
Into my varied verse! . . . (*Spring*, ll. 577–579)

He is confident that, in turning to nature, he will "touch a theme / Unknown to fame" and this desire for originality prompts a searching and comprehensive analysis of all that is offered. In the range of themes which Thomson mentions, the contributions being made by the scientists and natural historians to the growing understanding of nature play an important part. The revelations of the microscope arouse as much admiration in Thomson as they did in Diaper. The fascination with the infinitely descending chain of being is just as strong:

Gradual from these what numerous kinds descend,
Evading even the microscopic eye!
Full Nature swarms with life; one wondrous mass
Of animals, or atoms organized
Waiting the vital breath when Parent-Heaven
Shall bid his spirit blow. (*Summer*, ll. 287–292)

Thomsom also echoes Diaper in his insistence that the minutiae of nature are as worthy of consideration as its grander forms. This, it should be remembered, was not a theory which found favour with those who preferred the generality of Neo-Classicism. But Thomson argues that these low forms share some kinship with the Sun, or Apollo, the god of poetry:

Nor shall the muse disdain
To let the little noisy summer-race
Live in her lay and flutter through her song:
Not mean though simple—to the Sun allied,
From him they draw their animating fire. (*Summer*, ll. 236–240)

A similar awareness of the work being done in the scientific disciplines of astronomy, mineralogy, zoology and psychology, and the poet's indebtedness to these efforts is evident in the concluding panegyrical lines of *Autumn:*

O Nature! all-sufficient! over all
Enrich me with the knowledge of thy works;
Snatch me to heaven; thy rolling wonders there,
World beyond world, in infinite extent
Profusely scattered o'er the blue immense
Show me; their motions, periods, and their laws
Give me to scan; through the disclosing deep
Light my blind way: the mineral strata there;
Thrust blooming thence the vegetable world;
O'er that the rising system, more complex,
Of animals; and, higher still, the mind,
The varied scene of quick-compounded thought,
And where the mixing passions endless shift;
These ever open to my ravished eye—
A search, the flight of time can ne'er exhaust! (ll. 1352–1366)

In his search for poetic originality in the workings of nature, Thomson also turned to a fellow Scot, Martin Martin, the naturalist. Martin's account of the Western Isles and St. Kilda furnished Thomson with material which enabled him to combine his love of Scotland with his interest in the efforts of early naturalists.[28] Martin had devoted a considerable part of his work to the observation of sea birds and had written of their migration:

The several Tribes of Fowl here build and hatch apart, as if it were by consent. Some of the lesser Isles are so crowded with variety of Sea-fowl, that they darken the Air when the[y] flie in great Numbers after their coming, which is commonly in *February,* they sit very close together for some time, till they recover the fatigue of their long flight from their remote Quarters; and after they have hatched their Young, and find they are able to flie, they go away together to some other unknown Place.[29]

Thomson's use of this account of the mysterious comings and goings of the seabird population and the habits of their colonies is enlivened perhaps by a hint of his own ornithological observations:

Who can recount what transmigrations there
Are annual made? what nations come and go?
And how the living clouds on clouds arise,

---

[28] Martin Martin, a native of Skye, contributed a paper on the Western Isles to the Royal Society in 1697. It was published as *A Description of the Western Islands of Scotland* in 1703 and had several editions. In 1698, he published *A Voyage to St Kilda* which reached its 4th. edition by 1753. Martin's descriptions of Scotland are mentioned by Dr. Johnson.

[29] *A Description of the Western Islands of Scotland* (1703), pp. 374–375; See, A. D. McKillop, *The Background of Thomson's Seasons,* pp. 132–33; see also James Thomson, *The Seasons,* ed. James Sambrook pp. xxviii-xxxi.

Infinite wings! till all the plume-dark air
And rude resounding shore are one wild cry? (*Autumn*, ll. 866–70)[30]

Despite his grandiose diction and ambitious plans, it is Thomson the countryman who dominates in *The Seasons*. It is the simple secrets of nature, revealed by the close observation of one who loves the countryside, which entrance him. In the closing lines of *Autumn* he addresses nature in this intimate way:

under closing shades
Inglorious lay me by the lowly brook,
And whisper to my dreams. From thee begin,
Dwell all on thee, with thee conclude my song;
And let me never, never stray from thee! (*Autumn*, ll. 1367–1373)

The poet James Ralph was one on whom Thomson exerted a powerful influence, acknowledged by Ralph in his Preface to *Night* (1728). Like Thomson, Ralph was conscious that the unexplored areas of nature afforded original subjects for poetry. His choice was a poem on the mysteries of night. In the invocation he addresses the figure of Contemplation:

O thou, whose secret haunt is far remov'd
From all the restless, glaring, scenes of day,
Sweet contemplation, daughter of the night
O deign thy favour to th'adventurous muse,
And, on thy pow'rful pinions, safely guide
Her daring progress thro' the darksome round. (p. 2)

Although Ralph consciously follows Thomson, he also anticipates him by introducing aspects of winter that Thomson did not employ until 1730.[31] These include the scientific study of astronomy which, Ralph claimed, would supply an abundance of new ideas and themes as well as the thrill of the unknown and the excitement of discovery. Winter is the best time for this sort of astronomical research:

This is the time for such whose active Souls
Explore the twinkling glories of the sky;
This is the time for such t'ascend in thought,

---

[30] Further ornithological observations are: the migration of swallows *Autumn*, 11. 836–848, and storks: 1. 852. The signs of storm in winter, 11. 137–152 also bear the marks of Martin's influence. Apart from his impact on Dr. Johnson, the effects of Martin's investigations can be seen in William Collins's description of St. Kilda in *On the Popular Superstitions of the Highlands of Scotland* (c. 1749). Less frequently remarked is another poem, *Amyntor and Theodora: or The Hermit* (1747), which makes full use of Martin's description of St. Kilda; particularly of his information on the behavioural patterns of migrating flocks of seabirds returning to nest and breed there.

[31] W. P. Jones, *The Rhetoric of Science*, pp. 119–120.

And travel o'er the vast immense; to chase
The swiftest meteors with an equal wing,
And measure out the comet's vengeful blaze,
T'examine all the wand'ring stars that roll
Around the sun, the fountain of their beams!
To ken ev'n their attendant orbs, and watch
Their various motions, and their changing rays;
To sail thro' seas of fluid light, and search
The crowded splendours of the milky way;
To tow'r yet upwards, and be lost amid
New stars, and suns, and worlds, as yet unknown,
That fill the boundless space, and prove the pow'r
Of an Almighty Hand, thro' all the heavenly frame. (p. 39)

Like many of his contemporaries, Ralph was absorbed by the pursuit of originality. In its quest he was willing to strike out in any direction, however exotic. Thus he strayed not only in the heavens but across the oceans as well. In *Zeuma* (1729), he selected the history of South America—with the Indian as hero—in order to claim indubitable originality. The Preface to the poem is a charming amalgam of naive defensiveness and simple ingenuousness:

Should anyone object that I need not have laid the scene in so remote a country, or chosen such *Barbarians* for my Heroes; I answer, there is scarce any known story among the ancient *Greeks,* or *Romans,* but what is already exhausted, either in prose, or verse; consequently another entertainment of the same nature, would have wanted its due relish; and any obscure use, even among them, would be as liable to exceaption [sic] as this. Besides, 'tis to be presum'd that an *Indian* history may prove as effectual to fix the reader's attention, as any other; to awaken, and confirm his *Love* of *Liberty*, even better, when 'tis consider'd that those whom we esteem *Savages* could dye in it's defense; to entertain, and divert by the novelty of it's Scenes; and, in short to prevent any mischievous writer's drawing parallels to the author's disadvantage. (p. iv–v)

The same desire to acquit himself well in the struggle for originality informs the work of another occasional poet, James Kirkpatrick, better known, perhaps, for his translations of Tissot's medical treatises. In his one poem of note, *Sea-piece* (1750), Kirkpatrick chose a subject, the sea, which, for some reason, attracted few of his contemporaries.[32] In explaining his unusual choice, Kirkpatrick shows himself to be fully cognizant of current theories of the diversity of the human mind and the promise of originality inherent in each individual:

[32] Aubin, *Topographical Poetry in XVIII-Century England,* pp. 112–114. The desire for novelty occasionally pushed poets to strange feats. See, for example, William Goldwin, *A Poetical Description of Bristol* (1712) in the preface to which he claims that there is "nothing of this Sort among the Ancients" (sig. A1ᵛ); and Rev. Mr. James Ward, *Phoenix Park* in Concanen's *Miscellaneous Poems* (1724).

Nor servile trace the Path Another treads,
But follow Nature where my Genius leads.
Nature, our common Dame, has well supply'd
Somewhat to each, distinct from all beside;
Which who pursues, discovers, and obeys,
Shall stoop with Prudence, or ascend with Ease.
Why should I then this Spark of Nature quit,
To ape, assume, and pilfer Others Wit;
Which, when with Care I cull, with Art dispose,
Shall just adorn me like Another's Cloaths? (p. 35)

The mixed reception accorded *Sea-piece*, ranging from enthusiasm for its originality to condemnation of its "wretched cant terms", highlights the dilemma of the original poet who looked to "Working Nature" for inspiration.[33] However fervently he welcomed the potential of nature as new subject matter, he had still to face and solve the problem of how to shape and order his thoughts into an acceptable whole. Tradition, because it allotted only a minor, if necessary, place to description in the greater Kinds, offered little help. Lacking any model, the poet was forced to resort to his ingenuity. That he felt somewhat insecure in such a daring situation is clear from David Mallet's "Advertisement" prefixed to *The Excursion* (1728):

As my Intention, in the following Piece, was only to describe some of the most remarkable Appearances of NATURE, the Reader will not find in it that Unity and Regularity of Design, which are essential to Epic and Dramatic Writings. And this I readily acknowledge to be a Fault; tho' I hope it may be forgiven to a young Author, who, from Want of Skill and Experience in his Art, may sometimes find it necessary in a first Performance, to indulge a freer and more unconfined Range of Imagination. If the different Scenes, which these Verses attempt to describe, are introduced without Confusion, and drawn with some Degree of Spirit and Justness, perhaps the unprejudiced Reader will not be displeased even with this loose Essay, on a Theme so various and difficult. (pp. iii–iv)

The form proposed by Mallet, the long discursive poem in which observation, reportage and reverie combined with science, religion and philosophy, was a popular solution to the problem, especially for poets who were absorbed by the beauty and mystery of external nature and intrigued by the study of natural history.

But for many, the anatomy of "Working Nature", as revealed by experiment and the use of the telescope and microscope, was fast becoming too technical and abstruse. For them it became less important to understand the

---

[33] *The Monthly Review* (February 1750), in which Kirkpatrick's claims to originality are noted but his "wretched cant" deplored; *The Critical Review* (May 1751) notes "this very ingenious performance" but commends him for his imitation of Spenser. Note Johnson's remarks on the contemporary Spenserian preference in *Rambler* 121. See p. 135 below.

mechanics of nature as an object of study. A much higher priority was given to simply experiencing nature at first hand. In this they were encouraged by the Lockean stress on sight which Addison had popularised in his *Spectator* papers on the imagination (411–421). They came to believe that only through direct contact with nature could the poet undergo the prerequisite liberation and revitalization of the mind necessary to achieve inspiration. Thus, it is no longer nature itself that is of prime importance, but rather the poet's own burst of emotional lyricism when he confronts it. Although nature remains a vital element, it is the mind of the poet, in a state of inspiration, that now takes precedence.

The Inspired Poet

The figure of the inspired poet is as familiar to students of the eighteenth century as the cult of the sublime, with which it was, of course, associated. James Thomson, Mark Akenside and Joseph Warton dominate any discussion of the subject, but since scholars are acquainted with the works of these poets, a cursory survey drawing attention to their quest for originality in the inspiration of nature must suffice. [34]

Blessed with a vitality of perception and a receptivity to nature, it was the inspired poet's privilege to experience the awakening of his inner emotions and his duty to transmit the experience to his readers. This was the task that Mark Akenside proposed in *The Pleasures of the Imagination*. In its first version (1744) the opening lines of the poem read:

[34] In the following discussion I am particularly indebted to Joan Pittock, *The Ascendancy of Taste: The Achievement of Joseph and Thomas Warton* (1973). Other works which proved helpful were: Jeffrey Hart, "Akenside's Revisions of *The Pleasures of the Imagination,*" *PMLA*, 74 (1959), 67–74; John L. Mahoney, "Akenside and Shaftesbury: The Influence of Philosophy on English Romantic Theory," *Discourse*, 4 (1961), 241–47; Robert Marsh, "Akenside and Addison: The Problem of Ideational Debt," *MP*, 59 (1961), 36–48; John Norton, "Akenside's *The Pleasures of Imagination,*" *ECS*, 3 (1970), 366–383; Abbie F. Potts, *Wordsworth's Prelude* (Ithaca, N. Y. 1953), pp. 244–278; John E. Sitter, "Theodicy at Mid-century: Young, Akenside and Hume," *ECS*, 12 (1978–79), 90–106; John Butt, *The Mid-Eighteenth Century (Oxford History of English Literature* VIII: Oxford, 1979), 65 ff.; Arthur Fenner, Jr. "The Wartons 'Romanticize' their Verse," *SP*, 53 (1956), 501–08; W. D. MacClintick, *Joseph Warton's Essay on Pope: A History of the five Editions* (Chapel Hill, 1933); Alan D. McKillop, "Shaftesbury in Joseph Warton's *Enthusiast,*" *MLN*, 70 (1955), 337–339; David B. Morris, "Joseph Warton's Figure of Virtue: Poetic Invention in *The Enthusiast,*" *PQ*, 50 (1971), 678–683; George Baldwin Schick, "Joseph Warton's Conception of the Qualities of a True Poet," *Boston University Studies in English*, 3 (1957), 77–87. Since there are no scholarly modern editions of the works of Akenside or Warton, I have used a reprint of Alexander Dyce's *The Poetical Works of Mark Akenside* (Aldine Edition of the British Poets) 1834 (referred to as *Works*) and the first editions of Warton's Odes.

With what attractive charms this goodly frame
Of nature touches the consenting hearts
Of mortal men, and what the pleasing stores
Which beauteous Imitation thence derives
To deck the poet's, or the painter's toil,
My verse unfolds.[35]

In its later form (1757), the passage, like the rest of the poem is much inflated, but Akenside became more specific about the pleasures, the "raptures", which fill the breast of the unlearned poet who is only "with fancy's native arts endowed". Love of nature and appreciation of its beauty—innate good taste—is a universal gift, God-given in order to make the soul sensitive to the charms of nature. Gentlemanly education and learning are not necessary and Akenside chose the farm-labourer to personify these virtues:

His rude expression and untutored airs,
Beyond the power of language, will unfold
The form of beauty, smiling at his heart. (Bk.III, ll. 532–534)

The young Akenside was, incidentally, a radical Whig.

Despite his literary debt to Addison, Akenside felt that in attempting to investigate the mysterious relationship between nature and the mind of the poet, he had chosen an original theme. Other arts of poetry, he asserted, had merely propounded simple mechanical rules, but no one had so far examined the processes whereby Nature inspires the poet:

Oft have the laws of each poetic strain
The critic-verse employed; yet still unsung
Lay this prime subject, though importing most
A poet's name: for fruitless is the attempt,
By dull obedience and the curb of rules,
For creeping toil to climb the hard ascent
Of high Parnassus. Nature's kindling breath
Must fire the chosen genius; Nature's hand
Must point the path, and imp his eagle wings,
Exulting o'er the painful steep, to soar
High as the summer; there to breathe at large
Ethereal air, with bards and sages old—
Immortal sons of praise. (Bk. I, ll. 31–43, pp. 6–7)

Akenside is urged on to the enormous task of painting "the finest features of the mind" and giving "to most subtile and mysterious things" "colour, strength and motion", by his overpowering love of nature. It is again, this love that entices him to seek the "secret paths erewhile untrod by man", to

[35] *Works*, pp. 5–6.

"detect / Untasted springs, to drink inspiring draughts" and to bind the "unfading flowers" of originality, afforded by the inspiration of nature, into such a wreath as never poet gained before.

Alive to every "glad impulse" of the "congenial powers" of nature, the poet's imagination maintains a heightened degree of sensitivity, ever "responsive" to stimulus from without (Bk. I, ll. 116–124). In this state, nature is capable of kindling the spirit in a powerful surge of emotion, enabling "the feeling heart" to sweep away all that is trivial or mundane. This is the moment of perfect truth—the moment when nature and the poet are at one:

> Then Nature speaks
> Her genuine language, and the words of men,
> Big with the very motion of their souls,
> Declare with what accumulated force
> The impetuous nerve of passion urges on
> The native weight and energy of things. (Bk. II, ll. 150–55, p. 27)

Emotional responsiveness to nature is elevated to the status of a passion in the poetry of Joseph Warton. As one would expect, this reaction finds sustenance, not in the tamed landscape of the town poet (as Warton's repudiation of the school of Pope made clear), but in the distant recesses of the wilderness:

> Can gilt Alcoves, can Marble-mimic Gods,
> Parterres embroider'd, Obelisks, and Urns
> Of high Relief; can the long, spreading Lake,
> Or Vista lessening to the Sight; can Stow
> With all her *Attic* Fanes, such Raptures raise,
> As the Thrush-haunted Copse, whereby lightly leaps
> The fearful Faun the rustling Leaves along,
> And the brisk Squirrel sports from Bough to Bough;
> While from an hollow Oak the busy Bees
> Hum drowsy Lullabies? The Bards of old,
> Fair Nature's Friends, sought such Retreats, to charm
> Sweet *Echo* with their Songs.[36]

The process whereby the poet's love for the particularities of external nature is fused with his natural disposition or genius, provides a potential source for the strong feelings that stimulate originality of thought. For

---

[36] *The Enthusiast; or, The Lover of Nature* (1744), pp. 5–6. See also, Preface to *Odes on Various Subjects* (1746) and *Essay on the Writings and Genius of Pope,* I (1756), 2, 3–4, 36; Pittock, pp. 127, 144–45. Notice the rebuke administered to Warton by William Whitehead, who thought that Warton's rejection of society was both inhuman and antisocial, and admonished him to remember "That man was made for man", not for solitary wanderings: "The Enthusiast: an Ode" in *Poems on Several Occasions* (1754), rpt. in *Oxford Book of Eighteenth-Century Verse*, p. 421.

Warton, it was locations such as the "Pine-topt Precipice", the "bleak Heath" and, indeed, the exotic "Savannah's wild" that were most success-ful in encouraging the "correct" emotional response.[37] In such solitary and lonely places, his poetic imagination felt free of the restraint imposed by the evil confines of "smoaky Cities":

> Where never human art appear'd
> Nor ev'n one straw-rooft cott was rear'd,
> Where Nature seems to sit alone,
> Majestic on a craggy throne;[38]

The well-known conclusion to *An Ode to Fancy* reads like a royal petition from the original poet:

> O queen of numbers, once again
> Animate some chosen swain,
> Who fill'd with unexhausted fire,
> May rise above the rhyming throng.
> Who with some new, unequall'd song
> May boldly smite the sounding lyre,
> O'er all our list'ning passions reign,
> O'erwhelm our Souls with joy and pain,
> With terror shake, and pity move,
> Rouze with revenge, or melt with love.
> O deign t'attend his evening walk,
> With him in groves and grottos talk;
> Teach him to scorn with frigid art
> Feebly to touch th'unraptur'd heart;
> Like light'ning, let his mighty verse
> The bosom's inmost foldings pierce;
> With native beauties win applause,
> Beyond cold critic's studious laws:
> O let each Muse's fame increase,
> O bid BRITANNIA: rival GREECE![39]

It was a petition with which many other, more obscure, figures would have concurred, for the pursuit of originality was not confined to a few adventurous souls. In the first place, the cultivation of inspiration, and, in particular, that inspiration that was reputed to flow from a familiarity with nature, was part of the counter-attack on the idea of poetry as an elevated

---

[37] These were common preferences. See, for example, James Grainger, *Solitude* (1755), which, personified as a "romantic maid" is pursued by the poet and is associated with such sublime phenomena as towers, deserts, open tombs, the mountains of the Andes, volcanoes, ruins, the hidden source of the Nile etc. (*Oxford Book of Eighteenth-Century Verse*), pp. 405–407.

[38] *An Ode to Fancy* in Dodsley's *Collection* (1748), III, 78–84.

[39] Op. cit. pp. 83–84.

citadel of learning. To many authors this was a welcome release from the bondage of the past. The rules of art could be dismissed in favour of what was felt to be the greater powers of the untrammelled mind in its environment of genuine nature.

The idea was far from new, or particularly revolutionary. Indeed it had been sufficiently familiar to exercise the wit of the redoubtable and prolific Duchess of Newcastle. In *Of Poets and their Theft*, she fired off a volley at that category of poets, mostly men in her opinion, who regarded the craft of poetry as a means of airing their knowledge of the classics. True poets ignored such pretension. Like the birds of the air, they are "taught by Nature not Art". Their imagination is never obfuscated by the darkness of learning:

Fancies in the Braine that Nature wrought,
Are best, what imitation makes, are naught.[40]

Later poets were more specific in equating inspiration with the effects of nature. The opposition between the valuable simplicity of external nature and the useless complexity of learning was also noted. A certain egalitarianism appeared in statements such as Robert Gambol's that nature's very accessibility was a guarantee of its superiority over learning, the province of a privileged oligarchy:

The Book of Nature open lies to all
Let Man consult the great Original
Where, by one Page, he will more Knowledge gain,
Than all the Volumes in the World contain.[41]

In what may be merely another version of the same, the author was at pains to point his contention even more emphatically:

In nature's book the weakest brain may speed,
Th'untaught may learn it, and th'unlettered read;
Nor need of pedant, or of pedant's rod,
The book of nature is the book of God.[42]

At least one self-confessed "weaker brain" took advantage of the opposition between art and nature. Undaunted by her lack of formal education, Mary Masters proclaimed herself a poet and attributed her inspiration to the working of nature on her untrained mind:

---

[40] *Poems and Fancies* (1653), p. 123.
[41] Robert Gambol, *The Beauties of the Universe* (1732), p. 30.
[42] Quoted by Fitzgerald, as an anonymous contribution to the *Monthly Review*, III, 36 (1750), in *First Follow Nature*, p. 108.

Wholly unpractis'd in the learned Rules,
And arduous Precepts of the noisy Schools
Nature's strong Impulse gives my Fancy wings;
Prompted by her, I sing of various Things,
A flow'ry Meadow, or a purling Stream,
And Notes that differ with the diff'ring Theme.[43]

Her modest apology that her verses fail to capture the perfection of Nature but, in their clumsiness, are primarily "a true Picture of the Author's Mind" emphasises the intimate links she feels exist between external nature and her sensitivities. Her claim remains

What'er I write, whatever I impart,
Is simple Nature unimprov'd by Art.

In another of Mary Masters's poems, "Nature's strong impulse" is described as so powerful that even the poet's firm resolve to cease writing dissolves. The sight of fruitful nature, revealed in the ripening crops of wheat and barley, is irresistible:

I felt a Pow'r, too strong to be supprest
Move with Poetick Rapture in my Breast
Scenes all transporting set my Soul on fire
And Fields, and Meads their wonted Thoughts inspire.[44]

But, of course, it was not only women poets who felt they belonged with the unlearned and could therefore embrace the undemanding inspiration of nature with enthusiasm. The Scottish poet, Allan Ramsay, whose determinedly local poetry pointed the way to the steadily growing literary identity of the differing regions of Great Britain, displayed his ignorance of the classics with some pride. He attributed his self-confidence as a regional poet to the early advice from eminent friends who counselled, "Pursue your own natural manner, and be an Original".[45]

Another "unlearned poet" was more vociferous in defending his poetic inspiration and originality against charges of ignorance:

I'm ignorant, the Learned say,
That I write well, but not their Way.
. . . .
My free born Thoughts I'll not confine,

---

[43] "To a Gentleman" in *Poems on Several Occasions* (1733), pp. 44–45.
[44] "The Resolution broke", p. 94; see also, "To Clemene", pp. 34–38; "An Answer to Mr G's Invitation", pp. 118–119.
[45] Preface to *Poems on Several Occasions* (1776), p. iv. Cf. Walsh's reply to the youthful Pope's query on the subject of imitation: "The best of modern Poets in all languages, are those that have nearest copied the Ancients" (20 July, 1706), *The Correspondence of Alexander Pope* (Oxford, 1956), I, 20.

Tho' all Parnassus could be mine.
No let my Genius have its way,
My Genius I will still obey;
Nor, with their Stupid Rules, control
The sacred Pulse that beats within my Soul.

....
With Transport I the Pen employ,
And every Line reveals my joy.
   No Pangs of Thought I undergo...[46]

The obscure Edward Stephens was also a self-advertised and perhaps, more typical, "ignorant" poet. His "unlearned Muse" appears to have heeded Addison's advice and betaken itself to the rural retreats of inspiration, for, in the country, he had found himself so "excited by the various and enchanting Scenes of Nature" that the unpremeditated result was a series of descriptive poems modestly offered to the public.[47]

But even those of a learned disposition could fall prey to the charms of inspiration. In Oxford, the very heart of classical learning, one William Lux of Balliol College, appealed to the "sacred Pulse":

Let Fancy all her brightest Colours bring,
To Gild the Flow'rs, and Paint the purple Spring;
And whilst I write, may Nature rule my Lines,
As in those Flow'rs, unmixed with Art, she shines.
Nor let pale *Ivy* round my Temples twine,
But let the Nectar of the native *Vine,*
Which in the *Garden* grows, inspire my Lays,
To nobler Bards I leave the barren *Bays.*[48]

The inspired poet was also characterised by his pronounced aversion to society and the company of men. Only by fleeing their abodes and seeking the solitude of the wilderness, or, at least the vernal countryside, could he hope to experience the secret impulses of nature. Being deprived of this bliss and longing to experience it once again are constant themes in the works of these poets. James Thomson led the way to "the haunts of meditation" through "the falling glooms" or "with the rising dawn" to soar "excursive" "On fancy's eagle-wing". Those who wished to follow him there, were more modest. In "A Letter to a Friend in the Country", John Hughes compared the congenial environment of the countryside in which his friend is fortunate enough to live and work, with the uninspiring and oppressive atmosphere of the town:

[46] *Carribeana* (1741), quoted in M. M. Fitzgerald, *First Follow Nature,* p. 150.
[47] Preface to *Poems on Various Subjects* (1759).
[48] "The Garden" in *Poems on Several Occasions* (1719), sig. A1ʳ. The preface to this poem refers to the work of several contemporary natural historians.

Whilst thou art happy in a blest Retreat,
   And free from care dost rural Songs repeat,
Whilst fragrant Air fans thy Poetick Fire,
And pleasant Groves with Sprightly Notes inspire,
(Groves, whose Recesses and refreshing Shade
Indulge th'Invention, and the Judgment aid)
I, midst the Smoke and Clamour of the Town,
That choke my Muse and weigh my Fancy down,
Pass my unactive Hours;[49]

The town can only inspire the ephemeral sparks of wit, which, in its ignorance of feeling and passion, cannot qualify as true poetry:

In such an Air, how can soft Numbers flow,
Or in such a Soil the sacred Laurel grow?
All we can boast of the Poetick Fire,
Are but some sparks that soon as born expire.

It is only in the countryside, "where grateful Silence unmolested reigns", that the poet will find true inspiration. Only there can he satisfy his longing to "sing of rural Joys in rural Strains". However, in planning to share these joys with a carefully chosen friend, Hughes, it must be said, shows a closer kinship with those of Pomfret's inclination than with the solitary figure that roams through Thomson's or Warton's work.

A sense of belonging to a long tradition in which the inspiration of nature is responsible for the greatest steps mankind has taken, is apparent in the work of some of these nature poets. It is the reason given by Katherine Philips for choosing a country life in a poem of that name:

'Twas here the poets were inspir'd,
   Here taught the multitude;
The brave they here with honour fir'd,
   And civiliz'd the rude.

. . . .

In this retir'd and humble seat,
   Free from both war and strife,
I am not forc'd to make retreat,
   But chuse to spend my life.[50]

Reinforced by the growing cult of the sublime and the increasing appreciation of primitive and Hebrew poetry, the conviction that true poets drew their inspiration from close contact with the more awesome phenomena of nature became stronger. The well-known shift in taste in attitudes towards nature can be illustrated once again by comparing Charles Cotton's horrified

---

[49] *Poems on Several Occasions* (1735), pp. 111–113.
[50] "A Country Life" in *Poems by Eminent Ladies* (1755), II, 223–226.

diatribe against the mountainous scenery of the Peak district with an anonymous eulogy on the Southern Highlands of Scotland published in *The Gentleman's Magazine* (1743).[51] In Cotton's view, as we have already seen, the mountains of the Peak were nothing less than evidence of the corruption of the world. This author, on the other hand, though well aware of the beliefs that Cotton shared, cannot but regard the inspiring prospect from the top of the mountains as the means whereby man may be lifted into ecstasy:

> When plac'd on Grampian's lofty brow I stand,
> What solemn prospects strike on ev'ry hand!
> Here nature in majestic grandeur reigns,
> While from her throne she views her wide domains
> Hills pil'd on hills, and rocks together hurl'd,
> Sure, Burnet there the ruins of thy world! [sic]
> Trembling, I ask, what mighty arm could raise
> Those spiring summits from their rooted base?
> Whose cloudless points as high in Aether glow,
> As sink the caverns of the deep below;
> What awe, what thoughts these pathless wilds impart?
> They whisper omnipresence to the heart!
> Here meditation broods—and sheds around
> A pleasing stillness o'er the russet ground!
> I wonder not the bards of old inspir'd,
> Or prophets by celestial vision fir'd,
> To unfrequent'd scenes like these retir'd;
> On Sinai's top, possess'd with pious awe,
> Moses receiv'd the heav'n descended law;
> In Carmel's shades pursu'd by Abab's hate,
> The good Elijah shun'd his threaten'd fate.[52]

The poet asks nothing better than to be allowed to remain in this wilderness so that he too may partake of the sublime inspiration of the place:

> Here let me learn, as purer air I breathe,
> To scorn the bustling world that lies beneath!
> In wisdom's search the lovely walk improve,
> And view the realms of bliss that shine above.
>   See what romantic views surprize around;
>   Where'er I tread seems visionary ground.

The poet, it will be observed, resorts to the evocative words, "visionary" and "romantic" in his attempt to convey the significance the summit has for him. Rather than essaying his hand at the picturesque, he has chosen to convey his own feelings in the face of nature, an inclination which preoccupied the "inspired" poets.

[51] See above, p. 69.
[52] *The Prospect* (1743), quoted in M. M. Fitzgerald, pp. 140–141.

Long relegated to the lowest niche in the hierarchy of Kinds and burdened with more than its share of precedent and rule, pastoral poetry had become little more than a pedagogic exercise. Its strict conventions and citified dress—a constant prey to ridicule and parody—made it unpopular with poets who sought a more genuine contact with nature or who felt ill-equipped to deal with the affectation of learning that dogged the genre.

Nature itself and the countryside—once thought to lie beyond the pale of the civilised—were acquiring a new status. The Bible had always emphasised the beauties and joys of Creation. Scientific investigation had set about revealing its hitherto unrecognised complexity and mystery. Man's traditional role as lord of all was coming into question. Shocked voices were raised demanding an end to his cruel exploitation of what has since become known as the environment. Blood sports, eating meat and laying waste the countryside all elicited strong condemnation. The phenomena of nature, once deemed by many as alien and inhospitable, were now found to produce various ameliorative effects on the mind of man. In the face of nature many confessed to experiencing a raising of the spirits, calm of mind and, best of all, the inspiration to poetry.

The revelations of the early natural historians made their way into verse much as the early stirrings of scientific enquiry had done. But the subject of nature itself permitted and, indeed, encouraged those personal and lovingly detailed observations—the result of a long and dedicated love of nature—which science alone could not inspire.

But what is most striking about nature as a source of original themes is the phenomenon of the inspired poet who came to draw his emotional and poetic sustenance from a close and intimate communion with its wilder aspects. It was, it was claimed, from this inner activity that his originality came. Herein lay the key to originality, for this elusive quality was now thought to lie, not in the stimuli to be gained from without, but in the recesses of the poet's own heart itself.

In the following decade, this theme was seized on by the surprising figure of the veteran poet, Edward Young, who became its most outspoken apostle and whose treatise on the subject was the first avowed attempt to discuss at some length the implications for poetry of this discovery.

Chapter 4

"Thyself so reverence": Edward Young's *Conjectures on Original Composition* (1759)

With the publication of Edward Young's *Conjectures on Original Composi-tion* in 1759, the theory of originality is given its first extended brief.[1] After this date, too, the terms "original" and "originality" become firmly established in their modern meaning of new, independently creative and non-imitative.[2] Young was mistaken, of course, in believing that the subject of original composition was a new one, but it must be said that his discus-sion, although building on much that had already been said, opens up at least one scarcely explored dimension, that of "mental individuality".[3] Further-

---

[1] After more than a two and a half year gestation period the *Conjectures on Original Composition in a Letter to the Author of Sir Charles Grandison* was published anonymously in early May, 1759, in an edition of one thousand copies. Soon afterwards, in June of the same year, a second edition of the same size followed. It was republished in a supplementary volume of Young's works in 1767, after his death, and again in the *Complete Works* of 1770, 1774, 1778, 1798 and 1854. It was not separately printed again in England until 1918 when Edith J. Morley edited a reprint of the second edition collated with the first. This bibliographical information is from the Morley edition. See p. 50. All references in this chapter are from the Morley edition, hereafter referred to as Morley.

[2] The *OED* dates the term "original" in the sense of "made, composed or done by the person himself" to 1700, and in the sense of "having the quality of that which proceeds from oneself ... without imitation of or dependence on others" to 1756. "Originality" is dated 1787. However, Robert Wolseley used "original" as meaning "unlike anything that has been writ before" in Preface to *Valentinian* (1685), Spingarn, III, 8, and the term "originality" appears frequently in Young and his correspondents. See Pettit, op. cit. passim. It should be noted that the earliest English dictionaries of Robert Cawdrey (1604), John Bullokar (1616 and revision 1663) and Henry Cockeram (1623) define "original" as simply "the first beginning". In Thomas Blount's (1656 and many later eds.), Elisha Coles's (1676; reissued 10 times) and Edward Crocker's (1704), the additional meaning, "the first Draught of a Writing" appears. See also B. N. Defoe, *A Compleat English Dictionary* (1735). *A New General English Dictionary* (1735; 18 eds. by 1794) added "that from which another is taken or copied". Most of these definitions were incorporated in Johnson's *A Dictionary of the English Language* (1755). The only dictionary to offer a substantive was Nathan Bailey's *The New Universal English Dictionary* (1717; 5 eds. by 1760) which suggested "originalness": "the first source to rise; original nature or quality, primitiveness". It is clear that although both "original" and "originality" were early in common use, they did not sufficiently attract the compilers of dictionaries.

[3] In the *Conjectures* Young wrote, "I begin with *Original* Composition; and the more willingly, as it seems an original subject to me, who have seen nothing hitherto written on it". It is certainly true that the subject in general had never been treated before. The *Conjectures* appears to have been the only critical treatise of the period which incorporated the term "original" in its very title. But as we know other writers had attempted the subject, including Young himself. See his Prefaces *On Lyric Poetry* (1728) and to *Imperium Pelagi: A Naval Lyric* (1730).

more, nearing the end of his career as a renowned author and absolved from the need to court his audience, Young is able to treat of the subject of originality in general terms and as provocatively as he likes.[4]

The *Conjectures* is not a solemn work and its brevity and ill-arrangement have not endeared it to critics, but it has been underestimated.[5] It was never Young's intention to speak *ex cathedra*. Indeed he describes his work as the pastime of some leisure hours, although, as his correspondence with Samuel Richardson during the period of composition shows, a considerable degree of care and attention was lavished on the task.[6] Nevertheless, he takes care to present a very modest estimate of its value in the opening lines of the essay:

It is miscellaneous in its nature, somewhat licentious in its conduct; and, perhaps, not over important in its end. (p. 3)

It is certainly true that an artless unorthodoxy pervades the *Conjectures*. Enthusiasm for the craft of letters, somewhat unusual in a renowned author

---

[4] Young was born in 1683, five years before Pope and twenty-six years before Samuel Johnson. His reputation had been consolidated by the publication of *The Complaint: or, Night Thoughts*, 1742–1747, a poem of enduring popularity in Britain and Europe.

[5] In view of Young's great fame as a poet in his own time and later, the dearth of critical commentary on Young's *Conjectures* is surprising. But what this body of opinion lacks in volume is compensated by its variety. There is little unanimity to be found. Young's essay has been ignored, exalted or ridiculed and, less frequently it would seem, carefully examined. W. Thomas, the author of the most comprehensive biography of Young *Le Poète Edward Young* (Paris, 1901) called the *Conjectures* "une révolte ouverte contre les tendances littéraires qui avaient prévalu jusque-là", p. 477. Paul Kaufman regarded Young as one of the "heralds" of original genius, the treatise as a "manifesto" of liberty and found it difficult to speak of it "with moderation": "Heralds of Original Genius" in *Essays in memory of Barrett Wendell* (Harvard, 1926), pp. 201, 203; J. L. Kind, *Edward Young in Germany,* (N. Y., 1906) and Edith J. Morley in the edition noted above, both thought the *Conjectures* important, but not so much for any revolutionary quality as for the unique and interesting way in which Young was able to sum up and promulgate the most advanced critical opinion of the time (see p. 1 and Introd. pp. xv.-xvi in Kind and Morley resp.). Other critics have preferred to see Young as an isolated prophetic figure proclaiming his vision of the future to an inimical age. In "Richardson, Young and the *Conjectures,*" *MP,* 12 (May 1925), 391–404, A. D. McKillop noted his "radical romanticism" and his isolation. That quality, usually ascribed to the archetypal romantic poet, is underlined by René Wellek in *A History of Modern Criticism* (1955), p. 110. At odds with this enthusiasm is the criticism which pours scorn on Young's efforts: according to J. W. Draper, he merely jumped on the fashionable bandwagon of originality, but remained timebound by the conventions of his day ("Aristotelian Mimesis in England," *PMLA,* 36 (1921), 372–400). See also A. Bosker, *Literary Criticism in the Age of Johnson,* (Groningen, den Haag, 1930), pp. 207–208; W. K. Wimsatt and C. Brooks, *Literary Criticism. A Short History,* (N. Y., 1957), p. 290; Emerson R. Marks, *The Poetics of Reason* (N. Y., 1968), p. 86. All were agreed on the commonplace nature of Young's essay. Neither George Saintsbury nor W. J. Courthope saw fit to accord it a mention in their historical tomes on the period. For contemporary reactions, see Morley, pp. 50–53 and Note 29 below, p. 109.

[6] *The Correspondence of Edward Young. 1683–1765,* ed. Henry Pettit (Oxford, 1971), pp. 446–503. (Referred to hereafter as Pettit).

and elderly priest, characterizes the work. What is most striking about Young's attitude to literature is his passionate belief that the writing and the reading of it should be a pleasurable activity. With barely a token nod towards "the sacred interests of virtue, and the real service of mankind", Young extolls the charms and delights of all literary effort, irrespective of merit, with a generous and infectious enthusiasm.

Dr. Johnson had despaired of the period that he contemptuously dubbed "The Age of Authors", when the solid foundation of learning was neglected and every man considered himself qualified to instruct every other man. Even farmers and blacksmiths occupied their "hours of leisure with providing intellectual pleasures" for their countrymen.[7] Johnson assessed the resulting "multiplication of books" as nothing better than a modern pestilence in "an ignorant age".[8]

Not so Dr. Young. Though certainly one of Johnson's admirers, such opinions can have found little favour with him.[9] "The more composition the better", was his rallying cry (p. 4). He believed the function of literature to be solely escapist. It should serve as a necessary and blessed antidote to the turmoil and strife of modern life, bringing peace, activity, amusement and consolation. Unencumbered by any social or ethical message, its real worth and pleasure was to be found in its introspective nature—in the hidden potential of "the little world, the minute but fruitful creation "of man's own mind" (p. 5).

It was on this basis that Young approached the perennial question of originality and imitation. As might be expected of a thoroughgoing Whig, Young disputed any theory which sought to dethrone eighteenth-century man in favour of the lost perfection of the past.[10] He airily dismissed such dearly held beliefs as the post-diluvial denudation of the earth, the progressive decline of the mental faculties of men through the ages and the notion that the great Ancients had left nothing for the Moderns (pp. 10, 12, 32). The *Conjectures* is a testimony to the superiority of the individual and the ameliorative state of nature. Although elderly and ailing, Young was able to view his contemporaries without that distortion which arises from chronic nostalgia. He appears to have found each new generation rich in promise. For him the intellectual equality of all men in all times was a touchstone of

---

[7] *The Adventurer* 115 (1753).

[8] *The Idler* 85 (1759). The "contagion of authors" theme also appears in the *Grub-Street Journal* 55 (1731); *Weekly Register* 29 (19 Feb. 1732). Reports of both these articles appear in the *Gentleman's Magazine* for Jan. 1731 and February 1732.

[9] Young was hopeful that Dr. Johnson would read the *Conjectures*. See Pettit, pp. 500, 503.

[10] For an analysis of the typical Whig perspective on the past, see Herbert Butterfield, *The Whig Interpretation of History* (1931).

belief. "I think that human souls, thro' all periods, are equal", for "an impartial Providence scatters talents indifferently, as thro' all orders of persons, so thro' all periods of time" (pp. 10, 32).

He was, of course, aware that signs of contemporary inferiority were all too visible. But, he insisted, these should be assigned, not to "divine destination", but to more sublunary causes, for nature is ever bountiful. Her largesse renders us "as strong as our predecessors; and by the favour of time (which is but another round in nature's scale) we stand on higher ground" (p. 12). He acknowledges a belief in antediluvial perfection—but of nature, not man:

Are not our minds cast in the same mould with those before the flood? The flood affected matter; mind escaped. (p. 12)

There has been no golden age from which we are forever excluded. If such a state does exist, Young thought it much more likely to lie ahead—a goal towards which the present generation might strive—a heritage for future generations (p. 32).

Three main themes emerge from Young's patchwork of ideas. The first two—a comparison of originality and imitation in composition and an analysis of the respective merits of genius and learning—occupy the bulk of the essay. Although building on the arguments traditionally employed in these long-established feuds, Young's marked iconoclasm and his refreshing approach to the issues merits examination. But it is the third theme, Young's own contribution to the theory of original composition, which is most arresting. In the century or so before the *Conjectures* was written, authors and poets searched far and wide for ways in which to escape from the monolithic dominance of the classics. As we have seen, they often found what they sought in themes taken from the Christian religion, science or nature. But, increasingly, as the new theories of psychology put words to what men had long felt, the search for originality began to focus on that quality in man himself. His vagaries and eccentricities, his lawless imagination and his unique and distinct powers of perception, once outlawed, now cast him as the true original. These earlier hints were developed by Young into a full-blown theory of originality.[11]

---

[11] As we have seen, Isaac Watts thought the vagaries of his own mind of interest. See above, p. 27. Another author sharing similar views was Henry Baker. In his preface to *Original Poems: Serious and Humourous* (1725) he wrote that he hoped they "may serve for a natural History of myself, truly pointing out the Turn and Disposition of my Soul at the time it gave them Birth.—As I scarce ever have intentionally sat down to write, but only copied the Ideas, I know not how arising, accidentally, in my own Mind; as I have followed no Rules, nor at all consulted the Thoughts of others upon the same Subjects, it is very probable, there may be less of Art, and more of Nature,

Imitation and Originality

Young's definition of these terms, though cursory, is suggestive. Beginning with the simple distinction that imitation takes the work of other authors as its object, whereas the original writer is inspired directly by Nature, Young then enhances the difference by attributing to originality the virtues of Nature itself:

An *Original* may be said to be of a *vegetable* nature; it rises spontaneously from the vital root of genius; it *grows,* it is not made. (p. 7)

Imitation, meanwhile, partakes of the artificial, the man-made, and, most damning, the unnatural:

Imitations are often a sort of *manufacture* wrought up by those *mechanics, art* and *labour,* out of pre-existent materials not their own. (p. 7)

In a series of juxtapositions, a favourite technique of Young's, the superior quality of originality is repeatedly emphasised. Imitation simply increases "the mere drug of books" while the works of the original author, however indifferent, always enchant and inevitably expand the boundaries of "the republic of letters". There is a quality of magic energy about the productions of the original author, in comparison with which the efforts of the imitator seem stunted and fruitless:

The pen of an *original* writer, like *Armida's* wand, out of a barren waste calls a blooming spring: Out of that blooming spring an *Imitator* is a transplanter of laurels, which sometimes die on removal, always languish in a foreign soil. (p. 7)[12]

Regardless of the skill and art which may be apparent in an imitation, it will always rank second to even the most frivolous of new compositions, for though an imitator be "most excellent" (and Young here admits that such

than is usually found in Compositions of the like Sort: But to Those who have a just Taste of Poetry, which, Itself, is no more than a true Representation of Nature, this will give no Disgust" (pp. vi-vii—the latter is incorrectly numbered ix); see R. D. Havens, "Unusual Opinions in 1725 and 1726," *PQ,* 30 (1951), 447–48.

[12] Armida was the enchantress in Tasso's *Gerusalemme Liberata* (1581). An example of its frequent translation during the period is Elizabeth Rowe's "A Description of the enchanted palace and gardens of Armida, translated from the XVIth book of Tasso's Jerusalem" in her *Miscellaneous Works* (1739), I, 18–23. These particular lines from the *Conjectures* were adapted by Robert Lloyd in his poem *The Critic's Rules* thus:

True Genius, like Armida's wand,
Can raise the spring from barren land:
While all the art of Imitation,
Is pilf'ring from the first creation;
Transplanting flowers, with useless toil,
Which wither in a foreign Soil. etc. etc.

See the *Oxford Book of Eighteenth-Century Verse,* p. 411.

do exist), "yet still he but nobly builds on another's foundation; his debt is, at least equal to his glory; which therefore, on the balance, cannot be very great" (p. 7). Imitators, however fine, are a servile crew. They are always "diiminorum gentium" (p. 19). The "littleness" and "meanness" of the imitative mind, and its tendency to self-abnegation renders it constitutionally "somewhat of the pedestal kind" (p. 25).

Adoration of the Ancients is not a testimony of the imitator's great intellect or taste, but the result of a pathetic compound of ignorance and fear. It has, moreover, effectively hobbled the ambitions of the moderns, for, far from producing the well-read and learned writer, this leaden-eyed docility has resulted in "meanness of mind" and a frightening "prostration of our own powers" (p. 25). In attacking the period's supposed partiality for the Ancients, Young was out of date but only a little. That youthful authors ought to acquire a thorough knowledge of the classics remained a popular adage.[13] Young's dislike of this tenet was vehement. Even the slightest acquaintance with the great Ancients was, he suggested, a mistake, for they may "browbeat thy reason into too great a diffidence of thyself" (p. 24). It is all too easy to be blinded by these "illustrious examples".

They *engross* our attention, and so prevent a due inspection of ourselves; they prejudice our judgment in favour of their abilities, and so lessen the sense of our own; and they intimidate us with the splendour of their renown, and thus under diffidence bury our strength. Nature's impossibilities, and those of diffidence lie wide asunder. (p. 9)

Modern authors should certainly approach the Ancients in a spirit of admiration, but this admiration must be tempered with confidence in their own worth. While classical works should be accorded the just dues of posterity, for their charm is great and their status "inviolable", their influence must be curtailed. When the modern author picks up his pen he must bid his great precursors stand aside, "nor shade our Composition from the beams of our own genius; for nothing *Original* can rise, nothing immortal, can ripen, in any other sun" (pp. 10–11).

The aspiring author would do well to emulate the example of the scientists. Independent of the pernicious influence of the past, they have made striking progress. Their successes ought to dissuade those who believe the Age is one of decline. Young himself resorted to science for inspiration. From Bacon, the master of modern science, "under the shadow of whose great name" this "present attempt in favour of *Originals* is sheltered", Young borrowed the proof that genius in one area is evidence of a similar

---

[13] See *Rambler* 154; "An Advice to a Poet" in *The Whitehall Evening Post,* 12–15 Feb., 1731–32 and *Read's Weekly Journal or British Gazetter,* 29 Jan., 1732.

potential in others.[14] It is the insufferable habit of imitation rather than a fundamental inferiority which is the root cause of the present state of composition:

And since copies surpass not their *Originals,* as streams rise not higher than their spring, rarely so high; hence, while arts mechanic are in perpetual progress, and increase, the liberal are in retrogadation, and decay. *These* resemble pyramids, are broad at bottom, but lessen exceedingly as they rise; *Those* resemble rivers which, from a small fountain-head, are spreading ever wider and wider as they run. Hence it is evident, that different portions of understanding are not (as some imagine) allotted to different periods of time; for we see, in the same period, understanding rising in one set of artists, and declining in another. Therefore *nature* stands absolved, and our inferiority in Composition must be charged on ourselves. (p. 19)

Not only can the example of the sciences inspire the original author, but, claimed Young echoing earlier suggestions, he might also look to them for new subject matter:

... knowledge physical, mathematical, moral, and divine, increases; all arts and sciences are making considerable advance; with them, all the accommodations, ornaments, delights, and glories of human life; and these are new food to the genius of a polite writer; these are as the root, and composition, as the flower; and as the root spreads, and thrives, shall the flower fail? As well may a flower flourish, when the root is dead. (p. 33)

Young's enthusiasm for science was a legacy from his youthful days, when, as we have seen, such thoughts were not uncommon. But in making the suggestion that authors look to the sciences for inspiration and subject matter, he was, it must be confessed, a little behind the times. By mid-century the earlier suspicion of some true conservatives that the men of science were ill-educated, narrow-minded and absorbed with trifling, or dangerous, idiocies, had hardened into certainty. As interest in science among the upper classes waned, it became the preoccupation and enthusiasm of the lower social groups, in particular the Dissenting minorities.[15] In Young's declining years, therefore, few of his class would have shared his belief in the redemptive powers of science in literature.

Imitation not only deflects the natural thrust of progress, but, continues Young, it is also responsible for thwarting the very course of Nature itself. It is Nature's way to cultivate the individual and distinct and, according to Young, this produces a limitless and happy diversity in humankind. Unlike Dr. Johnson, Young saw no need to stress the common attributes of humanity. Johnson preferred to attribute what he regarded as the superficial unalikeness of individuals to such accidentals as time and place. In the

---

[14] For Young's debt to Bacon, see W. Thomas, *Le Poète Edward Young* (Paris, 1901), pp. 479–482.

[15] See J. H. Plumb, "Reason and Unreason in the 18th-Century", pp. 18–22.

greater cheme of things, these are irrelevant, and it is the writer's duty to ignore them.[16] The strength of Shakespeare's characters lies, he claimed, not in their idiosyncrasy, but in their universality; "they are the geniune progeny of common humanity, such as the world will always supply, and observation will always find"; they "act and speak by the influence of those general passions and principles by which all minds are agitated, and the whole system of life is continued in motion".[17]

Johnson abhorred the notion that men might be fundamentally different. His definition of nature is that which A. O. Lovejoy isolates as "the universal and immutable in thought, feeling and taste; what has always been known, what everyone can immediately understand and enjoy; usually connected with the assumption that the universally valued is also the objectively beautiful".[18]

In Young's opinion, however, the very opposite is true. According to him Nature "brings us into the world all *Originals*: No two faces, no two minds, are just alike; but all bear nature's evident mark of separation on them" (pp. 19–20). A belief in mutability and diversity, and a cheerful acceptance of their existence, is at the heart of his thinking. Nothing remains static; the world is a constantly changing place. The individual is ever evolving, and so is his language:

It is with thoughts, as it is with words; and with both, as with men; they may grow old, and die. Words tarnished, by passing thro' the mouths of the vulgar, are laid aside as inelegant, and obsolete. So thoughts, when become too common, should lose their currency; and we should send new metal to the mint, that is, new meaning to the press. (p. 8)

The practice of imitation, then, counteracts the very foundation of the human intellect—its intrinsic originality. To imitate is to thwart nature's intention. Young's summary brooks no compromise:

Born *Originals*, how comes it to pass that we die *Copies?* That meddling ape *Imitation,* as soon as we come to years of *Indiscretion* (so let me speak), snatches the pen, and blots out nature's mark of separation, cancels her kind intention, destroys all mental individuality; the letter'd world no longer consists of singulars, it is a medly, a mass; and a hundred books, at bottom, are but One. Why are Monkies such master of mimickry? Why receive they such a talent at

---

[16] *Adventurer* 95 (1753).

[17] *Preface* to Shakespeare (Yale edition, 1968), VII, 62; see also the famous Chapter X of *Rasselas,* but note Jean H. Hagstrum, *Samuel Johnson's Literary Criticism* (Minneapolis, 1952), pp. 22, 34, 37 & 54; Howard D. Weinbrot, "The Reader, the General, and the Particular: Johnson and Imlac in Chapter Ten of *Rasselas,*" *ECS,* 5 (Fall, 1971), 80–96; Arthur H. Scouten, "Dr. Johnson and Imlac," *ECS,* 6 (Summer, 1973), 506–8; R. G. Peterson, "Samuel Johnson at War with the Classics," *ECS,* 1 (Fall, 1975), 69–86.

[18] For definitions of nature current during the period, see A. O. Lovejoy's "Nature as Aesthetic Norm," *MLN,* 42 (1927), 444–450.

imitation? Is it not as the *Spartan* slaves received a licence for ebriety; that their betters might be ashamed of it? (p. 20)

Imitation is an activity, therefore, which perverts the human mind. Furthermore, it inhibits progress and development, the most fundamental movement in nature. Finally, it encourages a foolish expense of energy—of thinking little and writing much. The results of imitation are conspicuous in the telling bulk of boring and unreadable mediocrity that abounds.

Once during the essay Young does concede that imitation is probably the lot of most writers, but that it may be an "honourable lot" is admitted only in parenthesis. Those who take this path are often accused of having chosen to "move in the soft fetters of easy imitation" rather than opting for the more strenuous venture of soaring "in the regions of liberty" (p. 10). They will ever stand convicted in the eyes of posterity. Young singles out a couple of these felons. Ben Jonson, for example, is compared to Samson who was "very strong to his own hurt":

Blind to the nature of tragedy, he pulled down all antiquity on his head, and buried himself under it. (p. 35)

The supreme example of such pernicious prostration of self before the past is, of course, Young's long-dead rival and contemporary, Alexander Pope:

His taste partook of the error of his religion; it denied not worship to saints and angels; that is , to writers, who, canonized for ages, have received their apotheosis from established fame. (p. 30)

Neither Pope nor Jonson can claim a niche in the "republic of letters". In composition, hereditary dynasties are unacceptable. The imitator, although heir to a throne, is himself sterile and barren, however illustrious his descent may be. An original author, on the other hand, is more nobly born because he is born of himself, "is his own progenitor, and will probably propagate a numerous offspring of imitators, to eternize his glory; while mule-like imitators die without issue" (p. 30).

Young concludes his assessment of the respective merits of the two modes of composition in one more series of adamant juxtapositions:

One of these all writers must call to their aid; but aids they are of unequal repute. Imitation is inferiority confessed; emulation is superiority contested, or denied; imitation is servile, emulation generous; that fetters, this fires; that may give a name; this, a name immortal. (p. 29)

Genius and Learning

Although Young cites with apparent approval the Addisonian division of genius into the adult or unlearned and the infantine or learned, it is clear that he regarded learning and true poetry as fundamentally incompatible.[19] The influence of Longinus had considerably undermined the status of the learned and scrupulous poet.[20] By the time of the *Conjectures* the impatient and furious genius who disregards all the restraints of learning was a commonplace. Young was unequivocal in setting poetry and learning at loggerheads:

For unprescribed beauties, and unexampled excellence, which are the characteristics of genius, lie without the pale of *learning's* authorities, and laws; which pale, genius must leap to come at them. (pp. 13–14)

Learning is nothing but an excessive deference to tradition and the tutelage of reason, whereas "there is something in poetry beyond prose-reason" (p. 14). Reason and learning are inimical to true genius, which Young defines as "the power of accomplishing great things without the means generally reputed necessary to that end" (p. 13).

Like so many of his contemporaries, Young had fallen under the spell of the "unlearned" poet—he who has not been emasculated by learning. "Many a genius, probably, there has been, which could neither write, nor read" (p. 17).[21] The true genius is immune to the influence of the great Ancients for whom "too great awe" would lay any aspiring author under unwelcome restraint and deny him "that free scope, that full elbow-room, which is requisite for striking [the] most masterly strokes".

Learning resembles the well trained mechanic; genius partakes of the magical and divine. The one inhabits an artificial region of rules, authorities and "prose-reason". The other springs from "native force of mind" and abounds in that "*original*, unindebted energy". Genius requires no other assistance. Young chooses to praise Shakespeare, and a few other "adult" geniuses, including his friend Richardson, for having ignored the traps of learning and relied on their own powers and knowledge of nature and men.[22] Of Shakespeare he says, he "mingled no water with his wine, lower'd his genius by no vapid imitation" (p. 34).[23]

[19] See *Spectator* 160.

[20] See *Longinus: On the Sublime*, Ch. 33, "Superiority of Flawed Sublimity to Flawless Mediocrity", pp. 143–144.

[21] Young may well have known Stephen Duck, the most famous of the "unlearned" poets of the period. Duck was one of Joseph Spence's "most intimate Friends" as was Samuel Richardson, Young's friend and mentor. See Austin Wright, *Joseph Spence*, pp. 120–121; see also James M. Osborn, "Spence, Natural Genius and Pope," *PQ*, 45 (1966), 123–144.

[22] 'A friend of mine ... has relied on himself, and with a genius, as well *moral*, as *original* ... has made a convert to virtue of a species of composition, once almost its foe ... But you, I know, are sparing in your praise of this author ...", *Conjectures*, p. 34.

[23] Cf. with his supposed earlier opinion, recorded by Spence, that Shakespeare's work was mostly "trash", *Anecdotes*, I, 345.

Unlike some other writers on the subject, Young makes few concessions to the help which learning and tradition may afford the novice author. In this he probably confirmed Dr. Johnson's worst fears that "the mental disease of the present generation is impatience of study, contempt for the great masters...".[24] Young could only insist that the cultivation of learning was a serious danger to the writer. His individuality risked being smothered by "an indigested load" and he was in constant danger of being misled by "pedantic prejudice" for even "the best understanding" risked being "vitiated" by authority. This is because learning is "borrowed knowledge" while "genius is knowledge innate and quite our own". Like imitation, learning undermines the most important characteristics of the human mind—its individuality and uniqueness.[25]

Essentially a natural phenomenon, genius can most fittingly be compared "to the natural strength of the body". Learning can as appropriately be equated with "the super-induced accoutrements of arms" (p. 15). If the first is at all capable of the proposed exploit, the latter will act only as hindrance and encumbrance.

Resorting to yet another contrast in order to underline the inferior status of learning, Young compares genius to virtue and learning to riches:

As riches are most wanted where there is least virtue; so learning where there is least genius. As virtue without much riches can give happiness, so genius without much learning can give renown. (p. 14)

A final comparison involves the similarity between genius and conscience on the one hand and learning and the law on the other. The first pair are innate, natural and, therefore, superior. The second are, of course, superimposed, artificial and, consequently, inferior:

Genius can set us right in Composition, without the rules of the learned; as conscience sets us right in life, without the laws of the land: *This*, singly, can make us good, as men: *that*, singly, as writers, can, sometimes, make us great. (p. 15)

In sum, then, writes Young:

Learning we thank, genius we revere; That gives us pleasure, This gives us rapture; That informs, This inspires; and is itself inspired; for genius is from heaven, learning from man: *This* sets us above the low, and illiterate; *That*, above the learned and polite. Therefore, as *Bacon* observes, it may take a nobler name, and be called Wisdom; in which sense of wisdom, some are born wise. (p. 17)

To attempt to suppress genius is to oppose the most fundamental current of Nature—man's unique individuality.

---

[24] *Rambler* 154.
[25] Cf. Bacon's *Aphorisms* I, xxvi; II, xxxi.

Thyself so reverence

The fashion of imitation and learning is not only retrograde and counter to Nature's plan, it is also responsible for undermining confidence in man's greatest asset, his "mental individuality":

Forming our judgments, altogether by what *has* been done, without knowing, or at all inquiring, what possibly *might* have been done, we naturally enough fall into too mean an opinion of the human mind. (p. 22)

Although at times, it seems that by originality, Young meant little more than new subject matter, his whole theory is, in fact, based on the premise that originality is the activity of the self-exploring mind, the examination of man's "own stock and abilities" (p. 31). His brief but decisive analysis firmly establishes the special calibre of the poet as the true source of originality. It is, he asserts, every man's and, in particular, every author's, duty to cherish and cultivate his own talents and abilities. Self-respect and a fine disdain for the works of the great authors is the key to original composition: "Let not the blaze of even *Homer's* muse darken us to the discernment of our own powers" (p. 19).

In a new version of the spider and the bee parable so beloved by those who took sides in the perennial Ancients and Moderns controversy, Young writes that the original writer need not fear "a famine of invention". Such catastrophes can only affect the imitative writer who, starved of an inward harvest, must travel far afield in search of sustenance—"to the remote, and rich, Antients". The "inventive genius" meanwhile, "may safely stay at home" for "like the widow's cruse" he is "divinely replenished from within" and "affords us a miraculous delight" (p. 20).

Resorting to yet another metaphor to reinforce his enthusiastic advocacy of the poet's "mental individuality", Young finds that "there is a mine in man, which must be deeply dug ere we can conjecture its contents" (p. 21). Of the proportions and extent of this prodigious wealth little is known. But certain it is, that too many dearly held beliefs in our intellectual shortcomings are founded quite simply "on our ignorance of the possible dimensions of the mind of man" (p. 22). It is virgin territory, awaiting exploration and exploitation. For, challenges Young, "who hath fathomed the mind of man?":

Its bounds are as unknown, as those of the creation; since the birth of which, perhaps, not One has so far exerted, as not to leave his possibilities beyond his attainments, his powers beyond his exploits. (p. 22)

Young naturally assesses the riches of this treasure house as formidable, but hidden. So ignorant is man of his own abilities that he often remains quite oblivious of their existence. He is as unaware of his own powers as is the oyster of its pearl, or the rock of its diamond. These "dormant, un-suspected" gifts may lie unnoticed until "awakened by loud calls, or stung up by striking emergencies" on the "strong impulse of some animating occasion" (p. 23). Then, they burst forth, presumably to the surprise of all, not least of him who housed such divine powers.

Young's advice to all those who wish to rely on their own native energy and abilities is clear and trenchant. They must summon the aid of the two great rules of ethics, "Know thyself" and "Reverence thyself". These two offer a prescription to the original genius, which, if followed, will open up the hitherto uncharted world of the mind, as well as "the vast void beyond real existence". Thus empowered, the poet can unleash his secret strength, which is formidable: "so boundless are the bold excursions of the human mind, that, ... it can call forth shadowy beings, and unknown worlds, as numerous, as bright, and, perhaps, as lasting, as the stars; such quite original beauties we may call paradisaical" (p. 31). It is, furthermore, only in the ambitious path of literary experimentation, that true originality finds expression. Some of Young's most urgent exhortations direct the aspiring writer to choose this way rather than any other:

All eminence, and distinction, lies out of the beaten road; excursion, and deviation, are necessary to find it; and the more remote your path from the highway, the more reputable. (pp. 11–12)

Cultivating the uniqueness and originality of the individual mind pro-duces, as Young notes almost casually, a poetry characterised by the singu-lar and particular. Anticipating Blake's irritable marginalia on Reynolds's *Discourses,* Young states: " ... as for a general genius, there is no such thing in nature: A genius implies the rays of the mind concenter'd, and determined to some particular point" (p. 37).[26] In Young's view, the effect of generality in poetry is to dissolve its rhetorical power. When the mind dilutes itself into generalities, its rays "are scatter'd widely, they act feebly, and strike not with sufficient force, to fire, or dissolve, the heart" (p. 37). A lack of rhetorical effect is, therefore, an inevitable result of any attempt to pervert the natural inclination to singularity—the mark of the original genius. Generality stamps those who have abjectly followed in the footsteps of other, greater minds, and who think "in wretched unanimity with the throng". Earnestly Young urges his readers: "let not great examples, or

[26] "To generalize is to be an Idiot. To Particularize is the Alone Distinction of Merit. General Knowledges are those knowledges that Idiots possess", *Annotations to Sir Joshua Reynolds's Discourses* (1808) in *The Complete Writings of William Blake,* ed. Geoffrey Keynes (1966), p. 451. See also p. 453 (on the sublimity of "Minute Discrimination") and p. 778 (on Homer and Virgil).

authorities, browbeat thy reason into too great a diffidence of thyself'' (p. 24). To be forced into such debt merely results in the beggary of imitation (p. 18). To the original author who wishes to avoid such a fate Young's advice is clear:

Therefore dive deep into thy bosom; learn the depth, extent, bias, and full fort of thy mind; contract full intimacy with the stranger within thee; excite and cherish every spark of intellectual light and heat, however smothered under former negligence, or scattered through the dull, dark mass of common thought; and collecting them into a body, let thy genius rise (if a genius thou hast) as the sun from chaos; and if I should then say, like an *Indian, Worship it*, (though too bold) yet should I say little more than my second rule enjoins, (*viz.*) *Reverence thyself.* (p. 24)[27]

The rewards of this course of action are great, as Young frequently notes, for originality carries with it the promise of immortality:

The man who thus reverences himself, will soon find the world's reverence to follow his own. His works will stand distinguished; his the sole property of them; which property alone can confer the noble title of an *author;* that is, of one who (to speak accurately) *thinks,* and *composes;* while other invaders of the press, how voluminous, and learned soever, (with due respect be it spoken) only *read*, and *write*. (p. 24)

Towards the end of the essay, it transpires that there is yet another dimension which increases the attraction of originality as a goal. Young announces that originality is the characteristic of the true Englishman. The inhabitants of that blessed country, are, he declares somewhat partially, a special breed of supermen. They "seem not to be more sever'd from the rest of mankind by the surrounding sea, than by the current in their veins" (p. 33).[28] In strains of typical Whig euphoria, Young cites the numbers of British geniuses in the arts and sciences who have made even distant nations resound with their originality (p. 34). There are, of course, exceptions, but on investigation, those who seem by nature to be imitators and followers of tradition, are found to be black sheep—not truly English. They have re-

---

[27] It should be noted that the activity of "looking inward" had been recommended earlier. See, for example, Shaftesbury's "old Article of Advice" which he called "that main Preliminary of *Self-Study* and *inward Converse,* which we have found so much wanting in the Authors of our Time. They shou'd add the Wisdom of the *Heart* to the Task and Exercise of the *Brain,* in order to bring Proportion and Beauty into their Works. That their Composition and Vein of Writing may be natural and free, they must settle Matters, in the first place, with *themselves*": *Advice to an Author,* pp. 118–119. See also p. 123 ff. Note, too, the ironic advice proffered to the beautiful Belinda in *The Rape of the Lock,* "Hear and Believe! thy own Importance know" (Canto I, 1. 35). For Young's "egocentricity of perspective" in his poetry, see John E. Sitter, "Theodicy at Mid-century: Young, Akenside and Hume," *ECS,* 12 (1978–79), 90–106, esp. pp. 100–101.

[28] Significantly this became one of Dick Minim's favourite adages. See *Idler* 60 and also *Adventurer* 84.

jected the enlightenment and freedom which the mantle of English Protestantism offers. Forgetting that "true poetry, like true religion, abhors
idolatry", they have chosen the self-abasement of the imitator, which
closely resembles the perversion of adoring false gods. As we have already
seen, Young considered Pope the prime example of this deviousness. He, it
seems, grossly neglected the two golden rules of ethics, and instead of
looking into his own soul for inspiration, remained content to prostrate
himself before the icons of the past. In this he qualifies as a full member of
the servile throng:

> Incumbered with the notions of others, and impoverished by their abundance, he conceives not
> the least embryo of new thought; opens not the least vista thro' the gloom of ordinary writers,
> into the bright walks of rare imagination, and singular design; while the true genius is crossing
> all publick roads into fresh untrodden ground; he, up to the knees in antiquity, is treading the
> sacred footsteps of great examples, with the blind veneration of a bigot saluting the papal toe;
> comfortably hoping full absolution for the sins of his own understanding, from the powerful
> charm of touching his idol's infallibility. (p. 25)

If, however, the original genius is encouraged to cultivate his unique
"mental individuality" in the genial and happy climate of Protestant England, Young, ever-optimistic, prophesies that the country may be on the
threshold of another Augustan Age. Nor, indeed, is it unlikely, "that
heaven's latest editions of the human mind may be the most correct, and
fair; that the day may come, when the moderns may proudly look back on
the comparative darkness of former ages", and see Athens and Rome, not
as the zenith, but as the dawn of culture and civilization. This achievement
would be Young's "glorious revolution" (pp. 32–33).

As we know, Young's *Conjectures* was, by no means, the dawn of the
discussion on originality. To change the metaphor, it more nearly resembles
a watershed. Prior to its appearance, a desire to be original had impelled
many to attempt to expand the too confined limits of composition. Young's
suggestion that it was really in "mental individuality" that originality was to
be found accelerated the process. After the *Conjectures* the restraints of
tradition could more easily be abandoned. The efforts of poets from Isaac
Watts to Mary Masters were finally justified.

Despite its radical stance, the *Conjectures* was accorded a lukewarm
reception at best.[29] Although some readers appreciated to the full its

---

[29] Its reception was lukewarm among the pundits of the time. Edith Morley reviews many of
the reactions to it in her edition, pp. 50–53. But the general public seems to have enjoyed it. It
should be remembered that there were two editions of 1000 copies each, within a few months of
each other. Richardson describes what seems to have been a popular demand, "Mr Millar tells
me that he has but very few left: so small a number as was printed, I wonder he has any. Mr.
Dodsley's must surely be near gone. Be pleased, then, to send up your additions ...",
Richardson to Young concerning a second edition, 24 May 1759, Pettit, p. 498.

message of reform, others, particularily the traditionalists, chose to dismiss it with a measure of contempt. Some of the blame must lie with its loose structure and unpretentious style. But more significantly, the undoubtedly radical nature of Young's prescription for a "glorious revolution" in composition was perhaps obscured by his unconscious reiteration of what were becoming literary commonplaces. Indeed, so prevalent were these ideas that they are even to be found scattered through the pages of the ephemeral literary journals of the period, which provided amusement and intellectual provender for both the eminent and the obscure. An attempt to assess the popularity of the ideas we have been discussing would not be complete without a survey of their commercial promulgation.

Chapter 5

Originality in the "Physiognomy of the Age": the Literary Journals

Towards the end of the eighteenth century, Isaac D'Israeli noted that a "Review, conducted with skill, should present the literary physiognomy of the century", because,

In an age of refinement, the public taste is in a state of vacillation; and no mean art, or limited knowledge, can catch, with faithful resemblance, "the Cynthia of the minute". We abound with literary fashions, and have no other mode of recording and perpetuating our prevalent tastes, but in these useful archives of literature.[1]

The same may surely be said of the reviews' precursor, the literary journal or magazine. Born in the transition from seventeenth to eighteenth century, these early, but often excellent productions are a tantalizing reflection of many of the preoccupations of contemporary men and women.[2] More to the point, they often reveal a conscious effort and desire on the part of their authors to mould and direct public and literary opinion. The eighteenth-century journal's primary concern was always with the taste and moral values of the fast-growing reading public and it was never given over entirely to literary matters.[3] An interest in literature and art and a developed critical sense were, however, soon considered an essential element in the moral equipage of the man, or woman, of taste and the critical essay became a regular and popular feature in most journals.

Readers were frequently treated to disquisitions on many topics relating to the subjects discussed above. These were, at best, well-written essays which have found a place in the history of literary criticism or have been unaccountably neglected. At worst, they descend to bitter satire and personal polemic or simple-minded repetitions of half-understood clichés. It is, however, in these byways of literary criticism that one can observe the detailed physiognomy of the period. It is this detail which modifies and

[1] Preface to *Miscellanies; or Literary Recreations* (1796), pp. xviii-xix.
[2] For the development of the early journal see W. Graham, *English Literary Periodicals* (New York, 1930).
[3] See Addison's avowed aims in *Spectator* 10 (12 March, 1711) which served as a model for his successors. See also Clarence DeWitt Thorpe, "Addison's Contribution to Criticism," in *The Seventeenth Century*, ed. R. F. Jones (Stanford, 1951), pp. 316–29.

refines those dominating literary landmarks which, isolated by the flow of time, are too often accepted by subsequent generations as a comprehensive image of the life of a period.[4]

It should be mentioned that, as in the rest of this investigation, attempts to impose any chronological development on the material proved vain. Contrary to what the seeker after satisfying and clear cut lines of progression would wish, defenses of imitation are just as likely to occur at the end of the period as radical gestures on behalf of originality earlier. In fact, it is in two essays in journals from the latter part of the period that one finds the most vigorously defensive attempts to explain and justify the principle of imitation and its uses.

Rules and Imitation in the Journals

In *The Adventurer* (1753–54), edited by John Hawkesworth but with many contributors of differing opinions, "Z", the author of an essay on the sources of many of Pope's thoughts and expressions, makes a careful distinction between imitation and plagiarism.[5] Significantly, he accepts that it is to novelty and invention in poetry that the highest praise is due, but he excuses the frequency of imitation on the grounds that the fundamental uniformity of nature demands it: "want of originality arises frequently, not from a barrenness and timidity of genius, but from the invincible necessity and the nature of things" (*Adventurer* 63).[6]

He attempts to further explain the dilemma by defining imitation as the "faithful and just" description of "material or animate, extraneous or internal" objects, which, because they appear alike to all observers pre-empt the possibility of originality. Since it is only to "the first copier" that the "praise of priority" may be given, subsequent observers ought not to be condemned for plagiarism. There will always be a close resemblance between the original works of the great classical writers and later authors, because, in addition to the basic uniformity of nature, "the causes that excite and the operations that exemplify the greater passions will always

---

[4] J. H. Plumb has warned us of the dangers of "keeping one's eyes too fixedly on the peaks of culture or considering as typical those men whom subsequent generations have come to regard as symbolic of their time", *Reason and Unreason in the Eighteenth Century*, p. 72.

[5] *The Adventurer* ran to 140 nos. between 7 November 1753 – 9 March 1754. On the contributors to the journal consult David Fairer, "Authorship Problems in *The Adventurer*," *RES*, 25 (1974), 137–51.

[6] For the background to the problem of novelty in the eighteenth century, see Clarence DeWitt Thorpe, "Addison and some of his Predecessors on 'Novelty'," *PMLA*, 52 (1937), 1114–1129.

have an exact coincidence, though perhaps a little diversified by climate or custom".[7]

It is a telling comment on the vagaries of literary trends, that in the decade that produced the *Conjectures,* at least one author could regard the materials on which a poet may work, as well as his powers of perception, as permanent, unchanging and universally alike phenomena and claim that a "necessary resemblance and unavoidable analogy" was the premise of imitation.

The other late paper to espouse the defense of imitation was *The Gray's-Inn Journal.*[8] Its editor, Arthur Murphy, closely followed the model of the *Spectator* in both style and content, and the journal contained little that was new. What is striking however, is the apologetic and defensive tone which marks the discussion of the issues of imitation and originality.

Despite a decided enthusiasm for Shakespeare's originality, Murphy stoutly defends imitation, although he is careful to distinguish it from mere plagiarism. There are two modes of imitation which he deems acceptable. The first is part of the artist's freedom and right to draw on the vast storehouse of literary tradition to which he has fallen heir, and to do so without "incurring the ignominious appellations of a Plagiary or a transcriber". The availability of the works of great predecessors, close or distant, is part of the normal process of creation. The writer adopts an idea first hinted at by "some eminent example", exploits it by changing and diversifying it, and, in turn, inspires and stimulates successive writers:

This general and distant imitation, it will be readily owned, is allowable and just; is what cannot be easily avoided, where the subject is treated with propriety and according to the rules of art. (*The Gray's-Inn Journal* 16)

This has been the way of great writers since Virgil imitated Homer. At the present time, the essay informs us, aspiring writers regard Addison as the "eminent example" of "grave, or humorous speculation" and Fielding as the master of "comic Romance".

This was a form of emulation to which few of Arthur Murphy's predecessors or contemporaries would have objected, but he goes on to defend what

---

[7] Cf. Dr. Johnson's analysis of the same notion in *Adventurer* 95.

[8] There were 52 nos. of the journal between 29 September 1753 – 21 September 1754. These were reprinted together with 52 additional papers in 2 vols. in 1756 and the whole dated from 21 October 1752 – 12 October 1754. Its themes are varied: ill-natured and ignorant critics were attacked (No. 139); there is a vision of Parnassus with the usual metaphors of property ownership and cultivation (No. 4) and essays in praise of Shakespeare's originality (Nos. 51 and 94). See further, R. E. Aycock, "Shakespearian Criticism in the *Gray's-Inn Journal,*" *Yearbook of English Studies,* 2 (1972), 68–72.

so many others castigated as "servile imitation", which, in his words, "consists in adopting the sentiments and phrases of others". He is aware that this practice has been judged harshly as an indication of "poverty of thought and defect of imagination" and attempts to modify this severity by urging the advantages which may accrue to the language when this technique is applied to translation. For the "transfusion of wit" from one language to another, when executed "with elegance and ease" as well as the borrowing or revival of lost words and expressions, should lead to an enrichment of the language, "making it more exuberant, by introducing a succession of new Ideas; in proportion as the value of an ingot is superior to a single coin".

This form of literary imitation should not be slighted, for it is the lot of the great bulk of authors. These "authors of inferior genius" must be permitted resort to "easier methods" of composition—of selecting "the most agreeable and pleasing imagery", of giving "delicate and graceful turns to obvious and common thoughts" and of refurbishing the familiar with novelty of expression. Murphy fully endorses the principle that composition is only the "art of stealing wisely" for the uniformity of nature precludes original thinking. It is the procedure most authors must adopt and it is acceptable, Murphy argues, as long as some effort is made to transform the material.

He does concede, however, that there exists a superior category of authors to whom none of this applies. They are the chosen few, Nature's favourites, to whom "the creative power of the Imagination" has been vouchsafed. A free spirit, at odds with rules and learning, the true genius is the product of heaven. So commonplace had the definition of the natural genius become by this time, that Murphy, the defender of servile imitation, can nevertheless, opine:

... fruitless is the endeavour of the unborn poet who thinks to arrive at the heights of fame by painful vigils and the dint of labour and application. (*The Gray's-Inn Journal* 22)

Poetry demands the exercise of fancy and the energy of genius for its aim must be to stir the passions and the imagination:

Poetry requires warm and glowing colours; the language of it must be elevated above the diction of Prose; the expressions should be most animated and the imagination of the reader more immediately struck at than in any other kind of writing; and whoever has not the energy of genius to cultivate these qualities will be always sure to be neglected as a cold spiritless author. (*The Gray's-Inn Journal* 22)

It is clear that even the conservative editor of *The Gray's-Inn Journal* was not unscathed by over half a century's impatience with the restraints imposed on the original writer by the severity of tradition.

Grub Street in the Journals

This impatience had been fuelled, at least in part, by the tribe of comic figures that cavort through the pages of the literary journal from its earliest appearance. Ridiculous embodiments of many of the current literary fads, they illuminate more clearly than many a learned discourse some of the popular, acceptable and fashionable attitudes of the day. It is regrettable therefore, that pressure of space permits no more than a passing reference to such characters as the *Tatler's* Sir Timothy Tittle, the typical coffee-house critic, a not-so-distant relation of the *Idler's* Dick Minim and a far-off ancestor of the phrenetic critic in *Tristram Shandy*.[9] Nor should Ned Softly, the servile poet and his brethren who employ mechanical techniques of verse-making be totally forgotten.[10] The other face of the servile poet was the imperturbable pedant and he too received his due in many of the journals.[11]

But these, the denizens of that most infamous ghetto in literary history became the exclusive butt of the journal bearing the name of their demesne. *The Grub-Street Journal* (1730–37) was initially undertaken as a mouthpiece for Pope's personal self-glorification and as a weapon in his crusade against dullness and ignorance.[12] In its early stages at least, it breathed the spirit of the *Dunciad* and *Peri Bathos*. Its iconoclastic and irreverent tone and its savage satirical thrusts at would-be critics, false arbiters of taste and poetasters set it apart from the other journals of the time, and, it must be confessed, make its contents forceful and amusing, even to a twentieth-century reader.

Poets are divided into two groups according to which method of imitation they employ. The Parnassians, which include most of the great classical writers, advocated and practised a loose form of imitation which is in sharp

---

[9] See *Tatler* 165 for Sir Timothy Tittle and *Idler* 60 for Dick Minim. The critic in Tristram Shandy is he who measures the "length, height and depth" of all new works with "rule and compasses etc." and finds them "out of all plumb", "quite irregular" or "out" in every one of their dimensions (III, xii). See also *The Guardian* (1713), 12 and 37.

[10] *Tatler* 3, 106 and 163. For another image of the wretched yet conceited poet see *The Growler: or Diogenes Robbed of his Tub* (27 Jan. 1711): the poor creature would be pitiable "was he not so miserably wretched and idle, as to starve by devouring other men's labours and not being able to digest them". This fool "plumes himself nobly upon some scraps of French, Italian, Spanish, and thinks they are sufficent to have qualified him for an Interpreter to Babel's Bricklayers".

[11] See for example, *The Lay-monk* (1713), no. 8 and *The Censor* (1717), no. 33.

[12] *The Grub-Street Journal*, eds. R. Russel and J. Martyn ran to 418 nos from 8 Jan. 1730 to 29 December 1737; a selection was reprinted in 1737 as *Memoirs of the Society of Grub Street*. See J. T. Hillhouse, *The Grub-Street Journal* (Durham, North Carolina 1928), pp. 47 ff. No external evidence can be found to connect Pope with the journal according to Bertrand A. Goldgar, "Pope and the *Grub-Street Journal*," MP, 74 (1977), 366–80.

contrast to the Grubean approach:

a true Grubean imitator should follow his author step by step, quite contrary to that erroneous rule of Horace:

Nec verbum verbo curabis reddere fidus
Interpres. (*Grub-Street Journal* 5)

This principle would pose an almost insurmountable problem to the Grubean for so servile is his imitation that the result of his own efforts would be mere transcription. The solution, suggests the editor helpfully, is either to choose to translate a poem of the Parnassian kind from one language to another, or, if the would-be poet wishes to avoid such inconvenience, to adopt the simpler expedient of choosing a different subject from his author's:

Thus altho' the words may be Parnassian, yet the sense being Grubean, the whole poem will be so too; but much more so, as he can pick out such words as are Grubean also. (*Grub-Street Journal* 5)

Using this technique, even that most "vehement Parnassian" Milton, can be imitated in the "most profound Grubean". To prove his point the editor offers a selection of some of Milton's characteristic quirks, his digressions and archaisms, and shows how they have been transformed by Grubeans such as James Ralph and John Dennis.

The Scriblerian fascination with Grubean rhetoric figures prominently in the *Grub-Street Journal*. Its purely mechanical basis had been adequately illustrated by Swift in the prototypical literary computer proudly displayed to the astonished Gulliver in the Grand Academy of Lagado and this memorable fantasy is employed in one issue of the journal in which the butt of the satire is the writer of the false sublime. A letter from one "Puff" addressed to the learned society of Grub-Street, relates with satisfaction the benefits that can accrue to Grubeans from this splendid contraption. Puff had found his desire to participate in the competition of poems on Merlin's cave thwarted by discovering the difficulties involved in the craft of verse. [13] Nothing daunted, he acquired the machine:

... on which (with the assistance of some friends) I wrote down all the words in the English language in their several Moods, Tenses, and Declensions. I then set the engine to work, and in about six hours, to my great astonishment produced the following rhapsody. (*Grub-Street Journal* 324)

---

[13] *Gulliver's Travels* (Harmondsworth, England, 1972), p. 227. The poetry contest was run in the *Gentleman's Magazine*. For information on the contest, Merlin's cave and Queen Caroline, see Judith Colton, "Merlin's Cave and Queen Caroline," *ECS*, 10 (1967), 1–10, and "Kent's Hermitage for Queen Caroline at Richmond," *Architectura*, 2 (1974), 181–191.

116

What follows is a perfect example of "all the bombast and fustian, all the false and unintelligible Sublime" which characterises the writers of High Grub Street, that is, those who attempt to imitate the greater Kinds. For, just as "in the precincts of Parnassus there are valleys as well as mountains; so in these of Grub Street, strictly so-called, there are Hills as well as Dales" (*Grub-Street Journal* 216). Spun out of the jargon of the sublime and terrible and spiced with current literary clichés, a small part of this splendid nonsense deserves quotation:

> A rural Cote, venerably mean, with awful beauty
> and half-closed eyes with rising green,
> whose frugal windows diffused a solemn day over
> the dome, and checked the glaring ray.
> A heavy sage maintained his central seat, deep in the
> circuit of dread retirement (retreat).
> (*Grub-Street Journal* 324)

A spirit of what might be described as aristocratic contempt for the menials of Grub Street pervades the *Journal* and contributes greatly to its savage tone. This contempt is particularly reserved for the inhabitants of the lower levels of Grub Street, those who write "all the creeping, grovelling pieces in prose and verse". The *Journal* never misses an opportunity to point out their abject material poverty. In the unsentimental spirit of the time, this condition was felt to mirror a matching spiritual and literary paucity.[14] Withering scorn is poured on the literary remains of "brother Fannius, who lived up four pairs of stairs in the Strand". The paltry collection is nothing but a motley assortment of junk, worn clothes and broken furniture, all certain indications of his poetical bankruptcy:

A black coat and tye wig, both very valuable pieces of antiquity. An old silken purse, little used. All his linen, that is, the shirt on his back, and another at the washerwoman's. A tobacco box, two chairs and half a table with three legs, a flockbed, and a broken chamber pot. (*Grub-Street Journal* 216)

Fannius's poetry is, of course, nothing more than a mechanical imitation of his predecessors. It does not surprise us to learn that he has written "many copies of verses on Chloe's eyebrow, and Phillis's Cheek" and that

---

[14] Note Pope's opinion: " . . . poverty itself becomes a just subject of satyre, when it is the consequence of vice, prodigality, or neglect of one's lawful calling; for then it increases the publick burden, fills the streets and high-ways with Robbers, and the garrets with Clippers, Coiners, and Weekly Journalists", *The Dunciad Variorum: To the Publisher (The Poems of Alexander Pope*, ed. John Butt, 1963, rpt. 1965), p. 321.

he has a satire on Pope containing ingenious conceits—such as allusions to an ape and others "of the like Nature".[15]

A similar, if harsher, note occurs in another criticism of the classical ignorance of poets who set to work to copy mechanically in the fashionable exercise of modern Latin poetry. Such efforts are castigated as "the linsey-wolsey Anglo-Latin stuff of the Poet's own weaving and making up, patched in the most bungling manner with bits of Horatian velvet, which serve only to make the poorness and coarseness of the other more conspicuous" (*Grub-Street Journal* 302).[16]

From the foregoing it is evident that the figures of the imitative poet and his fellow, the rule-bound critic, were as much stock characters of comedy and satire in the literary journal as they were in contemporary comedy and mock epic. Such an awareness betokens a very real sensitivity to the evils of strict imitation or too great a subservience to the past. Much of the credit for the popularity of these attitudes must go to Joseph Addison. In the guise of the not-to-be gainsaid Mr. Spectator, he gave common currency to the image of the truly great poet as the man of free imagination and uncultivated genius, whose effect is to transport and astonish, unaided either by learning or conscious art.

The Spectator and the Cult of Originality

In *Spectator* 160 (September 3rd. 1711), Addison discusses the two types of genius, the learned and the natural.[17] Although the burden of the essay is not to suggest the superiority of one over the other, priority of place is given to the natural genius and three quarters of the essay is devoted to a description of it. Therefore, despite his assurances, the result is an apparent favouritism

---

[15] For attacks on Pope, see *Two Poems Against Pope* (Augustan Reprint Society 114, 1965), introd. by Joseph V. Guerinot. This introduction lists many such attacks on Pope.

[16] Attempts to write modern poetry in one or other of the classical languages were often lambasted. See, for example, the opinion of Jean Le Clerc as related in *Historia Literaria, or an Exact and Early Account of the most valuable Books published in the several Parts of Europe*, 2 vols. (1730–31): Moderns "have imitated the Ancients in the same manner that Apes imitate man, that is by copying their Faults and not minding their Beauties. . . . The Moderns are the mere Apes of the Ancients; they do not write out of their own stock; they are poets only by rote and imitation, without understanding the art they profess. Everyone ought therefore to write in his own language, which is the means to get rid of this servile spirit of Imitation. Then our Mind is not employed in recollecting the expression and thoughts of the Ancients; and as we are well provided with modern Worlds and Notions, everyone becomes himself an Original" (Ch. VIII, sect. xx); also *Parrhasiana* (1700), pp. 1–41. and, Ch. I, Note 22 p. 17 above.

[17] Addison thought his theme "so uncommon a subject" (No. 160, Bond, II, 126). On the fascination which the search for novelty aroused, see Clarence De Witt Thorpe, "Addison and some of his Predecessors on 'Novelty'," *PMLA*, 52 (1937), pp. 1114–1129.

118

of "those few" who "stand up as the Prodigies of Mankind, who by the meer strength of natural Parts, and without any Assistance of Art or Learning, have produced Works that were the Delight of their own Times and the Wonder of Posterity". These works are always "singular and inimitable", the result of nothing less than "the most unbounded flights of Nature" (No. 160, Bond, II, 126–7).

In describing the two kinds of genius, Addison makes copious use of the epithets and contrasts which became the familiar commonplaces of almost all subsequent discussions on genius. Thus the natural genius is "hurried on by a natural Fire and Impetuosity to vast conceptions of things, and noble Sallies of the Imagination" (p. 129). He is like productive soil in a salubrious climate, producing a "whole Wilderness of noble Plants rising in a thousand beautiful Landskips, without any certain Order or Regularity". He possesses something "nobly wild and extravagant", a freedom, which though uncouth, is significantly more sublime than "all the Turn and Polishing of what the *French* call a *Bel Esprit*". This "Turn and Polishing", on the other hand, is the hallmark of the correct genius—he who has followed the paths clearly marked by predecessors, to be found in the "Conversation, Reflection, and the Reading of the most polite Authors" (p. 127). At a time when this advice—the essence of Neo-Classicism—was frequently dispensed, it is interesting to note the depreciatory undertones it carried in the eyes of Mr. Spectator. Its negative connotations of the prosaic and readily accessible are epitomised in expressions such as, "being disciplined by the Rules of Art", or the telling remark:

The greatest Genius which runs through the Arts and Sciences, takes a kind of Tincture from them, and falls unavoidably into Imitation. (p. 127)[18]

Addison next considers the conflict which exists between those who are untouched and unbroken by the Rules of Art, the unlearned Geniuses, and those purveyors of strict imitation, the modern critics. The greatest geniuses, that is, the Ancients and those in the "more Eastern Parts of the World" are certainly lacking in decorum if measured according to "the Nicety and Correctness" of the critics. Addison was not entirely in favour of disregarding the whole body of the Rules. He thought it necessary for the

---

[18] That learning and sophistication undermine true art was a popular belief at the time. See especially that self-consciously "unlearned" journal, *The Gazette a la Mode, or Tom Brown's Ghost* (9 June, 1709): "the Multitude judge of Natural Wit and Humour with more impartiality and less depravity than men of letters do, whose Taste of Nature is often more vitiated by the Introduction of Art and Sophistry which is but too frequently taken for Wit and Humour, while Nature languishes in the Hand of Ars her handmaid is often passed upon us for the mistress, the Jugglers in this Affair, knowing well the Proverb that Joan is as good as my Lady in the Dark".

sensitive critic to be acquainted with certain rules, for example, "the Unities of Time, Place and Action", in order to acquire "a finished taste of good Writing". But he insisted that it was essential for the true critic to emancipate himself from "the Mechanical Rules which a Man of very little Taste may discourse upon", and to enter fully "into the very Spirit and Soul of fine Writing", or, in other words, to be receptive to the newness and originality of the writer, to that "something more Essential" that "elevates and astonishes the Fancy, and gives a Greatness of Mind to the Reader" (No. 409, Bond, III, 530). It is only in these modern times that the repressive inclinations of critics have conspired to dampen that "force and spirit" of the natural genius. Addison leaves his readers in no doubt about his feelings on the matter:

In short, to cut off all Cavelling against the Ancients, and particularly those of the warmer Climates, who had most Heat and Life in their Imagination, we are to consider that the Rule of observing what the *French* call the Bienseance in an Allusion, has been found out of latter Years and in the colder Regions of the World; where we would make some Amends for our want of Force and Spirit, by a scrupulous Nicety and Exactness in our Compositions. (No. 160, Bond, II, 128)

The difference between the natural and the learned genius hinges on the practice of imitation. The natural genius neither imitates nor is imitable. Shakespeare is the great example. In a later paper Addison describes one of his most original characteristics, his "Fairie way of Writing" (Bond, III, 570), a difficult Kind because the Author "has no Pattern to follow in it, and must work altogether out of his own Invention".[19] This kind of writing is especially suited to the English temperament, for English authors "are naturally Fanciful, and very often disposed by that Gloominess and Melancholy of Temper" to "many wild Notions and Visions". In such a difficult and original kind of composition, Shakespeare has "incomparably excelled all others":

That noble Extravagance of Fancy, which he had in so great Perfection, thoroughly qualified him to touch this weak superstitious Part of his Reader's Imagination; and made him capable of succeeding, where he had nothing to support him besides the Strength of his own Genius. (No. 419, Bond, III, 572–573)

The other kind of genius, "those that have framed themselves by Rules, and submitted the Greatness of their natural Talents to the Corrections and Restraints of Art", are characterised by their imitativeness and their imitability:

[19] The phrase, Shakespeare's "Fairie Way of Writing", is Dryden's in his Dedication (to the Marquis of Halifax) of *King Arthur* (1691). See Bond's note: III, 570.

The great Danger in these latter kind of Genius's, is, least they cramp their own Abilities too much by Imitations, and form themselves altogether upon Models, without giving the full Play of their own natural Parts. An imitation of the best Authors, is not to compare with a good Original; and I believe we may observe that very few Writers make an extraordinary Figure in the World, who have not something in their Way of thinking or expressing themselves that is peculiar to them and entirely their own. (No. 160, Bond, II, 129–30)

Here Addison's preference for the original is very specifically stated. His impatience with those who insist on rules and imitation as criteria of excellence is a theme to which he frequently returned in many of the *Spectator* papers. It had many variations. In *Spectator* 592, the ill-educated critic flourishing misunderstood jargon is the butt of his criticism and ridicule. This type of critic fails to understand "that there is more Beauty in the Works of a great Genius who is ignorant of all the Rules of Art, than in the Works of a little Genius, who not only knows, but scrupulously observes them" (Bond, V, 27).

In the same paper Shakespeare is again mentioned as the great example of an original writer. He is "a Stumbling-block to the whole Tribe of these rigid Criticks". Addison poses the rhetorical question:

Who would not rather read one of his Plays, where there is not a single Rule of the Stage observed, than any Production of a modern Critick, where there is not one of them violated? (V, 28)

In answering his own question, he combines praise and admiration of Shakespeare in a charming tribute to his originality:

Shakespear was indeed born with all the Seeds of Poetry, and may be compared to the Stone in *Pyrrhus's* Ring, which, as *Pliny* tell us, had the Figure of *Apollo* and the nine Muses in the Veins of it, produced by the spontaneous Hand of Nature, without any Help from Art.

Again, in his assessment of Milton's achievement in *Paradise Lost,* Addison accords the laurels of the original genius to the great poet who was more frequently praised for being a true son of Virgil. Addison does not ignore this aspect of the poet's genius. On the contrary, in his conclusion to his analysis of *Paradise Lost,* he tells his readers that he had endeavoured to show that "the Genius of the Poet shines by a happy Invention, a distant Allusion, or a judicious Imitation"; that he has "copied or improved" Homer and Virgil, and "raised his own Imaginations by the use which he has made of several Poetical Passages in Scripture" (No. 369, Bond, III, 392). But throughout his extended criticism of the great epic, Addison very often takes the opportunity to underline Milton's independent mode of imitation. This form of imitation has been countenanced by one of the great critical authorities, Longinus. To his list of the three constituents of poetic excellence that derive from art rather than nature, Longinus had appended the advice of Plato—to imitate and emulate the great poets and prose writers of antiquity. Leaving nothing to chance in his pedagogical crusade, Addison acquaints his readers with his version of Longinian reasoning on the matter:

Many are in this way inspired by the spirit of another, just as report says that the Pythian priestess on drawing near to the tripod where there is a chasm in the earth breathing forth a divine exhalation, is so filled with the heavenly power that she utters oracles under its influence.[20]

It is interesting that this version lays greater emphasis on the distinction between the original and the imitative than did Longinus. Addison adds what is, in effect, his own gloss: "By this means one great Genius often catches the Flame from another, and writes in his Spirit, without copying servilely after him". In this instance, at any rate, he is determined to possess Milton with the gift of natural genius: "his own natural Strength was capable of furnishing out a perfect work", although "by such an Imitation as that which Longinus has recommended, he has doubtless very much raised and ennobled his Conceptions".[21]

Another of the Addison's major undertakings was his crusade on behalf of the Imagination. To him must go credit for the rehabilitation of the Imagination as the principle element not only of the natural genius, but also of the man of taste. In his well-known series of *Spectator* papers on the pleasures of the Imagination, he insisted, with all the authority of Mr. Spectator, that the active perceptive Imagination was a basic necessity in life—this life (Nos. 411–421 (1712), Bond, III, 535–577). Significantly, Mr. Spectator's concerns were entirely temporal. It was not the moral but the aesthetic turpitude of his readers that perturbed him. Addison's crusade was aimed at an ill-educated readership whom he sought to release from the bondage of bad taste, not by filling the gaps in their formal education, but by awakening and nourishing their imaginations. Discarding the old watchwords of Learning, Reason and Judgment, he announced that his lectures on taste and the imagination would concentrate on that "something more essential" than a knowledge of merely "Mechanical Rules" that "elevates and astonishes the Fancy, and gives a Greatness of Mind to the Reader" (No. 409, Bond, III, 530).

In seeking to cultivate the imagination of his readership and to apprise them of the pleasures to be gained thereby, Addison was aware, as his

---

[20] Cf. Ch. 13 in *Longinus: On the Sublime*, p. 119. See also Elizabeth Nitchie, "Longinus and the Theory of Poetic Imitation in Seventeenth- and Eighteenth-Century England," *SP, 32* (1935), 580–597.

[21] *Spectator* 339 (Bond, III, 225). For other comments on Milton's method of imitation see Addison's essay on the 10th Book of *Paradise Lost* in *Spectator* 357 and 369 (Bond, III, 333 and 390).

readers must have been, of the novelty of his undertaking. He described the project as "entirely new", although at the same time, he acknowledged his debt to Longinus whose true heir he felt himself to be, for only Longinus had ignored formal rules of writing to consider audience effect and reaction and to emphasize the role of the passions in the experience of pleasure.

In arguing his brief for the validity of the pleasures of the Imagination, Addison picks and chooses from traditional thinking on the matter of the relative merits of the various faculties of the human mind. Thus, he accepts that the pleasures of the Understanding are superior because "they are founded on some new Knowledge or Improvement in the Mind of Man", but almost immediately qualifies this orthodoxy by claiming that the pleasures of the Imagination are "as great and transporting as the other".[22] He continues in their ardent support:

A beautiful Prospect delights the Soul, as much as a Demonstration; and a Description in *Homer* has charmed more Readers than a Chapter in *Aristotle*. Besides, the Pleasures of the Imaginaton have this Advantage, above those of the Understanding, that they are more obvious and more easie to be acquired. It is but opening the Eye, and the Scene enters. The Colours paint themselves on the Fancy, with very little Attention of Thought or Application of Mind in the Beholder. We are struck, we know not how, with the Symmetry of anything we see, and immediately assent to the Beauty of an Object, without enquiring into the particular Causes and Occasions of it. (No. 411, Bond, III, 538)

It is obvious that the pleasures of the Imagination are more beneficial than those of the Understanding because of their simplicity and accessibility. They are therefore, more salubrious than those of the Understanding which "are worked out by Dint of Thinking, and attended by too violent a Labour of the Brain". After such a verdict it hardly needed the authority of Bacon, to whom Addison refers at this point, to underline the therapeutic value of the action of the Imagination, especially on those minds with a melancholic or depressive inclination. But not content with this, Addison insists on the innocence, usefulness and positive qualities of the Imagination for men in general. Indeed, it is a gift from Heaven—given for the joy of man. Then, since the enjoyment of pleasure is so justified, it becomes almost a duty—"a Man should endeavour, therefore, to make the Sphere of his innocent Pleasures as wide as possible, that he may retire into them with Safety, and find in them such a Satisfaction as a wise Man would not blush to take" (No. 411, Bond, III, 529).[23]

[22] This decided inclination of Addison's to give priority to the Imagination has not been accorded sufficent credit. See, for example, Donald F. Bond, "'Distrust' of Imagination in English Neo-Classicism," *PQ*, 14 (1935), 54–69, in which Addison is enlisted on the side of those who "distrust" the Imagination. See also Note 16, p. 5 above.

[23] *Spectator* 411 (III, 529). This was a view shared by many, including Edward Young. See the *Conjectures*, pp. 4–5.

The satisfaction that is to be experienced by the Imagination's response to the well-known triad of qualities, the Great, the Unknown and the Beautiful is immediately apparent in the forceful and unequivocal language with which Addison describes it. "We are flung", he assures his readers, "into a pleasing Astonishment" by greatness; the new or uncommon "fills the Soul with an agreeable Surprise" and "gratifies its Curiosity" as well as diverting and refreshing us; Beauty "strikes the Mind with an inward Joy, and spreads a Chearfulness and Delight through all its Faculties". It, more than any of the other qualities, most directly affects the Soul, instantly diffusing "a secret Satisfaction and Complacency" through the Imagination. These pleasures are all of an immediate and violent character, but their effect is to soothe, and comfort while diverting and inspiring the mind. (No. 412, Bond, III, 540–542). Nor does Mr Spectator allow his readers to forget another dimension—the importance the Imagination has in the mutual attraction of the sexes.

Lest any vestiges of the older notion might still cling to the thoughts of his readers, Addison makes sure to trace the pleasures of the Imagination to the beneficient goodness of the Almighty. In the face of such enthusiasm, to argue for the guiding hand of Satan in the workings of the Imagination would have been somewhat churlish. According to the *Spectator* (413), the Imagination is the medium by which one can adore the Godhead and obey his Will. But, more importantly, the Imagination and its powers are a free gift, given to humanity by God in his largesse, in order to make human life more pleasant and agreeable. In order to perfect the gift, He has infused into the natural world the power to raise agreeable ideas in the Imagination. It is, therefore, impossible to contemplate the works of the Almighty without experiencing a secret satisfaction, a deep and real pleasure, which is the work of the Imagination. Without this imaginative intercourse, "what a rough unsightly Sketch of Nature should we be entertained with", for then we should see things only in "their proper Figures and Motions":

And what Reason can we assign for their exciting in us many of those Ideas which are different from any thing that exists in the Objects themselves, (for such are Light and Colours) were it not to add Supernumerary Ornaments to the Universe, and make it more agreeable to the Imagination? (No. 413, Bond, III, 546)

So complete is Addison's approbation of the Imagination that he can even exploit its much maligned sensual connection to its advantage. He hazards the possiblity that the soul divorced from the body may experience a shock when, bereft of the powers of the Imagination, it perceives the world as Reason dictates that it really is. It would be as "the disconsolate Knight" that finds himself on the breaking of a spell "on a barren Heath, or in a solitary Desart". The prospect must have struck him as too disagreeable, for he hastens to assure his readers that, since the pleasures of the Imagination are such a superior delight, "it is possible the Soul will not be deprived of them, but perhaps find them excited by some other Occasional Cause, as they are at present by the different Impressions of the subtle Matter on the Organ of Sight". The longing to free the soul from the corporeal trammels of the Imagination which many writers on the subject expressed are nowhere to be found in the *Spectator*. For Addison, Heaven will increase in perfection if the Imagination can add its delights to celestial bliss.

The Imagination, in particular the poetic Imagination, is characterised by a dynamic power and a forceful expansiveness. It will naturally find its inspiration in the boundlessness of nature, a God-given source, rather than in the narrower precincts of art (No. 414):

A Poet should take as much Pains in forming his Imagination as a Philosopher in cultivating his Understanding. He must gain a due Relish of the Works of Nature, and be thoroughly conversant in the various scenery of a Country Life. (No. 417, Bond, III, 563)

This is not, of course, a new idea, but what is interesting is Addison's wholehearted support and approval of the independence of this far-reaching and insatiable faculty.[24] Nowhere does he suggest that it could beneficially be reined in by the superior faculty of Reason. In a horticultural comparison, greatest pleasure is received from the unrestrained hand of nature:

There is something more bold and masterly in the rough careless Strokes of Nature, than in the nice Touches and Embellishments of Art. The Beauties of the most stately Garden or Palace lie in a narrow Compass, the Imagination immediately runs them over, and requires something else to gratifie her; but, in the wide Fields of Nature, the Sight wanders up and down without Confinement, and is fed with an infinite variety of Images, without any certain Stint or Number. For this Reason, we always find the Poet in love with a Country-Life, where Nature appears in the greatest Perfection, and furnishes out all those Scenes that are most apt to delight the Imagination. (No. 414, Bond, III, 549)[25]

The perennial problem of the untruth of the productions of the Imagination is easily solved by Addison. He has accepted that the satisfaction of man's yearning for an unreal perfection in life is a more than adequate compensation. Rather than merely supplying mirror images of reality or acting as a medium of moral precepts, it becomes the poet's duty to fulfill this basic human desire. Neither the desire, nor the fulfillment of it, is in any way reprehensible:

But because the Mind of Man requires something more perfect in Matter, than what it finds there, and can never meet with any Sight in Nature which sufficiently answers its highest Ideas

---

[24] See p. 75 above.
[25] But note the contrary view expressed a few lines later: " . . . yet we find the Works of Nature still more pleasant, the more they resemble those of Art" (p. 549).

of Pleasantness; or, in other Words, because the Imagination can fancy to itself Things more Great, Strange, or Beautiful, than the Eye ever saw, and is still sensible of some Defect in what it has seen; on this account it is the part of a Poet to humour the Imagination in its own Notions, by mending and perfecting Nature where he describes a Reality, and by adding greater Beauties than are put together in Nature, where he describes a Fiction. (No. 418, Bond, III, 569)

The poet need be neither truthful nor factual. "His Rose trees, Wood-bines, and Jessamines, may flower together, and his Beds be covered at the same time with Lillies, Violets, and Amaranths". If none of this satisfies, "he can make out several new Species of Flowers, with richer Scents and higher Colours, than any that grow in the Gardens of Nature".

In a later paper this power is compared with the art of Divine creation because it "bestows a kind of Existence, and draws up to the Reader's View, several Objects which are not to be found in Being. It makes Additions to Nature, and gives a greater variety to God's Works" (No. 421, Bond, III, 579). Far from dismissing these delusions, Addison is convinced that this power is the greatest asset of the poetic mind:

Thus we see how many ways Poetry addresses itself to the Imagination, as it has not only the whole Circle of Nature for its Province, but makes new Worlds of its own, shews us Persons who are not to be found in Being, and represents even the Faculties of the Soul, with her several Virtues and Vices, in a sensible Shape and Character. (No. 419, Bond, III, 573)

The objections raised by "Men of cold Fancies and Philosophical Dispositions" that these are improbable and therefore unacceptable cannot be taken seriously, argues Addison. Such is the state of knowledge at the moment that it is impossible to narrowly define the limitations of truth, for what is illusion today may well turn out to be reality tomorrow. Furthermore, the question of truth is hardly an issue of importance in this context. Most people happily accept a pleasing falsehood. Addison's example is the preoccupation of his contemporaries with the question of other forms of intellectual life as yet unknown. "We have all heard", he says, "so many pleasing Relations in favour of them, that we do not care for seeing through the Falshood, and willingly give ourselves up to so agreeable an Imposture" (No. 419, Bond, III, 571–572).

Addison's forthright analysis of the Imagination, though more eclectic than original, made few concessions to the opposition. Neither the restraining hand of Reason nor the limitations imposed by considerations of morality, were deemed fit to mar the justifiable pursuit of the pleasures afforded by the exercise of the finely tuned and sensitively aware Imagination. Furthermore, Mr Spectator gently intimated to his trusting readership, some of whom, as he well knew, were poorly educated and beyond the possibility of a close acquaintanceship with the classics, that the careful nurture and cultivation of their, as yet, unruly and impolite Imaginations would be

126

enough to equip them as irreproachable men, or women, of Taste. Their superiority to the dry pedantic critic was implicit. Consequently, the *Spectator*'s readers found the exercise of their Imagination—that less strenuous faculty—countenanced by the most popular literary and social pundit of the time. Indeed, Addison's influence remained a potent force. Long after the demise of the *Spectator* as a daily publication, the essays remained popular and widely read. Other, greater, men than Addison espoused the cause of the Imagination, but whether they knew it or not, their work, at least in its broad strokes, had already been done.[26]

The Anti-Classical Spirit of the Journals

After the *Spectator* it is not uncommon to find journals of the period tending to voice the same "liberal" attitudes, if more dogmatically expressed, to literary independence and creative freedom. An indication of this inclination is the pervasively anti-classical spirit to be detected in some of these ephemeral publications. It has already been noted that changes in the constitution of the reading public, and in taste and education, contributed to a waning of interest in and knowledge of, the classics. Authors and editors were not slow to grasp the implications of this decline. The journals carry frequent acknowledgement of public impatience with an outmoded legacy.

One of the most outspoken was *The Criticks* [sic] (1718).[27] A strange mixture of aggressive common sense and absurd superficiality, its author, probably Thomas Brereton, was successful enough to achieve a collected edition of his essays.

The more tactful approach of many of his predecessors is conspicuously absent in his writing. Brereton hits out at all who represent for him, learning and criticism. *The Censor* and its author, Lewis Theobald, for example, is ridiculed: "his excellence seeming to lie in the Art of using many words about nothing". Yet many of the author's own opinions resemble Theobald's. The pedant of Rymer or Dennis's stamp is attacked as harshly. Such critics, asserts Brereton, do not possess "any compass of judgment". They are merely "men who read old Books for no other Purpose than to censure

---

[26] On July 9, 1720, the *London Journal* carried an article or "editorial" in which the author calmly insists that men with lively Imaginations will have more pleasure in life "than those grovelling mortals, who walk very regularly, but very stupidly by the leading strings of common sense". He also suggests that the activity of building castles in the air may have its positive side. It certainly can neither corrupt or deprave. For the ways in which Addison anticipated Hutcheson see Clarence DeWitt Thorpe, "Addison and Hutcheson on the Imagination," *ELH*, 2 (1935), 215–234.

[27] There were 22 nos. from 8 January 1718– 28 May 1718. Rpt. 1719.

new", and who wage "War against all Mankind that were eminent for their Genius, only because they were so". Unlike this benighted group, he is determined, or so he believes, to give all noteworthy contemporary authors—"every growing genius"—their full due:

Let sour and servile Pedants (for they deserve not a more honourable Appelation) be still upon the Hunt for Errors; and hiding their unreasonable Prejudice against the Living, under a Shew of Reverence for the Dead, maintain Paradoxes of the Decay of human wit and understanding, and I know not what other extravagancies. (*The Criticks* 12)

True to his word he showers praise on Mr Fenton's *Epistle to Mr Lambrad;* "a masterpiece and little inferior to anything of that kind to be found in Horace himself". A similar encomium is meted out to Thomas Tickell's *Epistle from a Lady in England to a Gentleman at Avignon* (1717); "a sort of satire, for which the Ancients have no Parallel". But his most fulsome praise is reserved for one Mr Griffeth's Welsh epic, *Leek.* Although quietly ignored by subsequent generations, Brereton thought it deserved the extensive discussion to which he treated it. It is significant, however, that despite his protestations, he was obliged to fall back on the despised critical apparatus of Le Bossu in order to prove that his shining light, the redoubtable Mr Griffeth, was a great epic poet. To break away from the traditional critical approach required greater abilities than the "Critick" possessed.

The journal is steeped in anti-classical prejudice, remarkable until one permits the suspicion that the author may not have had the benefit of the classical education he purports to despise. The dictatorship of the classical languages and literature is treated to his fullest contempt. Beginning with an attack on Latin and Greek tags and irrelevant mottos, both merely "an Affectation of Learning", he proceeds to an analysis of "the Effect which the pedantic Spirit I have mentioned has upon the very life and Essence of our Modern Poetry" (*The Criticks* 17). His bane is the use of classical mythology, especially by minor poets who make the praise of desirable patrons their obsequious theme:

... all the World knows how their full-blown Panegyrick and best encomiums would but resemble a squeez'd Bladder, were it not for the Names of Alexander and Caesar with two or three other Greek and Roman Heroes, who stand here and there, as it were in their Niches, only serving to fill up the Void of Thought, which is apparently behind them. (*The Criticks* 17)

Indeed, even the "judicious Boileau" has shown himself a "Bigot to Antiquity" in all his works with the exception of his *Lutrin,* which, on these grounds alone, makes it compare favourably in Brereton's opinion, with "the otherwise inestimable Dispensary".

The classical mythology of the Ancients can have no place in modern poetry which should enshrine the popular and generally accepted beliefs of people now living. Dryden's suggestion in the Preface to *Juvenal,* that "the ministry of angels" should replace classical machinery in epic because angels are still accepted as part of popular belief, weighs heavily with Brereton. He finds therefore, that Pope's novel efforts in the *Rape of the Lock* are to be condemned because he introduced

a Fable which is only of the Study, and not in the least popular, as it ought to be; ... I cannot for my part but wish he had a little more interwoven his new Tradition with the common opinion of Fairys [sic]. (The Criticks 17).

Next to be impugned for slavish imitation are the pastoral poets who "not only continue strictly orthodox, with relation to the Divinity of Ceres, Pan, and the rest of the Sylvan Train; but make a Religion apart of keeping close to the Text of Virgil upon every occasion; even while they pretend not to imitate him, but write Originals of their Own". Even Philips, whose efforts are otherwise praiseworthy, has fallen prey to this evil, and has, consequently, failed to attune his pieces to "the rustic life of our island". The same applies to John Gay, considered by Brereton as the most successful author in this genre. But he has been so "blinded with this Prepossession as to call his Work The Shepherd's Week, at the same time that not one Shepherd is concerned in it".

Brereton's impatience with the current "idolization of former Impressions" is founded on his belief that neither Latin, "this deify'd tongue" nor Greek are as perfect as is popularly believed. He quotes Quintillian as one undisputed authority who was nevertheless aware of the "monstrous, inhuman and shocking" elements of these languages and draws attention to their "barbarous and disjointed constructions" in syntax. The English may with pride regard their language as second to none, insists the author, and adds, with characteristic chauvinism, that "there is an indisputable Affinity between the Honour of a Language, and of the People who speak it". However, until the present situation in which "our language is in a manner banished our own Universities, and Gentlemen train'd up in an habitual Contempt of it" changes for the better, he can only blush for the injustice done to the "fair sex", whose native merit is, in this situation, ignored or ridiculed. He singles out the translator of the *Tatler* mottos as especially praiseworthy for his pioneer efforts to render them accessible to the many who are unacquainted with the learned languages.[28]

In yet another essay on the same theme, the Critick brings to his readers a

---

[28] This translation was done by John Partridge (1644–1715), the author of *Titt for Tatt* (5 nos. between 2 – 11 March 1710). In *Titt for Tatt* 2 Partridge took the Tatler to task for his mottos and promised to oblige "the Fair Sex" with "good plain *English*".

reworking of Perrault's *Parallel of the Ancients and Moderns* of which he greatly approves.[29] Once again he argues that the general inability of his contemporaries to understand or read Greek or Latin should be enough to justify the superiority of English translations. Indeed, "the same salt and the same urbanity" characterises the English language which must be judged to be equal in quality: "every tongue has its proper elegance and in that the English yields to no other whatsoever" (*The Criticks* 18).[30] It is salutary to be made aware, as we are, by *The Criticks*, that eighteenth-century readers were not as unanimously appreciative of the classical languages as posterity sometimes appears to believe.

A similar impatience with the continued intrusion of the classics is evident in at least one number of *The Visiter* (1723), a journal mostly concerned with non-literary topics.[31] But in an essay which makes a strong demand for greater intellectual and literary freedom, for the exploration of previously untrodden paths and for tolerance on the part of critics and readers towards such experiments, the anonymous author rejects the blind following of custom and thus contributes further detail to the emerging picture of a society not generally sympathetic to the classics.

The Visiter also found the persistent habit of heading articles with a Greek or Latin motto quite absurd. In journals, such as *The Visiter* itself, addressed primarily to ladies, the addition of an incomprehensible classical tag is but an indifferent improvement. The author adds tersely and significantly, that, in any case, "there are very few people in Town at present that understand either language" (*The Visiter* 9). In such an environment, the fate of imitation was sealed.

In general, *The Visiter* argued, "the tyranny of Custom" is the enemy of progress and discovery in every field. Original thinking alone propels the

---

[29] Perrault and Boileau's quarrel was well covered by the English journals. See, for example, the *Muses Mercury* (January 1708) which published the text of Boileau's letter to Perrault "on their being reconciled, after a long dispute about the Ancients and Moderns". Incidentally, Boileau's tone was supremely conciliatory. He conceded happily that the Moderns easily outstrip the Ancients in the new genres that were unknown to them. They are particularly fortunate in the invention of the Romance for which no models exist so they are free to give rein to their own invention and originality and by so doing will guarantee their excellence as originals. English audiences were prepared to agree. See Joseph Spence's letter to Samuel Richardson in Wright, *Joseph Spence*, p. 122.

[30] *The Criticks's* linguistic chauvinism was a long established phenomenon in England. Cf. *Vindex Anglicus: Or the Perfections of the English Language* (1644): "Let us not therefore, with base and busy avarice, abuse our language with the dregs of others being possessed with the perfection of them already" (*Harleian Miscellany*, II, 63–65). These particular remarks of *The Criticks* called forth a vehement rebuttal published in full in No. 20, in which its critical efforts are dubbed "a pragmatic Incoherence of scurrilous Reproaches".

[31] *The Visiter* ran to 51 nos. from 18 June 1723 – 31 January 1723/24.

human race towards perfection. It is "to a singular way of Thinking that we owe all the greatest Genius's we ever had, and if Sir Isaac Newton had never ventured out of the common track, he had probably never been a greater man than Partridge" (*The Visiter* 9).

Equally abhorrent and dangerous is the tendency to close the mind against anything new, to cling to prejudices without giving a fair trial to the latest developments, like the lady who condemned "a certain modern author" without having read him.

In short, would we be wise, we must be singular; we must not look for wisdom and virtue, attended by a crowd of followers; they fly the multitude and are only to be overtaken by those who have resolution enough to pursue them through untrodden paths and thorny ways.[32]

In literary matters a dependence on rules produces an arid sterility—the hallmark of those who lack the fire of natural genius. It should be the critics' task to point this out, but all too often,

Criticks, and aged Beaux of Fancy chaste
Who ne'er had Fire or else whose Fire is past
Must judge by Rules, what they want Force to taste.
I would a Poet, like a Mistress try
Not by her Hair, her Hand, her Nose, her Eye,
But by some Nameless Power to give me joy. (*Visiter* 39)

In *The Visiter's* view, very many critics are insensitive to the truly original genius. They often display a frank preference for the "spurious offspring of the little scriblers" who are certainly possessed of judgment, but a judgment that only helps them to "borrow Beauties from other Authors", without teaching them that imagination must also have its say. To "the discerning Eye", of course, these borrowed beauties "only serve to make their own Faults more conspicuous" (*The Visiter* 39).

The belief that the modern method of imitation was responsible for much dull writing was a popular one. In one form or another this theme was part of the stock in trade of most writers on critical matters. A quarter of a century after *The Visiter* some little ingenuity was required, therefore, to render the wellworn theme more palatable. One of the most amusing attempts to refurbish it is to be found in *The Connoisseur* (1754–56) whose editors were Leo Colman and Bonnell Thornton.[33] Through their persona, Mr Town, Critic and Censor General, they evince a marked preference for the new and original. In one of the oldest of literary tricks, the allegorical dream, Mr Town makes this point in a new and charming way.

[32] The tendency to associate originality with moral rectitude was not new. See the opinions of Isaac Watts above, p. 29.
[33] There were 140 nos. between 31 January 1754 – 30 September 1756. Rpt. subsequently in collected editions in 1757 and 1793.

He chooses to fall asleep, not over the obligatory dusty copy of Virgil or Shakespeare: "I could never discover any opiate qualities in these authors", but over "some modern performance" which remains nameless. He is then transported to the shores of an immense sea of black ink, in which many ships and boats of different shapes and sizes ply to and fro. His cicerone is not an august personage of literary or historical fame, but a printing house demon, who competently guides him through the many navigational hazards of the ocean which include the "Eddies of Criticism" and the "strong current of Politics" (*Connoisseur* 3).

He notices that much of the maritime traffic is engaged in attempts to force a passage "without chart or compass" across a vast lake leading to two magnificent structures, erected apparently by the Tragic and Comic Muses. Among the multitude of vessels, a "triumphant Squadron" of first rate ships catches the eye immediately. They are not particularly modern. Indeed many of them were fitted out years previously, but

'Tho somewhat irregular in their make, and but little conformable to the exact rules of art, they will ever continue the pride and glory of the seas . . . .

His attention is then caught by "a large Fleet of Annotators, Dutch built, which sailed very heavy", and often ran aground or collided with each other. Such is the ponderous weight of pedantry! Needless to say, the whole ocean is infested with pirates, ever on the watch for booty. Having thoroughly ransacked any vessel which falls prey to them, they then endeavour to reach the "Coast of Gain" by sailing "under False Colours, or forging their Passports and pretending to be loaded by the most reputable merchants" (*Connoisseur* 3).

This then was Mr Town's vision of the contemporary literary scene—a seascape clogged for the most part with topheavy pedantry and rampant piracy. Under the not very original, if appropriate, motto, "O imitatores! servum pecus", he returns to the theme of the imitative poet in another number of the journal. This time his device is a letter from a poet who reverses Bayes's boast that he writes only what is new. The prevailing fashion among modern poets, and the reason for the growing number of absurdities in their writing, is found to be their practice of strict imitation. Unlike the comic Bayes, present day poets are

so far from endeavouring to elevate and surprize by anything original that their whole business is imitation; and they jingle their bells in the same road with those that went before them, with all the dull exactness of a packhorse. (*Connoisseur* 67)

The inevitable consequence of this near universal practice of imitation is a glut of dullness, "without the least wit, humour, or incident".

The Critic and Censor General attempts to stimulate his readers out of their apathy. To begin with he roundly attacks the implications of theories of the uniformity of nature. It is nothing but a feeble excuse, he maintains, for imitation has neither a philosophical nor a literary basis. It is merely a mindless following of fashion, a total servility to the prevailing mode and an effective stranglehold on originality. Writers should revolt against this stagnation, for needless shackles are being imposed on their imaginations. True genius, freed, will not fly into the "idle extravagant flights of imagination" so feared by some, he adds reassuringly, but neither should it be expected "to confine itself to the narrow track of imitation".

Authors are exhorted to cultivate new fields of originality, in which the dangers of being overwhelmed by the patterns of powerful predecessors is not so great. This was the practice of Swift, Pope, Gay, Addison and Bolingbroke, the great original writers of the last age. To urge his point he resorts to verse:

> Write from your own imagination,
> Nor curb your Muse by imitation,
> For copies shew, howe'er exprest,
> A barren genius at the best.

The juxtaposition of "imagination" and "imitation", it should be noted, crisply underlines the fundamental conflict that exists between the two modes of writing.[34]

By mid-century there were not many journals that attempted more than a defensive position on the merits of imitation, and then only as a useful expedient for the less gifted writer. By then, of course, that most influential successor to the *Tatler* and the *Spectator,* Dr. Johnson's *Rambler* had appeared.

The Rambler's Conjectures on Original Composition

Throughout its run, the *Rambler* maintained a fairly constant critical barrage against the sterility of imitation.[35] As might be expected considering the

[34] In *Connoisseur* 72, Mr. Town recalls the moral of these verses and uses Swift's verse-making machine and "other inventions wonderfully calculated for the promotion of literature" as a basis for a sardonic essay on the "regular and mechanical" craft of song writing. See also his attack on the mechanical devices of poetry in No. 83: "Poetry should seem at least to flow freely from the Imagination, and not to be squeezed from the droppings of the brain".

[35] There were 208 nos. of the *Rambler* which ran from 20 March 1750 – 14 March 1752. For information on the distribution of the journal see Roy McKeen Wiles, "The Contemporary Distribution of Johnson's *Rambler,*" *ECS,* 2 (December 1968), 155–171. See also Charles A. Knight, "The Writer as Hero in Johnson's Periodical Essays," *Papers on Language and Literature,* 13 (1977), 238–50, in which Johnson's dropping of the Addisonian persona is discussed.

reputation of the genre, the offensive opened with an attack on contemporary pastoral. Under fire since the days of Pope, it still managed to attract the attention of "numbers without number". But the *Rambler*'s opinion is uncompromising. The genre is anathema to originality. So similar are all current efforts in it that

he who reads the title of a poem, may guess at the whole series of the composition; nor will a man, after the perusal of thousands of these performances, find his knowledge enlarged with a single view of nature not produced before, nor his imagination amused with any new applications of those views to moral purposes. (*Rambler* 36)

Even that one attempt to infuse a little originality into the genre, the piscatory pastoral, deserves censure. It is too limited in its dimensions to permit much exercise of the individual imagination. Although Dr. Johnson's interpretation of the limits of pastoral was narrow, in making his judgment, he undoubtedly had the many imitations that gorged the period in mind.[36]

Under the inevitable motto, "O imitatores, servum pecus", in *Rambler* 121, he also took to task those dogged poets who persisted in clogging their verses with the mythological machinery of the Ancients. The problem is caused by the prestige still enjoyed by many Roman poets in whose writings appears "such a perpetual recurrence of allusions to the tales of the fabulous age, that they must be confessed often to want that power of giving pleasure which novelty supplies".

It is little wonder, Johnson tartly adds, that they achieved "so much in the graces of diction" since they appear to have done little else in their poetry, least of all cultivated a little originality in the form of "new thoughts". It is a distinguished group that attracted Johnson's ire, for Virgil is among their number. He is described as little more than a skilled compiler, uniting "the beauties of the *Iliad* and the *Odyssey* in one composition". Even in this uninspired activity his judgment often fails him. His "avarice of Homeric treasures" results in nothing more than a poor and inappropriate imitation of the great original. The most despicable example of Virgilian theft is, of course, the imitation of Ajax in the underworld in the figure of Dido.

Pointing his moral, Johnson concludes that if a poet of Virgil's undoubted stature "could be thus seduced by imitation" one can scarcely be surprised that lesser wits succumb. In their case it becomes a twofold imitation, for

---

[36] Earlier essays on the pastoral include the well-known *Guardian* essays, Nos. 22, 23, 28, 30 and 32. Pope's contribution to the subject was No. 40. See also J. E. Congleton, "Theories of Pastoral Poetry in England 1684–1717," *SP*, 41 (1944), 544–575 and the references in Note 3, Chapter 3, p. 66 above. On the subject of Pope and the pastoral see Daniel A. Fineman, "The Motivation of Pope's *Guardian* 40," *MLN*, 67 (1952), 24–28 and R. E. Tickell, *Thomas Tickell and the Eighteenth Century Poets* (1931), pp. 25–27.

besides following the "universal and acknowledged practice of copying the ancients" they copy each other. The consequence of this pernicious and destructive method of literary composition has been that each age has been dominated by whatever poetic practice is currently fashionable—now allegory, now visions, now pastoral—to the exclusion of other less popular kinds. This is a state of affairs which must disturb the original poet:

It is indeed easy to conceive why any fashion should become popular, by which idleness is favoured, and imbecility assisted; but surely no man of genius can much applaud himself for repeating a tale with which the audience is already tired, and which could bring no honour to any but the inventor. (*Rambler* 121)

According to Johnson, the current fashion is Spenserian imitation.[37] Not only the irreproachable "fictions and sentiments" of the older poet, but also his diction and stanzaic forms have become grist to the imitative mill of the present. The copying of Spenser's style is a perfect example of the purely mechanical imitation which Johnson so despises. Poets who uncritically adopt the older poet's eccentricities are clearly unaware that even in his own day, Spenser's style "was allowed to be vicious ... darkened with old words and peculiarities of phrase ... [and] remote from common use". In addition, his stanza form is an equally unfortunate model for Spenser ill-advisedly adopted it from the Italian "without due regard to the genius of our language". Johnson's conclusion is a moral one. Imitations of this nature are simply a waste of valuable time and vital human energy, for "life is surely given us for higher purposes than to gather what our ancestors have wisely thrown away, and to learn what is of no value, but because it has been long forgotten" (*Rambler* 121).

In other numbers of the *Rambler* Johnson turned his attention to the thorny question of the distinctions between the different forms of imitation—"not every imitation ought to be stigmatized as plagiarism" (*Rambler* 143)—and the legitimate uses to which the aspiring poet can put his literary heritage. Thus, plagiarism, that most damning of criticisms, cannot be levelled at the writer, "who imitates his predecessors only by furnishing himself with thoughts and elegancies out of the same general magazine of literature" any more than it can be charged that the architect is a "mean copier of Angelo or Wren, because he digs his marble from the same quarry, squares his stones by the same art, and unites them in columns of the same orders" (*Rambler* 143). Indeed it is of great importance that the aspiring writer should acquaint himself with the learning of previous ages that he "may not ascribe to himself the invention of arts generally known; weary his

[37] The *Monthly Review* praised James Kirkpatrick's *Sea-piece* as a commendable Spenserian imitation. See Note 33, p. 84 above.

attention with experiments of which the event has been long registered" or waste time on things "which have already succeeded or miscarried" (*Rambler* 154). But, cautions Johnson, such a study will by itself never be sufficient to produce literary merit. The author whom posterity will celebrate is he who adds "by his own toil to the acquisitions of his ancestors" or by "some visible improvement". Therefore, any dull following of precedent is to be discouraged. The young author is urgently counselled to shy away from all "beaten walks", for even "with all his diligence" the imitator can only hope to find a few flowers or branches untouched by his predecessors", which, if indeed they exist, can only be "the refuse of contempt" or their "omissions of negligence" (*Rambler* 86):

The Macedonian conqueror, when he was once invited to hear a man that sang like a nightingale, replied with contempt, "that he had heard the nightingale herself"; and the same treatment must everyone expect whose praise is that he imitates another. (*Rambler* 86)

The essence of great poetry is its originality, which in turn is the result of the free play of the imagination. The activities of the imagination need suffer none of the restrictions imposed, for example, by scientific investigation, the nature of whose object, being "fixed and limited" requires "the necessity of following the traces of our predecessors". Imagination, on the other hand, reigns over a boundless universe of fantasy, and therefore "should be subject to no such restraints":

... in the boundless regions of possibility, which fiction claims for her dominion, there are surely a thousand recesses unexplored, a thousand flowers unplucked, a thousand fountains unexhausted, combinations of imagery yet unobserved, and races of ideal inhabitants not hitherto described. (*Rambler* 121)

Those "collectors of fortuitous knowledge"—young students—may be allowed to absorb uncritically the opinions of their betters, but a severe judgment should be meted out to poets who have remained on these familiar paths.

Johnson's summing up of the value of originality, though well-known, deserves quotation as one of the most authoritative statements of the age:

No man ever yet became great by imitation. Whatever hopes for the veneration of mankind, must have invention in the design, or the execution; either the effect must itself be new or the means by which it is produced. Either truths hitherto unknown must be discovered, or those which are already known enforced by stronger evidence, facilitated by clearer method, or elucidated by brighter illustrations ... That which hopes to resist the blast of malignity, and stand firm against the attacks of time, must contain in itself some original principles of growth. The reputation which arises from the detail or transposition of borrowed sentiments, may spread for a while, like ivy on the rind of antiquity but will be torn away by accident or contempt, and suffered to rot unheeded on the ground. (*Rambler* 154)

Anything which acts as an obstacle to the free play of originality is suspect. Thus Johnson can dismiss the rules as but "the arbitrary edicts of legislators, authorised only by themselves" (*Rambler* 158). The young author must learn to distinguish between these dictates of custom and prejudice and the intrinsic organic rules of composition to which he must naturally subject himself. For although he should neither "violate essential principles by a desire of novelty", neither should he "debar himself from the attainment of beauties within his view, by a needless fear of breaking rules which no literary dictator had authority to enact" (*Rambler* 156). The rules cannot be condemned too strongly by Johnson. They were drawn up by critics whose only qualification is their attentive reading of the works of the past. Their severe and frigid application has encouraged the development of a literary atmosphere of "idleness and timidity". The result has been devastating, for this spirit of repression has

... prohibited new expressions of wit, restrained fancy from the indulgence of her innate inclination to hazard and adventure, and condemned all future flights of genius to pursue the path of the Meonian eagle. (*Rambler* 158)

In Johnson's thoughts on the subject of original composition, the link made by Isaac Watts and others between imitation and moral laxity reappears:

Moralists, like other writers, instead of casting their eyes abroad in the living world, and endeavouring to form maxims of practice and new hints of theory, content their curiosity with that secondary knowledge which books afford, and think themselves entitled to reverence by a new arrangment of an ancient system, or new illustration of established principle. The sage precepts of the first instructions of the world are transmitted from age to age with little variation, and echoed from one author to another, not perhaps without some loss of their original force at every repetition. (*Rambler* 129)

The mechanical repetition of established principles is an arid and sterile form of imitation which constrains the moral development of the individual, a parallel to the literary development. But boldness and defiance of "prejudice and censure" are the forces which change and mould society. It is not only the artistic, but also the moral duty of every man to attempt to step along untrodden paths, to seek the "qualities in the products of nature" as yet undiscovered, and the "combinations in the powers of art" as yet untried. Johnson's conclusion to this issue of the *Rambler* is a firm commitment to the forces of originality and progress:

It is the duty of every man to endeavour that something may be added by his industry to the hereditary aggregate of knowledge and happiness. (*Rambler* 129)

It is clear from these essays, which also established his reputation and brought about his friendship with Boswell, that Dr. Johnson was a committed believer in the value of originality. All forms of imitation—the pastoral, the anachronism of classical mythology in modern literature, and fashionable Spenserian verse, as well as the body of mechanical rules on which the practice rested—called forth his trenchant dismissal. In his opinion, any writer who followed precedent, even Virgil, was diminished as a result. Imitation produced, not memorable literature, but an atmosphere of timidity and ignorance which crippled the human psyche. It was only when the imagination was permitted full freedom that great literature, which is distinguished by its originality, emerges. Johnson's appreciation of originality culminated in *The Preface to Shakespeare* (1765). In this, the finest piece of Shakespearian criticism of the eighteenth century, he once again, and more thoroughly, vindicated the principle of originality. It has long been recognised, however, that in expressing these opinions he was following in the wake of others. The praise of natural genius, of Shakespeare in particular, was a favourite topic in eighteenth–century journals.

The Adulation of Natural Genius in the Journals

The image of the true genius frequently described in journals of the eighteenth century is as old as literature, and allowing for some modification and qualification, is as typical of any period of history. But the degree of enthusiasm and the frequency with which it appears in the popular press during this period is not perhaps fully realized. Repeatedly, the wild and undisciplined figure of the true genius makes his appearance in periodic essays—always treated with admiration, nostalgia and regret for what has passed. From the time of Addison's classification of genius into the two categories of natural and artificial (*Spectator* 160) to Arthur Murphy's apologetic defense of the lesser, imitative poet (*The Gray's-Inn Journal* 16), originality is defined as the most fundamental necessity of the true natural genius. As we have seen, no poet is ever accorded more than faint praise for faithful imitation.

The difference between the imitative poet and the original genius is often conveyed in the contrast between the pruned garden of neat borders and ordered paths and an untended, untamed wilderness of riotous growth and natural fertility. The imitative poet represents order, restraint and control, whereas the true genius is irrepressible. He disdains order and his richness of thought overflows all bounds. He neither imitates nor is imitable. It is he who will be remembered by posterity for having expanded man's mental horizon and for having contributed something new, whether in thought or expression, to the store of human wisdom. The imitator, on the other hand, may be applauded in his own time but is soon forgotten.

The true genius finds his strength in his passionate sincerity and strong feelings, for in him, neither has been compromised by the attenuated spirit of modern decorum and correctness. Purely mechanical imitation is abhorrent or unknown to him, for he chooses his subjects from his close knowledge of nature and humanity. These are then transformed and rendered unique by his creative individuality, and finally expressed in a strong spontaneous poetry, resonant with sincerity and passion and eschewing all refined rhetorical effects or eccentric extravagance.

The anonymous authors of the old English ballads are often cited as examples of this natural genius. Addison's well-known essays, *Spectator* 70 and 74, come to mind, but he had been anticipated by the sixth issue of the *Muses Mercury,* the first journal in the eighteenth century to publish a ballad. As Addison was to do later, the editor praises the old ballad of *Chevy Chase*. He notes its enduring popularity, but admits that he himself prefers a different sort of ballad. He differentiates between the heroic ballad and those which mirror "the truth and simplicity of Nature" and make their appeal to minds of a less warlike disposition. It is an example of the latter group that he offers to his readers, the ballad of the *Nut Brown Maid*. This little ditty, the editor assures his readers, describes nature in a way which cannot be excelled, despite its "antique colouring" which, however, finds favour with the editor as a guarantee of its originality. Displaying something of an antiquarian spirit, he evinces great pride in being able to reproduce in print what he claims to be the oldest available copy, including the old spelling. It is significant that the ballad is offered to the public without apology or deference, as though the editor is convinced that its primitive simplicity, sincerity and passion—the hallmarks of originality—will ensure the praise and sympathy of sensitive readers.

Aaron Hill, the author of *The Plain-Dealer,* was another who felt that the old English ballad enshrined poetic qualities lost to modern writers.[38] In keeping with the strongly moralistic tone of the journal, Hill displays a preference for a "sublime" religio-didactic poetry, infused with the atmosphere of what he calls, "Churchyard Terror". Naturally, he was little in sympathy with the poetic spirit of the Restoration tradition in which poets wilfully confounded "the serious with the Humorous, treating the most solemn subjects after a light and wanton manner" (*The Plain-Dealer* 36). He saw this as an unwise and unwarranted departure from the older English poetic tradition of simplicity and passion and deplores its substitution for a poetry which was a direct and unvitiated outpouring of elemental passion,

---

[38] *The Plain-Dealer* was a bi-weekly periodical by Hill and William Bond. It ran from 23 March 1724 to 7 May 1725. There were 117 nos.

unaffected by the repressive and disturbing shackles of civilization and essentially sublime and original.

Unfortunately, he appends much of this apologia for primitive, passionate poetry to David Mallet's poem *William and Margaret*, which he mistakenly believes to be one of these "nobler examples of the Sublime" written in the infancy of civilization. His comments do, however, constitute a definition of one aspect of originality, particularly that which was felt to be the essence of the primitive poet. He discovers a close and intimate contact between nature and the poet, who is, therefore, able to astonish and move the reader:

It [the ballad] is so powerfully filled throughout with that Blood-curdling, chilling Influence of Nature, working on our Passions (which cricticks call the sublime) that I never met it stronger in Homer himself. (*The Plain-Dealer* 36)

In contrast with Addison's attempt to square *Chevy Chase* with classical epic principles, Hill's appreciative criticism rests entirely on what he understands to be the poem's intrinsic qualities: its "air of impressive earnestness", its sincerity and passion, and, not least, its pathetic powers. All these he adduces as proof of its purity, age and simplicity. In fact, he takes its most original quality, its lack of tell-tale literary ornament, which would have betrayed imitation, to be one of the main reasons for its profoundly affecting pathos:

It is a plain and noble masterpiece of the natural way of writing, without turns, points, conceits, flights, raptures or affectation of what kind soever. It shakes the heart by the mere effect of its strength and passionateness; unassisted by those flaming ornaments which as often dazzle, as display, in Poetry. This was owing to the Author's native force of genius; for they, who conceive a thought distinctly, will, of necessity, express it plainly, because out of the words which arise, and offer themselves to embody a shadow'd meaning, they find no use for the superfluous, but to darken and confound their purpose. (*The Plain-Dealer* 36)[39]

But the towering figure of Shakespeare dwarfed all other examples of natural genius. Combined in him were the qualities of the primitive child of nature, great and untamed genius and, what was felt to be a crucial Englishness, an original and independent spirit.[40] Confronted by such a giant, few critics dared defend the rules and imitation. Lewis Theobald's analysis of

[39] Many of these opinions were repeated in Hill's other journal, *The Prompter,* a bi-weekly theatrical periodical, which ran from 12 November 1734 to 2 July 1736. See especially nos. 28, 29, 35, 39, and 51.

[40] Eulogising English freedom and comparing it with the less liberated states of Europe was a favourite theme during the period. See, for example, *The Honest Gentleman* 17 (25 Feb. 1718) in which the happy state of the country is compared with the Popish slavery which prevails in Europe and which is linked with the evils of absolute monarchy. The "great freedom of temper" and "unconstrained manner of living" to be found in England was generally held responsible for the unusual number of "striking genius's ... in the several arts and sciences"

Lear in *Censor* 7 is less well-known than many other pieces of eighteenth-century Shakespearian criticism, but it is typical of the disposition to respond to his pathetic power and to dismiss his transgressions against the rules.

Theobald's consideration of the play begins with a statement on the relevance of classical rules to native originality:

My Purpose at present is the Examination of a tragedy of Shakespeare's, which with all its Defects and Irregularities, *has still touch'd me with the strongest Compassion,* as well in my Study, as on the Stage: ... I do not intend to charge it with those Errors, which all this Author's Plays lie under, thro' his being unacquainted with the Rules of Aristotle, and the Tragedies of the Ancients; but to view it on the beautiful Side, to remark the Propriety of Lear's character, how well it is supported throughout all the scenes and what Spirit and Elegance reigns in the Language and Sentiments.

His faults, committed in ignorance or in spite of the rules, are negligible in comparison with his success as a dramatist: "I could without regret pardon a number of them for being so admirably lost in excellencies", Theobald wrote later. (*Censor* 10). His apparent ignorance of the classical rules has not detracted from his masterly portrayal of character, in particular, that of Lear. Like many of his contemporaries, Theobald's response to Shakespearian characters is full and unequivocal. Of the pathos of Lear's rhetoric he writes:

There is a grace which cannot be conceived in the sudden starts of his passion, on being controul'd and which best shows itself by forcing us to admire it ... I cannot sufficiently admire his struggles with his testy Humour, his seeming Desire of restraining it, and the force with which it resists his Endeavours, and flies out into Rage and Imprecations. (*Censor* 10)

As in most of the Shakespearian criticism that emphasised originality, Theobald allows his personal response, rather than the extraneous criteria of the rules, to dictate his critical stance. Indeed, in his discussion of *Julius Caesar,* he proposes this personal reaction as a more valid mode of criticism than the prescriptive and arid, although superficially more impressive, criticism of the pedant. The great works of literature, such as this play, are

(*Guardian* 144). See E. L. Mann, "The Problem of Originality in English Literary Criticism," *PQ,* 18 (1939), 97–118, who notes that this observation had become quite conventional by the time Young employed it in his *Conjectures.* Dr. Johnson had also taken issue with the belief that England "affords a greater variety of characters, than the rest of the world" because of the greater freedom to be found in the country. Perversely he insisted that not only a similar freedom but also a similar diversity would be found in foreign parts if the Englishman could be persuaded to break out of his insularity and inspect the state of other nations at close quarters (*Adventurer* 84, 1753). As far as Johnson was concerned, opinions regarding the originality and the freedom of the English character were worthy only of Dick Minim (*Idler* 60, 1759).

available to both "the Vulgar" and the "best Poets" alike. Its unclassical nature does not hinder a thorough enjoyment of it.[41]

Another reason for the inappropriateness of Neo-Classical criticism is that the restrictive forms permitted by that code inhibit the development of the original genius who should be attempting to find his own peculiar mode of expression. He should, therefore, always be judged on his own merits and not according to an extrinsic set of rules:

> As to particularities, it is not to be expected that a genius like Shakespeare's should be so judged by the laws of Aristotle, and the other Prescribers of the Stage; it will be sufficient to fix a character of excellence to his performances, if there are in them a Number of beautiful Incidents, true and exquisite turns of Nature and Passion, fine and delicate Sentiments, uncommon Images, and great boldness of expression. In this play of our Countryman, I think, I may affirm, tho' against the opinion of untasting Criticks, that all these beauties meet. (*Censor* 70)[42]

Many journals followed Theobald's example and singled out Shakespeare as the great original poet.[43] Addison's famous comparison of him with the stone in Pyrrhus's ring remains, however, the most memorable (*Spectator* 592).

The discussion of the merits of originality in the journals was not confined to the adulation of Shakespeare and the old ballad writers, and, in one instance at least, anticipates the ideas of Dr. Young himself. This unexpected foreshadowing of the *Conjectures* is to be found in the forgotten pages of *The Free-Thinker* whose firm and audacious stand for freedom and originality against authority and custom makes it one of the most interesting of the ephemeral papers of the time.

The Free-Thinker was one of the many journals to spring up and then wilt in the shadow of the greater *Spectator*.[44] The anonymous author introduces himself as a determined opponent of all "crude Notions in Science, vulgar Errors, wrong Principles, ill Manner and vicious Tast [sic]." He is, of course, a great "Lover of Vertue". He attributes the errors of the present to

---

[41] Richard Steele also substituted emotional response for agreement with the rules in criticism. See his essay on *Hamlet* in *Tatler* 106. See also J. H. Neuman, "Shakespearian Criticism in the *Tatler* and the *Spectator*," *PMLA*, 39 (1924), 612–623.

[42] See *Censor* 41 and 73 for Theobald's opinions on the dismal state of modern poetry—a state brought about by the practice of abject imitation.

[43] See, e.g., *Adventurer* 93 and *The Grey's-Inn Journal* 4 and 94. See also *Guardian* 37 in which *Othello* is described as a noble "Production of a Genius which has the Power of animating the Theatre beyond any Writer we have ever known".

[44] Only 6 nos. are known to have appeared, on Saturdays and Tuesdays, from 17 November to 3 December, 1711. See *Contemporaries of the Tatler and the Spectator* (Augustan Reprint Society, No. 47, 1954), introd. R. P. Bond. This journal should not be confused with the later *Free Thinker* (1718–21) by Ambrose Philips.

"that Credulity, which has obtained for many years, and is still industriously propagated". It is this unthinking acceptance of authority against which he intends to direct his "free-thinking" crusade:

It will be worth Enquiry, whether an easie Assent to everything upon the Credit of Authority or long Prescription has not given Rise to that Train of Delusions and Impostures which have taken footing in the World. (*The Free-Thinker* 1)

This state of affairs is evident in all spheres of life, but particularly in learning and art, where progress is hindered by timidity and fear of deviating from the well-trodden paths. The result is an art either "*Over-season'd or Insipid*", unoriginal and far removed from Nature. To alter this state requires energy and zeal for the tide of custom is strong:

All Innovations in Mode, Opinion or Custom, is in a Manner sailing directly in the Eye of the Wind with a strong Current against one, till Prejudice or Obstinacy be worn off, and after, once Reason is plac'd at the Helm we sail on with a settled easie Gale. (*The Free-Thinker* 1)

In explaining to his readers why he has entered the field of periodic publication, a field so dominated by the great *Spectator,* the author presents a programme of original composition which, in its simplicity, detailed clarity and depth, far exceeds anything of a similar nature from the same period. From his contention that the writer must be free to choose subjects and genres at will, he educes three principal areas of original composition: the manner of presentation, the selection of new subject matter and the fundamental originality of the creative consciousness of the individual author.

The first of these, the cultivation of a personal style of writing, is based on the premise that as each mind comprehends differently so each subsequent portrayal of nature will be original; "since every Man has an equal Propriety in Nature and the several Images which flow from thence may be delineated after a different Manner, and no certain Rule established".

New subject matter is permitted, and indeed demanded, by the infinite variety of human nature which should serve as a fruitful source of inspiration to the writer. The importance traditionally accorded the Neo-Classical precept of the uniformity of Nature—"Human Nature is the same in all reasonable Creatures" (*Spectator* 70)—is, in *The Free-Thinker,* displaced by a new emphasis on its diversity and complexity. Examination of these aspects reveals a wealth of new themes: "refinements upon, and the Deviations from" Nature, "the passions, resentments; the hot and cold Breezes of the Soul", all of which, because Nature is ever-changing, are "constant Resources" of originality for the poet. Even, he adds, the "single Topick of Love"—perhaps the most exploited passion of all—"yet wears many different Portraits than we have seen it hitherto cloth'd with" (*The Free-Thinker* 2). Endless permutations are possible:

The Incidents, Surprises, and variety of Circumstances and Temperaments give such un-accountable Turns to that Passion, as to render several Impulses of it new and astonishing. (*The Free-Thinker* 2)

Other possible sources of originality include a celebration of the individuality of "particular beauties", the numerous "*Foibles* of Human Kind" and the "Errors of the Mind". Again these afford such "large Funds of Reflexion ... that we are under no great Apprehensions of wanting Matter". Even the chance that two writers will choose a similar subject should not cause anxiety, for, as he had noted earlier, such is the distinct individuality of human nature that it is possible for two authors to "*tread the same round* without exchanging Hands". Should such an unlikely coincidence occur, it is his opinion that the subject may perhaps "be improv'd by such a gentle Collision".

It is his discussion, however brief, of the final source of original composition which is of greatest interest, and which serves as a link between the beginning of this period and Edward Young's conclusion to it. *The Free-Thinker* maintains that originality is essentially a result of what Edward Young later termed "mental individuality"—the nature and activity of the human mind:

There is as much Curiosity in Thoughts, as in Flowers with different Colours and Variegations, and all Images that present themselves receive different Modification from distinct Minds. (*The Free-Thinker* 2)

This is a guarantee of perpetual originality in art. It is impossible to exhaust the subjects available as long as the transforming mind of the individual is the decisive factor in composition.

In so trenchantly pointing to the individual in all his diversity, not only as an unlimited source of material for original composition, but also as a unique imagination rendered creative by virtue of his natural "Curiosity in Thoughts"—his mental individuality—the author of *The Free-Thinker* is one of the earliest, perhaps the earliest, theorist of innate originality in the eighteenth century.

From this survey of the discussion of originality and imitation in the literary journals of the period it is evident that it was a subject which interested and amused the general reader. The authors of these essays rarely went beyond what might be expected of critics discussing what was, rather than what ought to be, the state of contemporary poetry, but then, their audience were mostly consumers not producers of poetry. Directives to explore new areas of composition would have been out of place.

Instead the essays were intended as guides to, and arbiters of, good taste. Most of the ideas to be found in them were well-thumbed; some were sprightly and inspiring; a very few managed to say something quite unexpected. To the general reader, they were, however, a veritable storehouse of treasures. From them he would have learned to laugh at the benighted figures of pedant, imitative poet and superficial critic. He would have found encouragement to appreciate Shakespeare's independent spirit and to allow his fondness for old ballads to appear in polite society. Rumours of literary controversy would have filtered through to him, but he would also have sensed the growing impatience with the dominion of the present by the now distant classical past.

From Dr. Johnson he would have gleaned something of the seriousness of earnest literary effort and, from Addison, a certainty that what mattered was the operation of the well-tuned and sensitive imagination and that the true natural genius was one who relied on his own resources and ignored or disregarded the ballast of tradition.

These, and a myriad other details, would have made him familiar with the issues surrounding the question of literary independence and would, perhaps, have made him welcome with interest, the efforts of poets who aspired to follow the bent of their imaginations.

In conclusion, it may not be inappropriate to try to recapture some of the fun authors and readers of these literary journals had with what have since become the leaden topics of historical analysis. When John Gay wanted to amuse his readers on the subject of original composition, he devised the "great Genius in dress" (*Guardian* 149). This dandified equivalent of the natural genius was not to be confused with those mere pretenders who, like Horace's patchwork poets, "strike out but by halves", favouring "the Scarlet Stocking and the Red Heel" but neglecting "all the superiour Ornament of [the] body". True to his species, the great sartorial original, on the other hand, "cannot content himself with meerly Copying from others", but when the opportunity arises, will strike out in the sartorial equivalent of the boundless flight of genius: "the long Pocket, slash'd Sleeve, or something particular in the disposition of his Lace, or the flourish of his Embroidery", displaying at all costs "a Manner of his own".

As far as John Gay was concerned, poets engaged in the quest for originality had become so ubiquitous as to merit the status of a public joke.

Conclusion

Whereas many of the more eminent literary figures of the period 1650–1760 (and others less distinguished) regarded themselves as the loyal custodians of the classical tradition they had inherited, to a large section of the reading public and those authors who sought to gratify its demands, there was little in this legacy that attracted or inspired. To them its secular and aristocratic basis, its backward-looking aspect, its elements of fantasy and outworn folktale and, finally, its cosmopolitan non-English inclination rendered it more and more unpalatable.

Often ill-equipped by either education or tradition to understand or appreciate the languages and literatures of Greece and Rome, this new group of readers and authors sought a poetry which would reflect their immediate concerns and interests. Gripped by a desire to assert their own identity they preferred to exploit more accessible resources. These resources were found to lie in the lore of the Bible and related religious themes, in the discoveries of science, in a new appreciation of nature and, lastly, in the very mind of man itself.

Divine poetry, which has always enjoyed a constant, if unfashionable popularity, acquired a new significance in the hands of those who sought originality. Its foundation, the tenets of Christianity and, in particular, the Bible, offered an unrifled store of subjects and themes of intrinsic worth and unfingered novelty. As great as the works of the Ancients, Holy Writ possessed the additional advantages of immunity to the classical rules, relevance to the present time and the key to the greater passions—for what could be more pathetic than man's search for salvation?

In the highly individual religious verse of Isaac Watts, an astonishingly popular poet of the age, the cultivation of singularity and the pursuit of originality are his main preoccupations. In keeping with his Dissenting inclination, Watts expressed the belief that the poet must defy accepted conventions and cultivate his own uniqueness. Only in this way will he fulfill his humanity.

By the 1740's divine poetry had become respectably modish. The passion and sublimity of the Bible was an axiom of the best taste. Finally, so many poets had tried their hand at the genre that claims to originality were dropped and the earlier devotional impulse again took precedence.

146

The new revelations of science also fired the imagination. Their impact on the popular mind was enormous. Old fears and anxieties about the decay of the world and post-diluvian corruption were dissipated by the remarkable, thought-provoking and seemingly endless discoveries of the pioneer scientists and the host of lay-folk who followed their example with microscope, telescope and experiment.

To many, such as Bishop Sprat, it seemed that a whole new order had been instated. It was this order, in all its pristine novelty that he urged aspiring poets to celebrate. Unlike the fantastic notions of the Ancients, science could supply the poet with factual truth, at the same time romantic, inspiring, mysterious and original. All he had to do was to study what, with diligence, he would find around him, "new *Virtues* and *Qualities* of things".

Early on, however, it was noted that the matter of science might be intractable and difficult to render into verse. To some extent this proved to be the case, for many of the poets who turned to science did so merely to illustrate, within the confines of physico-theological verse, the might and magnanimity of the Godhead.

The machinery of science and its empirical method of investigation may well have contributed to another, more enduring, inspiration for poets—the unveiled face of real nature. What had been disguised for centuries by the citified dress of pastoral or kept at bay by a distaste for its discomforts, now emerged.

To poets who had been excluded from "Neo-Classical" verse by the apparatus of learning and tradition on which it rested, the new vision of raw nature was alluring. It seems that these "unlearned" poets accepted gratefully the freedoms that the freshness of the subject permitted them. As many acknowledged, sometimes apologetically, sometimes happily, they could write no other verse but that to which their emotions gave inspiration. The new subjects inspired by close observation of nature in the countryside—plants, animals, the weather and the changing seasons—seemed to offer unlimited scope to those emotions.

The poet's emotional reaction to nature could also provide a pretext for the exploration of his own feelings. Indeed, a keen interest in the complexity and uniqueness of the individual mind was fast becoming the common property of Polite conversation. Side by side with what is frequently accepted as more typical Neo-Classical notions, such as the uniformity of nature and the superior virtues of generality, there existed a growing pleasure in unearthing and defending the endless variety of mankind. By the time of Edward Young's *Conjectures,* this interest had developed the descriptive term "mental individuality" which had become inextricably linked with the originality and personal merit of the poet. By then, originality was deemed the goal of the aspiring author. To achieve it, he was to ignore what tradition offered, disregard the principle of imitation and the rules and look inward on the mysteries of his own mind and unique nature. "Know Thyself and Reverence Thyself" was Dr. Young's advice.

It is my contention then, that the urge to be original, to cast off the burden of the past, was expressed, not, of course, by a consolidated group, school or movement, but by a multitude of individuals. They sought literary freedom in the opportunities offered by themes derived from the Christian religion, scientific researches, nature and the countryside and the human mind itself. Their achievement may have fallen short of their ambitions. But they were far from being a few eccentric revolutionaries. Rather they were responding to a popular demand for a modern, accessible and relevant poetry. This is evidenced by the fact that their enthusiasms—interest in originality, distaste for the classical past and contempt for rulebound poets and critics—were themes which found a frequent airing in the popular press.

The many journals and magazines which proliferated, particularly during the latter half of the period, were aimed, in most cases, at the general reader and designed to school him and form his taste. Both trivial and serious journal alike, devoted space to the question of literary originality. Few disputed its superior merit and then only defensively. The average reader would have learned to despise the petty critic and uninspired poetaster. He would have admired appreciatively the free originality of Shakespeare and the old ballad writers. He would have understood too, that, in comparison with the perceptive and finely tuned Imagination and the related faculty of Taste, a scholarly knowledge of the classical languages and their literatures counted for little. It was to him that the original poet made his appeal.

It seems that Shaftesbury's assessment of the literary efforts of many of his contemporaries was correct. They did disobey the rules of art. They were ignorant of the past. But their defiance was founded on a justifiable desire for novelty and freer personal expression, for the Neo-Classical age was, equally, an age of Experiment.

Bibliography

Place of publication is London unless otherwise stated.

Primary Sources

Abercromby, David. *A Discourse of Wit*. 1685.

Addison, Joseph. *The Miscellaneous Works of Joseph Addison*. Ed. A. C. Guthkelch. Vol. II. 1914.

The Adventurer. 1752–54.

Akenside, Mark. *The Poetical Works of Mark Akenside. Aldine Edition of the British Poets*. Ed. Alexander Dyce. 1834. Undated reprint.

Amyntor and Theodora: or The Hermit. 1747.

Armstrong, John. *The Art of Preserving Health; a Poem*. 1744.

— *Sketches; or Essays on Various Subjects. By Launcelot Temple, Esq. In Two Volumes*. 1758. Vol. VIII of *Harrison's British Classics*. 1787.

Aristotle. *Aristotle's Theory of Poetry and Fine Art*. Trans. S. H. Butcher. 1895. 4th. ed. 1927.

The Athenian Oracle. Being an Entire Collection of all the Valuable Questions and Answers in the old Athenian Mercuries. 4 vols. 2nd. ed. 1704 and 3rd. ed. 1728.

Bacon, Francis. *Works*. Ed. James Spedding et al. 1870; rpt. N. Y., 1968.

Bailey, Nathan. *The New Universal English Dictionary*. 1717.

Baker, Daniel. *Poems upon Several Occasions*. 1697.

— *The History of Job: A Sacred Poem*. 1706.

Baker, Henry. *Original Poems: Serious and Humourous*. 1725.

— *The Universe. A Poem intended to restrain the Pride of Man* 1720 or 1734.

— *The Microscope made Easy*. 1742. 2nd. ed. 1743.

[Baker, Thomas] *Reflections upon Learning. Wherein is shewn the Insufficiency thereof, in its several Particulars. In order to evince the Usefulness and Necessity of Revelation. By a Gentleman*. 1699. 3rd. ed. 1700.

Beattie, James. *Essays*. Edinburgh, 1776.

[Benson, William.] *Letters concerning Poetical Translations, and Virgil and Milton's Arts of Verse*. 1739.

Blackmore, Sir Richard. Preface to *Prince Arthur*. 1697.

— *A Paraphrase on the Book of Job,* etc. 1700.

— *Creation. A Philosophical Poem in seven books*. 1712.

— and John Hughes. *The Lay-Monk*. 1713–1714. Publ. as *The Lay-Monastery*. 1714.

— *Essays upon Several Subjects*. 1716.

— Preface to *Redemption: A Divine Poem in Six Books*. 1722.

Blackwall, Anthony. *The Sacred Classics Defended and Illustrated: or, An Essay Humbly offer'd towards proving the Purity, Propriety, and true Eloquence Of the Writers of the New Testament. In two Parts*. 1725.

Blake, William. *The Complete Writings of William Blake*. Ed. Geoffrey Keynes. 1966.

Blount, Thomas. *Glossographia or a Dictionary interpreting all such Hard Words . . . now in use . . . .* 1656.

Blount, Sir Thomas Pope. *Essays on Several Subjects*. 1691. 3rd. ed. 1697.

Bowden, Samuel. *Poems on Various Subjects*. Bath, 1754.

149

Brereton, Jane. *Hymn to the Creator*. 1744.

Brereton, Thomas. *The Criticks*. 1718, rpt. 1719.

[Brooke, Henry.] *Universal Beauty. A Poem*. 1735.

Browne, Isaac Hawkins. *Of Design and Beauty*. 1734.

— *The Fire Side: A Pastoral Soliloquy*. 1735.

— *The Immortality of the Soul. A poem*. Trans. William Hay. 1754.

Browne, Moses. *Poems on Various Subjects*. 1739.

— *The Works and Rest of the Creation*. 1752.

Bullokar, John. *An English Expositour, or Compleat Dictionary teaching the Interpretation of the hardest words, and most useful terms of Art used in our Language*. 1616. Revised 1663.

Burn, J. H. *Catalogue, Part I of Ancient and Modern Books*. 1822–30.

Burton, Robert. *The Anatomy of Melancholy*. 2nd. ed. Oxford, 1624.

Campbell, John. *The Rational Amusement*. 1754.

Casaubon, Meric. *A Treatise Concerning Enthusiasm*. 1665.

Cawdrey, Robert. *A Table Alphabeticall of Hard Usual English Words*. 1604.

Chudleigh, Lady Mary. *Poems on Several Occasions*. 1703. 4th. ed. 1722.

Classical Literary Criticism. Trans. T. S. Dorsch. Harmondsworth, England. 1965.

Cobb, Samuel. "A Discourse on Criticism and the Liberty of Writing" in *Poems on Several Occasions*. 1707. Introd. Louis I. Bredvold. Augustan Reprint Society. Los Angeles, 1946.

— *Of Poetry*. 1710.

Cockeram, Henry. *The English Dictionarie*. 1623.

Coles, Elisha. *English Dictionary*. 1676.

Collins, William. *On the Popular Superstitions of the Highlands of Scotland*. c. 1749.

Comberbach, Roger. *A Dispute; consisting of a Preface in Favour of Blank Verse*. 1755.

Commendatory Verses, on the Author of the Two Arthurs and the Satyr against Wit, By some of his particular Friends. 1700.

Congreve, William. *An Essay Concerning Humour in Comedy to Mr. Dennis*. 1695.

Constable, John. *Reflections upon Accuracy of Style*. 1731.

Contemporaries of the Tatler and Spectator. Introd. Richmond P. Bond. Augustan Reprint Society. Los Angeles, 1954.

The Connoisseur. Eds. Leo Colman and Bonnell Thornton. 1754 – 56.

[Cooper, J. G.] *The Power of Harmony*. 1745.

— *Letters concerning Taste*. 1755.

Cotton, Charles. *The Wonders of the Peak*. Nottingham, 1725.

Cowley, Abraham. *The Advancement of Experimental Philosophy*. 1661.

— *Davideis*. 1668.

— *Pindaric Odes*. 1677.

— *Poems* etc. Ed. A. R. Waller. Cambridge, 1905.

— *The Essays and other Prose Writings*. Ed. Alfred B. Gough. Oxford, 1915.

The Country Life; or, A Passionate Invitation of the Soul to Retirement being A Divine Soliloquy on Canto VII, ii. 1721.

Critical Essays of the XVIIIth-Century. Ed. W. H. Durham. New Haven, 1915.

The Critical Review. May 1751.

Crocker, Edward. *Crocker's English Dictionary*. 1704.

Critical Essays of the Seventeenth Century. Ed. J. A. Spingarn. Oxford, 1908–9, rpt. 1957.

The Daily Post. 12 April, 1744.

Dalton, John. *A Descriptive Poem addressed to Two Ladies, At their Return from Viewing the Mines near Whitehaven*. 1755.

Defoe, B. N. *A Compleat English Dictionary*. 1735.

Denham, Sir John. *Poems and Translations; with the Sophy, a Tragedy.* 1668. 7th ed. 1769.

Dennis, John. *The Critical Works of John Dennis.* Ed. Edward N. Hooker. 2 vols. Baltimore, 1939, 1943.

Derham, William. *Physico-Theology: or, a Demonstration of the Being and Attributes of God, from his Works of Creation.* 1713. 3rd. ed. 1714.

Desaguliers. J. T. *Lectures of Experimental Philosophy.* 2nd. ed. 1719.

Diaper, William. *Dryades; or, The Nymphs Prophesy. A Poem.* 1713.

D'Israeli, Isaac. *Miscellanies; or, Literary Recreations.* 1796.

Divine Wisdom and Providence; An Essay occasion'd by the Essay on Man. 1736.

Dodsley, Robert. (Ed.). *A Collection of Poems by Several Hands. In Three Volumes.* 1748. Vol. IV, 1749.

— *Agriculture.* Bk. I of *Public Virtue: A Poem.* 1753.

Dryden, John. *The Essays of John Dryden.* Ed. W. P. Ker. 1900. Rpt. N. Y., 1961.

— *The Works of John Dryden.* Gen. Ed. H. T. Swedenberg, Jr. 12 vols. to date. Berkeley, Los Angeles and London, 1956–1979.

Dyche, Thomas. *A New General English Dictionary.* 1735.

Dyer, John. *Grongar Hill.* 1726.

Edwards, Samuel. *The Copernican System. A Poem.* 1728.

Elizabethan Critical Essays. Ed. G. G. Smith. Oxford, 1904.

Eighteenth-Century Critical Essays. Ed. Scott Elledge. 2 vols. Ithaca, N. Y., 1961.

Ellwood, Thomas. *Davideis.* 1712.

An Essay Concerning Critical and Curious Learning. T. R. 1698. Introd. Curt A. Zimansky. Augustan Reprint Society. Los Angeles, 1965.

Essays upon Pastoral. 3rd. ed. 1730.

Evans, Abel. *Vertumnus. An Epistle to Mr Jacob Bobart.* 1713.

Farquhar, George. *Works.* 2 vols. 2nd. ed. 1711.

Felton, Henry. *A Dissertation on Reading the Classics and Forming a Just Style.* 1713.

Fénelon, François De Salignac de la Mothe. *Dialogues sur l'Eloquence.* Paris, 1718. Trans. William Stevenson. *Dialogues Concerning Eloquence* etc. 1722.

Fontenelle, Bernard le Bovier, Sieur de. *Entretiens sur la pluralité des Mondes.* 1686. Trans. Aphra Behn. 1688; Joseph Glanvil. 1695; W. Gardiner. 1715.

Fortescue, James. Science: *An Epistle on it's* [sic] *Decline and Revival.* 1750.

— *On the Passions.* 1752.

— *Essays Moral and Miscellaneous.* Oxford, 1754.

Four Pastorals. 1751.

[Gambol, Robert.] *The Beauties of the Universe. A Poem.* 1732.

The Gazette a la Mode, or Tom Brown's Ghost. June 9, 1709.

The Gentleman's Magazine. March 1732.

Gildon, Charles. *Miscellaneous Letters and Essays, on Several Subjects.* etc. 1694.

— *The Complete Art of Poetry.* 2 vols. 1718.

[Goldsmith, Oliver.] *An Enquiry into the Present State of Polite Learning in Europe.* 1759.

— and John Newbery. *The Art of Poetry on a New Plan.* 2 vols. 1762.

Goldwin, William. *A poetical Description of Bristol.* 1712.

The Gray's-Inn Journal. 1753–1754.

Green, Matthew. *The Spleen.* 1737.

[Gregory, John.] *A Comparative View of the State and Faculties of Man with those of the Animal World.* 1765.

The Growler: or Diogenes Robbed of his Tub. 1711.

The Grub-Street Journal. Eds. R. Russel and J. Martyn. 1730–1737.

The Guardian. 1713. 2 Vols. 1714.

The Harleian Miscellany. Ed. T. Park. 10 vols. 1808–1813.

Hay, William. *Mount Caburn. A Poem Humbly Inscribed to her Grace The Dutchess of Newcastle.* 1730.

Hawling, Francis. *Miscellany of Original Poems on Various Subjects.* 1752.

Higgons, Bevill. *A Poem on Nature: In Imitation of Lucretius.* 1736.

Hill, Aaron. *Prefaces* etc. 1720. Introd. Gretchen Graf Pahl. Augustan Reprint Society. Los Angeles, 1949.

— and William Bond. *The Plain-Dealer.* 1724–1725.

— *Advice to the Poets. A Poem.* 1731.

— *The Prompter.* 1734–1736.

— *The Works of the Late Aaron Hill, Esq.* 4 Vols. 1753.

Historia Literaria, or an Exact and Early Account of the most valuable Books published in the Several Parts of Europe. 2 vols. 1730–1731.

The Honest Gentleman. No. 17. Feb. 25. 1718.

[Howard, Edward.] Preface to *The Womens Conquest. A Tragi-Comedy.* 1671.

— *An Essay upon Pastoral.* 1695.

Howard, Sir Robert. Preface to *The Great Favourite.* 1668.

Hughes, John. *An Ode to the Creator of the World.* 1713.

— *The Works of Edmund Spencer.* 2 vols. 1715.

— *The Ecstacy. An Ode.* 1720.

— *Poems on Several Occasions.* 2 vols. 1735.

Hume, David. *A Treatise of Human Nature.* 1739.

Hurd, Richard. *Letters on Chivalry and Romance.* 1762. Ed. E. J. Morley. 1911.

Husbands, John. Preface to *A Miscellany of Poems by Several Hands.* 1731.

An Hymn to the Creator of the World. The Thoughts taken chiefly from Psalm. civ. To which is added in Prose, An Idea of the Creator from his Works. 1750.

An Hymn to God. 1746.

Jacob, Hildebrand. *Of the Sister Arts, An Essay.* 1734.

Jenyns, Soame. *Poems.* 1752.

Johnson, Samuel. *The Rambler.* 1750–1752.

— *A Dictionary of the English Language* etc. 2 vols. 1755.

— *The Idler.* 1758–1760. 2 vols. 1761.

— *The Prince of Abissinia. A Tale.* 2 vols. 1759.

— *Mr. Johnson's Preface to his Edition of Shakespeare's Plays.* 1765.

— *Lives of the English Poets.* Ed. G. Birkbeck Hill. 3 vols. Oxford, 1905.

Jones, Henry. *Poems on Several Occasions.* 1749.

[Keach, Benjamin] *The Glorious Lover.* 1679.

King, Dr. William. *An Historical Account of the Heathen Gods and Heroes; Necessary for the Understanding of the Ancient Poets.* 1711.

Kirkpatrick, J. *The Sea-piece.* 1750.

Leapor, Mary. *Poems upon Several Occasions.* 1748.

Le Clerk, Jean. *Parrhasiana: or, Thoughts upon Several Subjects,* etc. 1700.

Literary Criticism—Plato to Dryden. Ed. Allan H. Gilbert. N. Y., 1940.

Locke, John. *Some Familiar Letters between Mr Locke, and Several of his Friends.* 1708.

The London Journal. July 9, 1720.

Lowth, Robert. *De Sacra Poesi Hebraeorum praelectiones academenica Oxonii habitae,* etc. 1741–1750. Trans. G. Gregory. 1787.

Lux, William. *Poems on Several Occasions.* Oxford, 1719.

Mallet, David. *The Excursion. A Poem.* 1728.

Manwaring, Edward. *An Historical and Critical Account of the most Eminent Classic Authors in Poetry and History.* 1737.

Martin, Martin. *A Voyage to St. Kilda.* 1698.

— *A Description of the Western Islands of Scotland.* 1703.

Masters, Mary. *Poems on Several Occasions.* 1733.

Melmoth, William, the younger. *Letters on Several Subjects. By the late Sir Thomas Fitz-osborne, Bart.* 1748. Harrison's *British Classics.* Vol VIII. 1787.

Memoirs of the Society of Grub Street. 1737.

Milton, John. *Complete Prose Works.* Gen. Ed. Don M. Wolfe. Vol. I. New Haven and London. 1953.

— *A Variorum Commentary on the Poems of John Milton.* Gen. Ed. Merritt Y. Hughes. Vol. IV. 1975.

Miscellaneous Poems and Translations. By Several Hands. Published by Richard Savage. 1726.

Miscellaneous Poems, original and translated. By Several Hands. Published by Matthew Concanen. 1724.

Miscellany Poems and Translations by Oxford Hands. 1685.

Mitchell, Joseph. *Jonah.* 1720.

Montaigne, Michaell de. *The Essayes, or Morall, Politike and Millitarie Discourses.* Trans. John Florio. 1603.

The Monthly Review. Feb. 1750.

Morris, Corbyn. *An Essay Towards Fixing the True Standards of Wit, Humour, Raillery, Satire and Ridicule.* 1744. Introd. James L. Clifford. Augustan Reprint Society. Los Angeles, 1947.

The Muses Mercury. 1708–1709.

Nature. A Poem. 1747.

Needler, Henry. *The Works of Mr. Henry Needler. Consisting of Original Poems, Translations, Essays, and Letters. Published* by Mr. Duncombe. 1724. 2nd. ed. 1728.

[Nevile, Thomas.] "Remarks on Mr Mason's Elfrida" in *Letter to a Friend.* 1752.

Newcastle, Margaret Cavendish, Duchess of. *Poems and Fancies.* 1653.

Newcomb, Thomas. *The Last Judgment of Men and Angels. A Poem in twelve books: After the Manner of Milton.* 1723.

— *A Miscellaneous Collection of Original Poems* etc. 1740.

News from Newcastle. 1651.

Norris, John. *A Collection of Miscellanies: Consisting of Poems, Essays, Discourses and Letters, Occasionally Written.* 1678. 4th ed. revised and corrected 1706.

Oldmixon, John. *Amintas.* 1698.

— *An Essay on Criticism.* 1728.

The Oxford Book of Eighteenth-Century Verse. Ed. David Nichol Smith. Oxford, 1926. Rpt. 1963.

Paget, Thomas Catesby Page. *Essay on Human Life.* 1734.

Partridge, John. *Titt for Tatt.* 1710.

Patrick, S. *Paraphrase on Ecclesiastes, and the Song of Solomon.* 1685.

Pemberton, Henry. *Observations on Poetry, especially the Epic.* 1738.

Pennecuik, Alexander. *Streams from Helicon: or, Poems on Various Subjects.* 2nd. ed. 1720.

Philips, Ambrose. *A Reflection on our Modern Poesy,* 1695.

— *The Poems of Ambrose Philips.* Ed. M. G. Segar, Oxford, 1937.

A Philosophic Ode on the Sun and the Universe. 1750.

Plattes, Gabriel. *A Discovery of Subterraneall Treasure*. 1639.

Poems Divine, Moral and Philosophical. Gloucester, 1746.

Poems by Eminent Ladies. 2 vols. 1755.

Poems by Several Hands and on Several Occasions collected by Nahum Tate. 1685.

The Polite Gentleman: or reflections upon several kinds of wit, viz. in conversation, books, and affairs of the world. Done out of French. Trans. Henry Barker. 1700.

Pomfret, John. *The Choice*. 1700.

Poole, Joshua. *The English Parnassus*. 1657.

Pope, Alexander. Gen. En. John Butt. *The Twickenham Edition of the Poems of Alexander Pope*. Vol. I: *Pastoral Poetry and An Essay on Criticism*. Ed. E. Audra et al.; Vol. II: *The Rape of the Lock*. Ed. G. Tillotson; Vol. III i: *An Essay on Man*. Ed. Maynard Mack; Vol. V: *The Dunciad*. Ed. James Sutherland. London and New Haven, 1939–1961.

— *The Poems of Alexander Pope*. Ed. John Butt. 1963. Rpt. 1965.

— *The Prose Works of Alexander Pope*. Ed. Norman Ault. Vol. I. *The Earlier Works, 1711–1720*. Oxford, 1936.

— *The Correspondence of Alexander Pope*. Ed. George Sherburn. Vol. I. Oxford, 1956.

The Present State of the Literati. A Satire. 1752.

The Present State of Poetry. A Satyr addres'd to a Friend. By B. M. 1721.

Prior, Matthew. *Poems on Several Occasions*. 1718.

Purney, Thomas. *The Works of Thomas Purney*. Ed. H. O. White. Oxford, 1933.

— *A Full Enquiry into the True Nature of Pastoral*. 1717. Introd. Earl Wasserman. Augustan Reprint Society. Los Angeles, 1948.

Ralph, James. *Night. A Poem*. 1728.

— *The Muses' Address to the King*. 1728.

— *Zeuma: or the Love of Liberty. A Poem*. 1729.

— *The Taste of the Town: or, a Guide to all Publick Diversions*. (Rpt. of *The Touchstone*, 1728). 1731.

Ramsay, Allan. *Poems on Several Occasions*. 1776.

Rapin, René. *De Carmine Pastorali, prefixed to Thomas Creech's translation of the Idylliums of Theocritus. 1684*. Introd. J. E. Congleton. Augustan Reprint Society. Los Angeles, 1947.

Read's Weekly Journal or British Gazetter. Jan. 29. 1732.

[Reynolds, John.] *Death's Vision Represented in a Philosophical Sacred Poem*. 1709.

— *Memoirs of the Life of the late Pious and Learned Mr John Reynolds. Chiefly extracted from his Manuscripts. To which is added, His View of Death*: etc. 3rd. ed. 1735.

Richardson, Jonathan. Father and Son. *Explanatory Notes and Remarks on Milton's Paradise Lost*. 1734.

Rouquet, André. *The Present State of the Arts in England*. 1755.

Rowe, Elizabeth. *The History of Joseph. A poem*. 1736.

— *The Miscellaneous Works in Prose and Verse of Mrs. Elizabeth Rowe. . . . By Mr. Theophilus Rowe*. 2 vols. 1739.

Rymer, Thomas. *The Critical Works of Thomas Rymer*. Ed. Curt A. Zimansky. New Haven, 1956.

A Satyr upon a Late Pamphlet Entituled A Satyr against Wit. 1700.

Savage, Richard. *The Wanderer: A Poem in five Canto's* [sic]. 1729.

Settle, Elkanah. *Farther Defence of Dramatick Poetry*. 1698.

Shaftesbury, Anthony Ashley Cooper, Third Earl of. *Sensus Communis: An Essay on the Freedom of Wit and Humour*. 1709.

— *Characteristics of Men, Manners, Opinions, Times*. 3 vols. 1711.

Sheridan, Thomas. *British Education: Or, The Source of the Disorders of Great Britain*. 1756.

Sidney, Sir Philip. *Defense of Poesie*. Ed. Albert Feuillerat. Cambridge, 1923.

Silvester, Tipping. *Original Poems and Translations consisting of The Microscope, Piscatio, or Angling*, etc. 1733.

Slater, Samuel. *Poems in Two Parts*. 1679.

Smith, Adam. *The Early Writings of Adam Smith*. Ed. T. R. Lindgren. N. Y., 1967.

— *Essays on Philosophical Subjects*. 1795.

Some Remarks on the Tragedy of Hamlet, Prince of Denmark, Written by Mr William Shakespeare. 1736. Introd. Clarence DeWitt Thorpe. Augustan Reprint Society. Los Angeles, 1947.

The Spectator. Ed. Donald F. Bond. 5 vols. Oxford, 1965.

Spence, Joseph. *Observations, Anecdotes, and Characters of Books and Men collected from Conversation*. Ed. James M. Osborn. 2 vols. Oxford, 1966.

Spingarn, J. E. *A History of Literary Criticism in the Renaissance*. 1899. 2nd. ed. N. Y., 1908.

Sprat, Thomas. *Three Poems upon the Death of . . . Oliver, Lord Protector . . . .* 1659.

— *The Plage of Athens*. 1659.

— *The History of the Royal Society of London, For the Improving of Natural Knowledge*. 1667.

— "An Account of the Life and Writings of Mr Abraham Cowley". Prefixed to Cowley's *Works*, 1668.

Stephens, Edward. *Poems on Various Subjects*. 1759.

Sterne, Lawrence. *Tristram Shandy*. 1760.

Swift, Jonathan. *A Tale of a Tub with Other Early Works 1696–1707*. Ed. Herbert Davis. Oxford, 1939.

— *Gulliver's Travels*. Harmondsworth, 1967.

Tasso, Torquato. *Gerusalemme Liberata*. 1581.

Taste, An Essay. By J. S. D. S. P. 2nd. ed. 1739.

The Tatler. 1709–1711.

Theobald, Lewis. *The Censor*. 1717.

Theologie Ruris sive Schola et Scala Naturae. 1686. Introd. H. S. V. Ogden. Augustan Reprint Society. Los Angeles, 1956.

Thomson, James. *The Complete Poetical Works of James Thomson*. Ed. J. Logie Robertson. 1908; rpt. 1963.

— *James Thomson (1700–1748). An Annotated Bibliography of Select Editions and the Important Criticism*. Ed. Hilbert H. Campbell. N. Y. and London, 1976.

— *The Seasons*. Ed. James Sambrook. Oxford, 1981.

Trapp, Joseph. *Praelectiones Poeticae: In Schola Naturalis Philosophiae Oxon. Habitae*. 1711. Trans. William Boyer and William Clarke. 1742.

Two Poems Against Pope. Introd. Joseph V. Guerinot. Augustan Reprint Society. Los Angeles. 1965.

The Visiter. 1723–1724.

Warton, Joseph. *The Enthusiast, or, The Lover of Nature*. 1744.

— *Odes on Various Subjects*. 1746.

— *An Essay on the Genius and Writings of Pope*. Vol. I. 1756. 5th. ed. 1806.

Warton, Thomas. *Observations on the Faerie Queene of Spencer*. 1754.

— *The History of English Poetry from the close of the Eleventh to the Commencement of the Eighteenth Century*. 3 vols. 1774; 1778; 1781.

Watts, Isaac. *Horae Lyricae. Poems chiefly of the Lyric Kind in Two Books*. 1706. 10th. ed. corrected. 1750.

The Weekly Register. 1732.

Welsted, Leonard. *A Dissertation Concerning the Perfection of the English Language prefixed to Epistles, Odes etc. Written on Several Subjects*. 1714. 2nd. ed. 1725.

Wesley, Samuel. *Preface, Being an Essay on Heroic Poetry. etc.* 1693; 2nd. ed. 1697.

— *The Life of Our Blessed Lord and Saviour.* 1694.

— *Epistle to a Friend concerning Poetry. 1700.* Introd. Edward N. Hooker. Augustan Reprint Society. Los Angeles, 1947.

The Whitehall Evening Post. 12–15 Feb., 1731–32.

Woodford, Samuel. *A Paraphrase upon the Psalms of David.* 1667.

— *A Paraphrase upon the Canticles.* 1679.

Woodward, George. *Poems on Several Occasions.* Oxford, 1730.

Young, Edward. *A Paraphrase on part of the Book of Job.* 1719.

— *Conjectures on Original Composition in a Letter to the Author of Sir Charles Grandison.* 1759. Ed. E. J. Morley. 1918.

— *The Complete Works of the Reverend Edward Young.* Ed. J. Doran. 2 vols. 1854.

— *The Correspondence of Edward Young. 1683–1765.* Ed. Henry Pettit. Oxford, 1971.

Secondary Sources

Achievements of the Left Hand: Essays on the Prose of John Milton. Eds. Michael Lieb and John T. Shawcross. Amherst, 1974.

Atkins, J. W. *English Literary Criticism: The Renascence.* 1947.

Aubin, Robert A. *Topographical Poetry in XVIII-Century England.* 1936; rpt. N. Y., 1966.

Aycock, Roy E. "Shakespearian Criticism in the *Gray's-Inn Journal.*" *Yearbook of English Studies,* 2 (1972), 68–72.

Baldwin, C. S. *Renaissance Literary Theory and Practice.* N. Y., 1939.

Baroway, Israel. "The Bible as Poetry in the English Renaissance: An Introduction." *JEGP,* 32 (1933), 447–481.

Battestin, Martin C. "The Transforming Power." *ECS,* 2 (1969), 183–204.

Bond, Donald F. "'Distrust' of Imagination in English Neo-Classicism." *PQ,* 14 (1935), 54–69.

— "The Neo-Classical Psychology of the Imagination." *ELH,* 4 (1937), 245–264.

Bosker, A. *Literary Criticism in the Age of Johnson.* Groningen, den Haag, 1930.

Bray, René. *La Formation de la Doctrine Classique en France.* Paris, 1931.

Bredvold, Louis I. "The Tendency toward Platonism in Neo-Classical Esthetics." *ELH,* 1 (1934), 91–119.

— *The Intellectual Milieu of John Dryden.* Ann Arbor, 1935.

— *The Literature of the Restoration and Eighteenth Century 1660–1798.* Vol. III of *A History of English Literature.* Ed. Hardin Craig. 1950; rpt. N. Y., 1962.

Brett, R. L. "The Third Earl of Shaftesbury as a Literary Critic." *MLR,* 37 (1942), 131–146.

Brewster, Dorothy. *Aaron Hill. Poet, Dramatist, Projector.* N. Y. 1913.

Broadbent, J. B. *Some Graver Subject. An Essay on Paradise Lost.* 1960.

Bundy, Murray W. *The Theory of Imagination in Classical and Mediaeval Thought.* Univ. of Illinois Studies in Language and Literature, Vol. XII. Urbana, 1927.

— "'Invention' and 'Imagination' in the Renaissance." *JEGP,* 29 (1930), 535–545.

Butt, John. *The Augustan Age.* 1950; rpt. N. Y., 1966.

— *The Mid-Eighteenth Century.* Vol. VIII of *The Oxford History of English Literature.* Oxford, 1979.

Butterfield, Herbert. *The Whig Interpretation of History.* 1931.

Chalker, John. *The English Georgic.* Baltimore, 1969.

Clark, A. F. *Boileau and the French Classical Criticism in England.* Paris, 1925.

Cohen, Ralph. "Thomson's Poetry of Space and Time." In *Studies in Criticism and Aesthetics, 1660–1800*. Eds. Howard Anderson and John S. Shea. Minneapolis, 1967, pp. 176–192.
— *The Unfolding of The Seasons*. Baltimore, 1970.
Colton, Judith. "Merlin's Cave and Queen Caroline: Garden Art as Political Propaganda." *ECS*, 10 (1967), 1–10.
— "Kent's Hermitage for Queen Caroline at Richmond." *Architectura*, 2 (1974), 181–191.
Congleton, J. E. "Theories of Pastoral Poetry in England." *SP*, 41 (1944), 544–575.
— *Theories of Pastoral Poetry in England. 1684–1798*. Gainesville, 1952.
Corder, Jim W. "A New Nature in Revisions of *The Seasons*." *N & Q*, 211 (1966), 461–464.
Crane, R. S. "An Early Eighteenth-Century Enthusiast for Primitive Poetry: John Husbands." *MLN*, 37 (1922), 27–36.
— "A Neglected Mid-Eighteenth-Century Plea for Originality and its Author." *PQ*, 13 (1934), 21–29.
— "Suggestions toward a Genealogy of the 'Man of Feeling'." ELH, I (1934), 205–230.
— "On Writing the History of English Criticism, 1650–1800." *UTQ*, 22 (1952), 376–391.
Crum, Ralph B. *Scientific Thought in Poetry*. N. Y., 1931.
Das, P. K. "James Thomson's Appreciation of Mountain Scenery." *ES*, 64 (1929), 65–70.
Davies, Gordon L. "The Concept of Denudation in Seventeenth-Century England." *JHI*, 27 (1966), 278–284.
Dillenberger, John. *Protestant Thought and Natural Science*. N. Y., 1960.
Dobrée, Bonamy. *English Literature in the Early Eighteenth Century*. Oxford, 1959.
Draper, J. W. "Aristotelian Mimesis in England." *PMLA*, 36 (1921), 372–400.
Drennon, Herbert. "Scientific Rationalism and James Thomson's Poetic Art." *SP*, 31 (1934), 453–471.
— "James Thomson's Contact with Newtonianism and his Interest in Natural Philosophy." *PMLA*, 49 (1934), 71–80.
— "Newtonianism in James Thomson's Poetry." *ES*, 70 (1936), 358–372. Reviewed in *PQ*, 14 (1935), 175–76.
Duncan, Carson S. *The New Science and English Literature in the Classical Period*. 1913; rpt. N. Y., 1972.
Durling, Dwight L. *Georgic Tradition in English Poetry*. N. Y., 1935.
English Studies Today. Eds. C. L. Wrenn and G. Bullough. Oxford, 1951.
Essays in Memory of Barrett Wendell. Harvard, 1926.
Fairchild, Hoxie Neale. *Religious Trends in English Poetry*. 2 vols. N. Y., 1939, 1942.
Fairer, David. "Authorship Problems in *The Adventurer*." *RES*, 25 (1974), 137–151.
Fenner, Arthur, Jr. "The Wartons 'Romanticize' their Verse." *SP*, 53 (1956), 501–508.
Fineman, Daniel A. "The Motivation of Pope's *Guardian* 40." *MLN*, 67 (1952), 24–28.
Fitzgerald, M. M. *First Follow Nature*. N. Y., 1947.
Forsgren, Adina. *John Gay. Poet "Of A Lower Order"*. Stockholm, 1964.
Goedgar, Bertrand A. "Pope and the *Grub-Street Journal*." *MP*, 74 (1977), 366–380.
Grabo, Carl. "Science and the Romantic Movements." *Annals of Science*, 4 (1939), 191–205.
Graham, Walter. *English Literary Periodicals*. N. Y., 1930.
Grant, Douglas. *James Thomson: Poet of The Seasons*. 1951.
Green, C. C. *The Neo-Classical Theory of Tragedy*. Cam. Mass., 1934.
Hagstrum, Jean H. *Samuel Johnson's Literary Criticism*. Minneapolis, 1952.
— *The Sister Arts: The Tradition of Literary Pictorialism and English Poetry from Dryden to Gray*. Chicago, 1958.
Hart, Jeffrey. "Akenside's Revisions of *The Pleasures of the Imagination*." *PMLA*, 74 (1959), 67–74.

Havens, R. D. *The Influence of Milton on English Poetry*. Cambridge. Mass., 1922.
— "Primitivism and the Idea of Progress in Thomson." *SP*, 29 (1932), 41–52.
— "Unusual Opinions in 1725 and 1726." *PQ*, 30 (1951), 447–448.
Heuston, Edward. "Windsor Forest and *Guardian* 40." *RES*, 29 (1978), 160–168.
Hillhouse, J. T. *The Grub-Street Journal*. Durham, North Carolina, 1928.
Hoyles, John. *The Waning of the Renaissance 1640–1740*. The Hague, 1971.
Humpreys, A. R., "A Classical Education and Eighteenth-Century Poetry." *Scrutiny*, 8 (1939), 193–207.
Jones, R. F. *Ancients and Moderns. A Study of the Background of the Battle of the Books*. St. Louis, 1936.
— "Science and Criticism in the Neo-Classical Age of English Literature." *JHI*, I (1940), 381–412.
— et al. *The Seventeenth Century*. 1951; rpt. Stanford, 1969.
Jones, W. P. "The Vogue of Natural History in England, 1750–1770." *Annals of Science*, 2 (1937), 345–352.
— "Science in Biblical Paraphrases in Eighteenth-Century England." *PMLA*, 74 (1959), 41–51.
— "Newton Further Demands the Muse." In *Studies in English Literature 1500–1900*. Vol. III Rice University, 1963, pp. 287–306.
— *The Rhetoric of Science: A Study of Scientific Ideas and Imagery in Eighteenth-Century English Poetry*. Berkeley and Los Angeles, 1966.
Kiernan, Colm. "Swift and Science." *Historical Journal*, 14 (1971), 709–722.
Kind, J. L. *Edward Young in Germany*. N. Y., 1906.
Knight, Charles A. "The Writer as Hero in Johnson's Periodical Essays." *Papers on Language and Literature*, 13 (1977), 238–250.
Loiseau, Jean. *Abraham Cowley's Reputation in England*. Paris, 1931.
Lovejoy, A. O. "The Parallel of Deism and Classicism." *MP*, 29 (1931–32), 281–299.
— "'Nature' as Aesthetic Norm." *MLN*, 42 (1927), 444–450. Rpt. in *Essays in the History of Ideas*. Baltimore, 1948, pp. 69–77.
MacClintick, W. D. *Joseph Warton's Essay on Pope: A History of the Five Editions*. Chapel Hill, 1933.
McKillop, A. D. "Richardson, Young and the *Conjectures*." *MP*, 12 (1925), 391–404.
— *The Background of Thomson's Seasons*. Minneapolis, 1942.
— "Shaftesbury in Joseph Warton's *Enthusiast*." *MLN*, 70 (1955), 337–339.
— *James Thomson: The Castle of Indolence and other Poems*. Lawrence, Kansas, 1961.
MacLean Kenneth. *John Locke and English Literature of the Eighteenth Century*. New Haven, 1936.
Mahoney, John L. "Akenside and Shaftesbury: The Influence of Philosophy on English Romantic Theory." *Discourse*, 4 (1961), 241–247.
Man Versus Society in Eighteenth-Century Britain. Ed. James L. Clifford. Cambridge, 1968.
Mann, Elizabeth L. "The Problem of Originality in English Literary Criticism, 1750–1800." *PQ*, 18 (1939), 97–118.
Marks, Emerson R. *The Poetics of Reason*. N. Y., 1968.
Marsh, Robert. "Akenside and Addison: The Problem of Ideational Debt." *MP*, 59 (1961), 36–48.
Mayo, Thomas F. *Epicurus in England 1650–1728*. Dallas; Texas, 1934.
Meyer, G. D. *The Scientific Lady in England. 1650–1760*. Berkeley, 1955.
Miller, G. M. *The Historical Point of View in English Literary Criticism from 1570–1770*. In *Anglistische Forschungen*, 35. Heidelberg, 1913.

Monk, Samuel H. *The Sublime: A Study of Critical Theories in Eighteenth-Century England.* N. Y., 1935.

Moore, C. A. "A Predecessor of Thomson's *Seasons.*" *MLN*, 34 (1919), 278–281.

Morris, David B. "Joseph Warton's Figure of Virtue: Poetic Invertion in *The Enthusiast.*" *PQ*, 50 (1971), 678–683.

Neff, Emery. *A Revolution in European Poetry. 1660–1900.* N. Y., 1940.

Neuman, J. H. "Shakespearean Criticism in the *Tatler* and the *Spectator.*" *PMLA*, 39 (1924), 612–623.

Nicolson, Marjorie, and Nora M. Mohler. "The Scientific Background of Swift's *Voyage to Laputa.*" *Annals of Science*, 2 (1937), 299–334.

Nicolson, Marjorie. *Newton Demands the Muse.* Princeton, 1946.

— *Science and Imagination.* 1956; rpt. Ithaca; N. Y., 1962.

— *Mountain Gloom and Mountain Glory: The Development of the Aesthetics of the Infinite.* Ithaca; N. Y., 1959.

Nitchie, Elizabeth. "Longinus and the Theory of Poetic Imitation in Seventeenth- and Eighteenth-Century England." *SP*, 32 (1935), 580–597.

Norton, John. "Akenside's *The Pleasures of Imagination.*" *ECS*, 3 (1970), 366–383.

Parker, William R. "On Milton's Early Literary Program." *MP*, 33 (1935–36), 49–53.

Perdeck, Albert A. *Theology in Augustan Literature.* The Hague, 1928.

Peterson, R. G. "Samuel Johnson at War with the Classics." *ECS*, 1 (1975), 69–86.

Pittock, Joan. *The Ascendancy of Taste: The Achievement of Joseph and Thomas Warton.* 1973.

Plumb, J. H. *Reason and Unreason in the Eighteenth Century: The English Experience.* 1971.

— *The Commercialisation of Leisure in Eighteenth-Century England.* The Stenton Lecture, 1972. Reading, 1973.

Potter, G. R. "Henry Baker. F. R. S." *MP*, 29 (1931–32), 301–321.

Potts, Abbie F. *Wordsworth's Prelude.* Ithaca; N. Y., 1953.

Price, Martin. *To the Palace of Wisdom: Studies in Order and Energy from Dryden to Blake.* N. Y., 1964.

Reed, Amy L. *The Background of Gray's Elegy. A Study in the Taste for Melancholy Poetry 1700–1751.* 1924; rpt. N. Y., 1962.

Rosenberg, Albert. *Sir Richard Blackmore.* Lincoln; Nebraska, 1953.

Rossky, William. "Imagination in the English Renaissance: Psychology and Poetic." In *Studies in the Renaissance.* Vol. V. 1958, pp. 49–73.

Røstvig, Maren-Sofie. *The Happy Man: Studies in the Metamorphoses of a Classical Ideal.* 2 vols. Oslo, 1954, 1958.

Sayce, R. A. *The French Biblical Epic in the Seventeenth Century.* Oxford, 1955.

Schick, George Baldwin. "Joseph Warton's Conception of the Qualities of a True Poet." In *Boston University Studies in English*, 3, Boston, 1957, pp. 77–87.

Scouten, Arthur H. "Dr. Johnson and Imlac." *ECS*, 6 (1973), 506–508.

Scurr, Helen M. "Henry Brooke". Diss. University of Minnesota 1922.

Sewell, Margaret E. *The Orphic Voice: Poetry and Natural History.* New Haven, 1960.

Sherwood, John C. "Dryden and the Rules: The Preface to *Troilus and Cressida.*" *CL*, 2 (1950), 73–83.

— "Dryden and the Critical Theories of Tasso." *CL*, 18 (1966), 351–359.

Simon, Irene. "Robert South and the Augustan." In *Essays and Studies* (1975), 15–28.

Simpson, H. C. "The Vogue of Science in English Literature. 1600–1800." *UTQ*, 2 (1933), 143–167.

Sitter, John E. "Theodicy at Mid-Century: Young, Akenside and Hume." *ECS*, 12 (1978–79), 90–106.

de Sola Pinto, V. "Issac Watts and the Adventurous Muse." In *Essays and Studies by Members of the English Association,* 20. Oxford, 1935.

Some Aspects of Eighteenth-Century England. Introd. Maximillian E. Novak. Los Angeles, 1971.

Sorelius, Gunnar. 'The Giant Race before the Flood': *Pre-Restoration Drama on the Stage and in the Criticism of the Restoration.* Uppsala, 1966.

Spacks, Patricia M. *The Varied God: A Critical Study of Thomson's The Seasons.* University of California English Studies 21. Berkeley and Los Angeles, 1959.

— *The Poetry of Vision.* Cam. Mass., 1967.

Spencer, Jeffrey B. *Heroic Nature: Ideal Landscapes in English Poetry from Marvell to Thomson.* Evanston, 1973.

Stephen, Sir Leslie. *History of English Thought in the Eighteenth* Century. 3rd. ed. 1927.

Sutherland, James. *A Preface to Eighteenth-Century Poetry.* 1948; rpt. Oxford, 1968.

Swedenberg, jr., H. T. "Rules and English Critics of the Epic." *SP,* 35 (1938), 566–587.

Thale, Mary. "Dryden's Dramatic Criticism: Polestar of the Ancients." *CL,* 18 (1966), 36–54.

Thomas, Walter. *Le Poète Edward Young (1683–1763).* Paris, 1901.

Thorpe, Clarence DeWitt. "Addison and Hutcheson on the Imagination." *ELH,* 2 (1935), 215–234.

— "Addison and some of his Predecessors on 'Novelty'." *PMLA,* 52 (1937), 1114–1129.

Tickell, Richard E. *Thomas Tickell and the Eighteenth-Century Poets. 1685–1740.* 1931.

Tuveson, Ernest L. *The Imagination as a Means of Grace.* Berkeley, 1960.

Wedel, T. O. "On the Philosophical Background of *Gulliver's Travels." SP,* 23 (1926), 434–450.

Weinberg, Bernard. "L'Imitation au XVIe et au XVIIe Siècles." In *Actes du IVe Congrès de l'Association Internationale de Littérature Comparée. Fribourg. 1964.* Ed. F. Jost. The Hague, 1966.

Weinbrot, Howard D. "The Reader, the General and the Particular: Johnson and Imlac in Chapter Ten of *Rasselas." ECS,* 5 (1971), 80–96.

Wellek, René, *A History of Modern Criticism.* 1955.

Whelan, Sister M. Kevin. *Enthusiasm in English Poetry of the Eighteenth Century. 1700–1774.* Washington, D. C., 1935.

Whitney, Lois. *Primitivism and the Idea of Progress.* Baltimore, 1934.

Wiles, Roy McKeen. "The Contemporary Distribution of Johnson's *Rambler." ECS,* 2 (1968), 155–171.

Willey, Basil. *The Seventeenth-Century Background.* 1936.

Williams, Raymond. "Nature's Threads." *ECS,* 2 (1968), 45–57.

Williamson, George. "The Restoration Revolt against Enthusiasm." *SP,* 30 (1933), 571–606.

Wimsatt. W. K., and Cleanth Brooks. *Literary Criticism. A Short History.* N. Y., 1957.

Wright, Austin. *Joseph Spence. A Critical Biography.* Chicago, Illinois, 1950.

Index

162